The Meaning of Work
in Israel

THE MEANING OF WORK IN ISRAEL

Its Nature and Consequences

ITZHAK HARPAZ

PRAEGER

New York
Westport, Connecticut
London

HD
8660
H37
1990

Copyright Acknowledgments

We gratefully acknowledge permission to reprint extracts from the following sources:

MOW-International Research Team, *The Meaning of Working*. Copyright © 1987 by Academic Press Inc. (London) Ltd.

Itzhak Harpaz, "The Meaning of Working Profiles of Various Occupational Groups," *Journal of Vocational Behavior* 26 (1985), pp. 25–40, including Tables 12.1 and 12.2. Copyright © 1985 by Academic Press Inc. (London) Ltd.

Itzhak Harpaz, "The Factorial Structure of the Meaning of Working," *Human Relations* 39, no. 7 (1986), pp. 595–614, including Figure 1 and Tables 6.1 and 6.2. By permission of Plenum Publishing Corp.

Itzhak Harpaz, "Variables Affecting Non-financial Employment Commitment," *Applied Psychology: An International Review* 37 (1989), pp. 235–248, including Tables 7.4 and 7.5. Copyright by the International Association of Applied Psychology.

Library of Congress Cataloging-in-Publication Data

Harpaz, Itzhak.
    The meaning of work in Israel : its nature and consequences /
Itzhak Harpaz.
        p.   cm.
    Includes bibliographical references.
    ISBN 0–275–92475–0 (alk. paper)
        1. Work ethic—Israel.   2. Work—Psychological aspects.
    I. Title.
HD8660.H37   1990
306.3′6—dc20   89–48748

British Library Cataloguing in Publication Data is available.

Copyright © 1990 by Praeger Publishers

Library of Congress Catalog Card Number: 89–48748
ISBN: 0–275–92475–0

First published in 1990

Praeger Publishers, One Madison Avenue, New York, NY 10010
An imprint of Greenwood Publishing Group, Inc.

Printed in the United States of America

The paper used in this book complies with the Permanent Paper Standard issued by the National Information Standards Organization (Z39.48–1984).

10 9 8 7 6 5 4 3 2 1

To Bill England,
my mentor, colleague, and friend,
who taught me the meaning of working.

Responsibility and creativity distinguish human beings from all other animals. Animals other than people can live only off what is available or off prey; only human beings can create something new—indeed create at all; and only humans know the taste of creation, the joy of creation and the supreme light of creation. . . .

. . . Work is not merely intended to make life technically better. It is intended to create or to reveal a new interest, a new purpose in life.

—A. D. Gordon, 1911

Contents

Preface

As we approach the end of the twentieth century, most people's association with work is as it was in the past: a fundamental and basic activity in their lives. To put it succinctly, the centrality of work is pervasive. The outcome of work determines one's social and economic status as well as the nature of the society we create and perpetuate. Nevertheless, work and the workplace are in a state of flux. Dramatic social and technological transformations, especially in the second half of this century, have altered the structure and fashion of work, and in some respects its meanings. Extensive social, demographic, and economic factors are still exerting a profound effect on the manner in which people encounter work in the industrialized world. It would be too facile a conclusion, however, to say that such changes have diluted the importance of work for the individual.

It is only in the last few decades that we have had fairly objective, empirical accounts of the meaning of work for the average individual. Evidence of the "common person's" conception of work in earlier times is barely available. Some hints regarding various historical meanings of work are found in philosophical and religious writings; these, though, mostly pertain to the ideal of work adhered to by elite groups.

The aim of this book is to outline and discuss some of the important considerations and conceptual, theoretical research issues and problems related to work as a major aspect in human life. The study reported here is part of a comprehensive international project conducted in eight countries on the meaning of working (MOW). The present work focuses on data collected in Israel and deals with Israeli society. The international comparative results were published earlier in *The Meaning of Working* (MOW-International Research Team 1987).

It was not easy to write a book on the meaning of work in Israel after having taken part for many years in such an international cooperative endeavor as the MOW-International Research Team. The problem was to come up with novel ideas not previously expressed. Especially problematic was presenting issues or chapters dealing with theory and concepts (Chapter 4) and designing a methodology for the study (Chapter 5), areas that had been developed jointly with the international team. Hence, in many instances, the "wheel" was not reinvented in the present book; ideas, issues, and concepts found in the international comparative volume (MOW-International Research Team 1987) are also utilized here, obviously with a specific focus on Israeli data not presented previously.

Consequently, special thanks and sincere gratitude are due my MOW colleagues for many years of fruitful cooperation and teamwork on the MOW project. Their basic ideas, thoughts, insights, and effort influenced my own ideas and contributed immensely to the development of this book. While responsibility for the present book rests solely with the author, I acknowledge with deep appreciation my MOW colleagues: J.H.T.H. Andriessen, Free University of Amsterdam, Netherlands; Vojko Antončić, Institute of Sociology, Ljubljana, Yugoslavia; Pol Coetsier, Ghent State University, Ghent, Belgium; Pieter J.D. Drenth, Free University of Amsterdam, Netherlands; George W. England, University of Oklahoma, Norman, OK, USA; Frank A. Heller, Centre for Decision Making Studies, Tavistock Institute of Human Relations, London, England; Marnix Holvoet, Ghent State University, Ghent, Belgium; Rob N. van der Kooij, Netherlands Railways Ltd., Utrecht, Netherlands; Jyuji Misumi, Osaka University, Osaka, Japan; S. Antonio Ruiz Quintanilla, Technical University of Berlin, Berlin, FRG; Rita Spoelders-Claes, Ghent State University, Ghent, Belgium; William T. Whitely, University of Oklahoma, Norman, OK, USA; Bernhard Wilpert, Technical University of Berlin, FRG.

I am very much indebted to Bill England, who read the first draft of the manuscript and made many valuable suggestions. His detailed comments were as helpful as was his unfailing encouragement during this long and laborious project. This book is dedicated to him as an expression of my genuine esteem.

Many thanks are due other individuals: Nurit Weiss and Miriam Kuljic, for their research assistance; Baruch Nachmany, for his assistance with computer data analysis; and Reneé Ben-David, for typing the manuscript. The research reported here was supported by a grant from the United States–Israel Binational Science Foundation (BSF), Jerusalem; its support is gratefully acknowledged, as is that of the Research Authority of the University of Haifa. Finally acknowledgments are also due Academic Press, Plenum Press, and the International Association of Applied Psychology for permission to reproduce certain previously published material.

The Meaning of Work
in Israel

1

Introduction to the Study

Work plays a central and fundamental role in the life of the individual (MOW-International Research Team 1987). Support for this assertion may be found in the absolute commitment individuals make to work in terms of time, in the significance working has in an individual's life, and in the social and economic consequences of work in organizations and society. There is also much evidence of the active roles individuals and groups have adopted in structuring and changing their work, work institutions, and societies.

In most industrialized societies, people spend nearly a third of their waking hours at work. In addition, much time is spent in training and preparation for work as well as concern about being out of work or in planning for a better work situation. Thus, work encompasses a great part of our adult life.

In modern industrial countries work is an important link between human beings and their society. Through work individuals procure resources from the environment to secure their sustenance. Proficiencies can be tested through work. This, in turn, can provide a measure of abilities and competency in various skills. Work also provides social relationships at the workplace. Consequently, work is a central constituent of life, enabling people to exist as private and social beings.

So important is the role attributed to the work people do that the familiar greeting of "How do you do?" could be altered to "What do you do?" Willingly or not, adults in modern industrialized societies are "located" and receive some initial identity on the basis of their job. People are asked about their jobs to discern where they stand in the social system. The assumption is that every adult "works at" something. The replies given enable us to place people approximately. We can broadly estimate the range of income, size of family, place of residence, leisure activities, and even friends individuals are likely to have on the basis of their work. Work may, then, be typically regarded as a fundamental part of life, determining status and social position for the whole family.

Work is so prominent that in Western societies rewards and status are allocated according to one's position in the workplace, degree of attachment to the labor force, and type of occupation. Because factors associated with work affect how rewards are distributed, very few people can actually stay away from work, although work cannot be imposed in any formal manner. In addition, society inflicts a social stigma on those who do not work, which usually causes them to be placed on its margins.

A different aspect of the importance of work in the life of an individual may be seen in the vast amount of research on the consequences of unemployment and retirement on active employees (e.g., Friedman & Havighurst 1954; Jahoda 1979; Kaplan & Tausky 1974; Warr 1984). The literature points in general to the negative impact of unemployment and retirement on healthy and active workers and to their demoralizing effects.

Any attempt to discuss the topic of work and its implications for other life roles and society must deal with the notion of why people work and what work means to individuals. Various writings indicate that for most people the meaning of work has generally been expounded by three propositions. The most prominent is the *economic* or *instrumental*, which asserts that people work in order to secure a livelihood and to satisfy their material needs (Anderson 1961; Dubin 1958; Friedman & Havighurst 1954; Kaplan & Tausky 1974; Miller 1980; Neff 1968). The second concerns the commitment to work as part of *human nature* and *human needs* (Garson 1977). This position has been advanced by social and developmental psychologists and relies on concepts such as the "work instinct" (Hendrick 1943; Levitan & Johnson 1982), the "work personality" (Neff 1971), and "socialization" (Erikson 1963; Lantos 1952). This approach points to the prevalence of an underlying human desire to exert effort, an urge to learn, develop, and accomplish, and to structure one's environment.

The third proposition on the importance of work in the lives of people is *socio-psychological*. According to this view, work is essential in imparting meaning to our lives. Not only does work contribute to our sense of who we are, it also provides this awareness with a stability and continuity once it has been formed. It thus plays a crucial role in helping us to achieve and maintain our personal identities by the opportunities it offers for contacts and companionship with other people (Friedman & Havighurst 1954; Steers & Porter 1983). It can also give us a sense of having an impact on our environment. It thereby enhances our feelings of personal competence and self-esteem (Chestang 1982). Additionally, work can confer status and prestige (Kaplan & Tausky 1974; Steers & Porter 1983), or it can be an intrinsically satisfying activity from which we derive enjoyment and a sense of accomplishment (Kaplan & Tausky 1974; Neff 1971). Work may also serve as a means of winning approval and of achieving self-actualization and self-fulfillment (Menninger 1964; Steers & Porter 1983). It may also foster the feelings of being part of society and being in the mainstream of social life (Morse & Weiss 1955; Wilensky 1964).

H. R. Kaplan and C. Tausky (1974) suggested a typology of six meanings and functions of work that seem to embody the findings of most of the research. These are divided into two categories: expressive and instrumental.

A. *Expressive*

1. *Work as an intrinsically satisfying activity*. Enjoyment and a sense of accomplishment may be derived from performing a work task, for example, rendering a service to others. There may be a desire for new experience, to learn more, and to utilize and develop abilities through a job, that is, to self-actualize. There may be a need for responsibility and autonomy at the workplace.

2. *Work as a status- and prestige-bestowing activity*. There may be a desire for status achievement in monetary or social terms. A job may be valued for the prestige that accrues to the person performing a specific task. Status or prestige may be sought from one's co-workers, friends, or relatives. The pursuit of money in this context is an outward sign that signifies achievement of status.

3. *Work as a morally correct activity*. Work is seen as an activity that fulfills a prescribed role in society, thus carrying prescriptions about the ''rightness'' and ''correctness'' of working.

4. *Work as a source of satisfying interpersonal experiences*. Satisfaction may be derived from associations with others in work and from working with patrons, clients, patients, or co-workers. The satisfaction is not from services rendered, but from affiliative relations in one's job.

B. *Instrumental*

5. *Work as an economic activity, a means of survival*. Work is sought for money. It is prized for the opportunities it provides for obtaining satisfaction away from the job.

6. *Work as a scheduled or routinized activity that keeps one occupied*. It consumes time and energy and may be viewed as a vehicle for avoiding negative consequences associated with laziness and idleness, for example, hustling or illegal activities. (Kaplan and Tausky, 1974:186)

WHY STUDY THE MEANING OF WORK?

Given the diversity of work and the differences among individuals, no single conceptualization can account fully for why people work. Most people's work behavior is influenced by various combinations of the factors presented here.

Studies on the meaning of work and work values have received increased attention in the past few decades. Some of the major reasons for this and for the present study are the following:

• Social and technological changes have altered the structure and style of work and in some respects may also have influenced its meaning.

• Concern over the possible decline of the work ethic in Western society has been expressed since the mid–1960s (Juzanek 1978). Social observers and researchers have detected a weakening in the traditional work and business ethic while noting a growing preoccupation with leisure, quality of working life, comfort, and the avoidance of risk (Etzioni 1979).

- Productivity slowdown and decline of output per worker have been noted in most industrialized countries, including Japan (Reynolds, Masters & Moser 1986). This may be related to global economic trends but may also be associated with how employees perceive their work and with various aspects of the work context.

- Dramatic changes have taken place in many industrialized countries with regard to the legal and societal conceptions about "working rights" of women, minority groups, protected-age categories, and a variety of disadvantaged groups. These have certainly modified employment policies and practices substantially (MOW-International Research Team 1981).

- Increasing educational levels of many special groups, along with that of the general population, have led to changes in the composition of the labor force. Of particular note is the increase in the number of women. Another development is the rise in the proportion of those employed in the services sector as compared with those employed in manufacturing, construction, and agriculture (Levitan & Johnson 1983).

- The sweeping change that has occurred in industrial development with reference to the opportunities to work in general and certain types of work in particular have most likely had an effect on the meaning and significance of work. This issue is especially note-worthy in Israel, where intensive industrialization of a new society took place in a rapidly developing country. Moreover, since its creation in 1948, Israel has absorbed millions of immigrants (about 2 million of its 4.5 million current inhabitants arrived from other countries). Integration of individuals who had brought cultures, work habits, and work ethics with them from their countries of origin is an ongoing task.

The focus of this book is to explore the meaning, significance, and values that individuals and groups in Israeli society attach to work. These themes are developed conceptually, identified empirically, and understood in terms of how they have developed in the past and what their consequences are for the future.

Within this framework, the goals of the book are as follows:

1. Identification of major patterns of meanings that individuals and significant target groups attach to working.

2. Understanding of how individuals and groups have developed particular work meanings.

3. Comprehension of the consequences of meaning of work (MOW) patterns to individuals, organizations, and society in general.

4. Development of policy implications based on the findings.

More specifically we will consider the following issues and topics:

- A literature review of the role and meaning of work in Israel through the ages. This includes the concept of work in the Bible, in the Judaic sources (Oral Law), in Zionist writings, and in the empirical findings from modern Israel. (Chapter 2)

- Basic background information about the status of social and economic conditions, as well as the industrial relations system in Israel. (Chapter 3)

- A heuristic model on the meaning of work specifying the critical antecedents and consequences of the central domains. The model presented comprises the major variable sets and the most direct and straightforward relationships initially considered to be of primary importance in the study of the meaning of work. (Chapter 4)

- The heuristic model empirically developed to identify and understand the structure of the meaning of work. The MOW structure and its consistency is determined for ten different target groups as well as for the national sample of the labor force in Israel. (Chapter 6)

- The work centrality concept, focusing on the importance of work for people. The exploration of this concept focuses on the role of work in comparison with other important life roles. It also examines the centrality of work in absolute terms. (Chapter 7)

- Societal norms about work and working. Two central concepts are presented: (1) entitlements (or work opportunities), that is, what everyone may expect from work; and (2) obligations, that is, what everyone is expected to contribute to organizations or society via working. (Chapter 8)

- Valued work outcomes. The relative importance of the broad functions of work to the individual is assessed and consideration is given to the general desired outcomes to be obtained through working, along with their relative importance. Related to this theme are work roles and the determination of which work roles one identifies with. (Chapter 9)

- Focus on a uniform set of work goals or facets of work to ascertain how important each is to individual workers. Here is a useful way of understanding what is important to people in their working life. (Chapter 10)

- Defining the concept of work. Three classes of concepts are treated: (1) broad rationales for engaging in work: (2) personal outcomes or states resulting from performing working activities; (3) constraints or controls related to the context or performance of working activities. (Chapter 11)

- Dimensions of work meaning combined so that certain patterns associated with work meanings emerge. It is possible to identify different MOW patterns or profiles that may characterize the population. Such patterns may also be used for classification of occupational groups. (Chapter 12)

- Consequences of holding certain patterns of beliefs, values, and preferences regarding work. Some fundamental questions considered include these: Why do people work? What are the correlates of working? What might explain different levels of working intensity? (Chapter 13)

- Conclusions and implications. Based on empirical findings presented throughout this volume, conclusions are drawn and implications for organizations as well as society are presented. (Chapter 14)

The central theme of the book is the meaning of work and working. The research presented here sheds light on work values of the Israeli worker and provides a unique picture of a variety of work-related issues.

2

Work and Its Meaning in Israel through the Ages

In order to gain some understanding of the special meaning work has had in Israel through the ages and to attain a better appreciation of the data on Israel in the 1980s presented here, it will prove helpful to trace the roots and significance of work as depicted in various Jewish-Israeli writings as well as in empirical studies conducted in Israel. The review focuses only on Jewish-Israeli thoughts about work and its meanings, not on the evolution or history of work in the world, which has been elaborated and described elsewhere (e.g., Neff 1977; Shostak 1980; Tilgher 1962). Accordingly, the chapter is divided into four major sections, each describing a prominent era or characteristic feature related to work and its meaning: (1) work as portrayed in the Bible, (2) work according to Judaic sources, (3) work in Zionist writings, and (4) work in modern Israel.

A vast amount of literature is available on the first three of these topics. Necessarily only the essence of these writings can be presented here in order to permit the reader to savor each period's uniqueness with regard to the concept of work. The fourth category, based on empirical research, discusses findings taken from studies on work values, work centrality, and the meaning of work in modern Israel.

A fifth section deals with the findings of studies conducted on the kibbutz. The value and organization of work in kibbutz society are unique, their effects spilling over into Israeli society at large. Although this book does not include a kibbutz sample, for the reader's benefit it does include a brief review of kibbutz philosophy on work as well as a discussion of major findings from relevant research on the collectives.

WORK IN THE BIBLE

Many verses and proverbs in the Bible deal with work, most of them proclaiming the high regard in which work and workers should be held. Some are explicit, such as "Man goeth forth unto his work and to his labor until the evening" (Psalms 104:23). Others are implicit, as in the case of the sluggish son who is directed to the humble ant to acquire some of its virtues: "Go to the ant, thou sluggard, consider her ways, and be wise. Which having no guide, overseer, or rule provideth her meat in the summer and gathereth her food in the harvest" (Proverbs 6: 6–8).

The notion of one's being entitled to enjoy life only after fulfilling some useful activity is also expressed: "And the Lord God took the man and put him into the Garden of Eden to dress it and to keep it" (Genesis 2:15). A Talmudic exegesis on this verse goes as follows: Rabbi Shimeon Ben-Elazar said: "Adam tasted nothing until he worked. For it is written: ' . . . to dress it and to keep it,' and only later, 'of every tree of the garden thou mayest freely eat' " (Tractate Avot 11:1).

A fundamental disagreement exists between the Jewish and Christian notions of work in relation to the Garden of Eden story. Christian writings view toil as a curse and punishment imposed upon Adam for his sin of disobedience to God (Agrell 1976; Tilgher 1962). Jewish writers, on the other hand, assert that the punishment was restricted only to the expulsion from the Garden of Eden. In their view, work was and has remained the domain of human beings (Le'sham 1964; Sela 1984). According to I.H. Weisfeld (1974), when God told Adam, "In the sweat of thy face shalt thou eat bread" (Genesis 3:19), Adam understood that human beings were superior to animals and that their labor was both purposeful and dignified. Moreover, work would provide new meaning to life.

Another important, fundamental verse in the Bible also points out that people have to work before they may rest and/or worship God: "Six days shalt thou labor and do all thy work. But the seventh day is the Sabbath of the Lord thy God, in it thou shalt not do any work" (Exodus 20:9–10). Weisfeld considered it rather odd that while this dictum forbids working on the Sabbath day, it also emphasizes the importance of working during the rest of the week.

The moral value of work, its positive functions, and the special meanings it has (that is, a sense of achievement) may be found in the following biblical extracts:

They that sow in tears shall reap in joy. He that goeth forth and weepeth, bearing precious seed, shall doubtless come again with rejoicing, bringing his sheaves with him. (Psalms 126:5–6)

For thou shalt eat the labor of thine hands: happy shalt thou be, and it shall be well with thee. (Psalms 128: 2)

The sleep of a laboring man is sweet, whether he eat little or much: but the abundance of the rich will not suffer him to sleep. (Ecclesiastes 5:11)

The contrast between diligence and idleness is especially emphasized in the Book of Proverbs. The superiority and virtues of hard work may be found in such maxims as "Half-hearted effort makes for poverty but diligence makes for wealth" (Proverbs 10:4); "Diligent men wield authority, but slackness leads to slavery" (Proverbs 12:24); "You have seen a man who is skillful at his work?

It is with kings that he will hold office; he will not hold office with obscure men'' (Proverbs 22:29).

The opposite of diligence is sluggishness, a phenomenon harshly decried: "How long, O' sluggard, will you lie there? When will you rise from your sleep? A little sleep, a little slumber, a little folding of the hands to lie down, and poverty will come to you like a vagrant, and want like a beggar'' (Proverbs 6:9–12). "A son who gathers crops in summer is competent, but one who sleeps through the harvest is a disgrace'' (Proverbs 6:9–12). "Laziness induces deep sleep, and a lethargic man goes hungry'' (Proverbs 19:15). "Through sloth the ceiling sinks, and through slack hands the house leaks'' (Ecclesiastes 10:18).

Work takes on an entirely different meaning in the Bible in relation to God. In that case work means daily prayer accompanied by devout study of the holy scriptures. One example of this ideology is found in the Book of Joshua: "This book of the law shall not depart out of thy mouth but thou shalt meditate therein day and night, that thou mayest observe to do according to all that is written therein'' (Joshua 1:8). In other words, the only right work is worship of God. (And, indeed, the Hebrew word for work—*avodah*—is also the word for worship.)

Jewish women, too, received in the Bible special attention with regard to work. The "woman of valor'' is one who is industrious, kind, wise, and happy (Weisfeld 1974):

Who can find a virtuous woman? For her price is far above rubies. . . . She seeketh wool, and flax, and worketh willingly with her hands. She is like the merchants' ships; she bringeth her food from afar. She riseth also while it is yet night, and giveth meat to her household, and a portion to her maidens. She considereth a field, and buyeth it: with the fruit of her hands she planteth a vineyard. She girdeth her loins with strength and strengtheneth her arms. She perceiveth that her merchandise is good; her candle goeth not out by night. She layeth her hands to the spindle, and her hands hold the distaff. She stretcheth out her hand to the poor; yea, she reacheth forth her hands to the needy. She is not afraid of the snow for her household; for all her household are clothed with scarlet. She maketh herself coverings of tapestry; her clothing is silk and purple. (Proverbs 31:10–22)

In the ancient world the inferiority of slaves was their accepted status, but the Bible legislated scrupulously in their favor. Weisfeld (1974) claims that nowhere in the Bible can it be found that Jews treated their slaves barbarically or harshly. Indeed, the injunction was as follows:

If a fellow Hebrew, man or woman, is sold to you, he shall serve you six years, and in the seventh year you shall set him free. When you set him free do not let him go empty-handed; furnish him out of the flock, threshing floor, and vat, with which the Lord your God has blessed you. (Deuteronomy 15:12–14)

Moreover, slaves were treated and taken care of just like members of the family. In many instances, slaves were even asked for their opinion or advice

(Weisfeld, 1974). That they be treated humanely is a biblical injunction further illustrated by the following sentences:

Observe the Sabbath day . . . in it you shall not do any work, you, or your manservant, or your maidservant . . . that your manservant and your maidservant may rest as well as you. (Deuteronomy 5:12–14)

In summary, the concept of work appears in the Bible in four different situations:

1. *Work of the soil.* "And there was no man to till the soil" (Genesis 2:5). "So the Lord God banished him from the Garden of Eden to till the soil from which he was taken" (Genesis 3:23). "He who tills his soil has his fill of bread, but he whose pursuits are empty has no sense" (Proverbs 12:11).

2. *Work as enslavement.* "The Egyptians ruthlessly imposed upon the Israelites the various labors that they made them perform. Ruthlessly they made life bitter for them with harsh labor, mortar and bricks and with all sorts of tasks in the field" (Exodus 1:14–15).

3. *Work as laboring for a wage.* "Laban said to Jacob, just because you are my kinsman, should you serve me for nothing? Tell me, what shall your wages be?" (Genesis 29:15).

4. *Work as worshipping God.* "Let my people go that they may worship me in the wilderness" (Exodus 7:15). "Now therefore fear the Lord and serve him in sincerity and in truth" (Joshua 24:14).

WORK IN THE JUDAIC SOURCES

Work is discussed in several Jewish sources written after the biblical period, including the Talmud (known as the Oral Law and composed of Mishnah and Gemarrah), Midrash, and Tosefta. The first two compilations were edited and written down mainly between the first and fifth centuries c.e., though studied orally long before that period. The third compilation is a late medieval commentary on the Talmud. In addition, many values and norms elucidated in the Judaic sources were institutionalized and became laws during the Middle Ages. These can be found in codifications such as those of the Maimonides (known as the "Rambam") and Joseph Caro's *Shulchan Aruch.* M. Ayali (1987), who conducted an extensive review of Judaic sources, described five positive aspects of work emanating from these writings:

1. *Work prevents poverty.* "If one does not work, one does not eat" (Bereshith Raba 94).

2. *Work saves one from sins.* Idleness may bring a person to commit crimes or desecrate the Sabbath.

3. *Work averts boredom.* Idleness creates problems for people. "Rabbi Yossi says, people die only out of idleness" (Bereshith Raba 49:33).

4. *Work acts as a restraint on relying on the favors of others.* A person should do any kind of work so as not to need support from others. "Make your Sabbath secular (profane) and do not rely on the public [for support]" (Tractate Sabbath 118:71).

5. *Work averts the suspicion of the public.* "If one does not work, people may wonder from where one gets [money] to eat or drink." (Adar'n 101).

Surveying biblical and talmudic laws relating to labor, Weisfeld (1974) found that, contrary to other ancient civilizations and religions, Judaism endowed human labor with dignity and that no person, regardless of position, was to feel above manual labor ("Skin a carcass in the market place to earn a wage and say not, 'I am a Priest; I am an important personage and this type of work is degrading to me,' " Tractate Baba Batra 140a). Weisfeld also reviewed the positive place work holds in the Judaic sources, with such prescriptions dealing with the rights of workers, work contracts, and laborers' justification for breaking these contracts, the responsibility of employers to pay wages on time, and respect toward work: "One who is honestly engaged in trade is regarded as if he observed the whole Torah" (Mekilta 47b).

The writings of early Jewish scholars, according to Y. Fogel (1978), showed an emphasis on work as fulfilling a commandment and God's wish. The importance these scholars attributed to work, to love of work, and to the obligation of educating for work is illustrated in an apothegm like "He who does not teach his son a craft, teaches him brigandage" (Tractate Kiddushin 29a).

Fogel (1978) focused on the dilemma between the obligation to study Torah and the duty to work. He concluded that, according to the early Jewish sages, the solution lay in their integration. For example, "Any (study of the) Torah which is not carried out along with work will end up in idleness and will create crime" (Tractate Avot 2:2).

The author pointed out that these Jewish scholars not only talked about the importance of work and workers, they themselves or most of them, were also engaged in manual jobs and occupations. Many were even identified by their profession (Ayali 1984). For example, Hillel was a woodcutter (Faderbush 1973), Shamai was a builder (Tractate Shabbat 31), Rabbi Akiva carried wood (Tractate Avot), Rabbi Yehuda was a baker, Rabbi Yochanan a shoemaker, Rabbi Meir a clerk (Tractate Eiruvin 13), Rabbi Yossi Ben Halfath processed leathers (Tractate Shabbat 49), Rabbi Yehuda was a tailor, Rabbi Avoha made women's scarves (Faderbush 1973), Rabbi Hona was a farmer (Megilla 28), Rabbi Itzhak a blacksmith (Tractate Peshachim 113), and Rabbi Avin a carpenter (Tractate Shabbat 23).

In discussing basic moral issues in the Bible and in the writings of early Jewish philosophers, C. W. Reines (1979) offered evidence that work was viewed as a central element of human culture. It was, in addition, thought to have a moral value, since work was said to tie people to society and save them from wrongdoing and other negative outcomes resulting from idleness.

M. Fyindling's (1945) survey of the *Shulchan Aruch,* the works of the Rambam, and other sources led him to conclude that work in Jewish tradition is intended for the development of the world, not for the needs of the individual. The purpose of work is to reach the ultimate goal, which is to "mend the work in God's kingdom." Hence, work is of religious importance. He also concluded that in order to achieve this goal, Jewish religious law (or Halachah) mandates that people elevate their work to levels of high morality and sanctity.

A unique study was conducted by A. Sela (1984), who investigated work values according to "Judaic sources." Sela collected and analyzed over 700 quotations drawn from talmudic and midrashic sources, grouping them into seven categories: (1) God's will (religious aspects), (2) substance of work (personal-moral), (3) work ethic, (4) egoistic values (intrinsic and extrinsic), (5) collective values (humanistic and altruistic), (6) Torah and work (conflict between devoting time to studying Torah and work), (7) work organization (different forms of organization). Most quotations, he found, fell into the work ethic and collectivistic values categories. The former category includes such values as expressing loyalty to an employer, fairness toward the employer and fellow workers, diligence, avoidance of time loss and causing damage to the employer, commitment to work, and role set (for example, "Employer may change work duties only to easier jobs but not to the contrary," Tosefta for Tractate Baba-Metzia 7:3). The latter category contains statements dealing with a humanistic orientation toward the individual as well as altruistic statements (for example, "A person processing skins can set up shop only on the eastern edge of town," Tractate Baba-Batra 2:8; the reason is that eastern winds are moderate and will not carry the bad smell of the skins to town). Sela (1984) also found that most of the quotations dealing with the conflict of time devoted to the study of Torah versus work recommended a combination of the two.

G. Alon (1967) identified four criteria that guided the attitude of early Jewish philosophers toward the topic of work:

1. *Social Meaning.* "A man has to set up the settlement, to say that he participated in the building of the society, and whoever does not deal in work does not belong to the settlement and helps its hindrance."

2. *Personal-Moral.* "The one who turns himself to idleness corrupts his soul." Work stabilizes the soul and protects the individual from destruction and crisis.

3. *Humanitarian.* An idler betrays his role as a human being and violates the holiness of his humanistic world. "A worker who does his duty determines his exclusivity in the world."

4. *Spiritual.* Work is a means for the spiritual uplift of a man and his joining with God. Work is a prayer: "A man who repeats two laws in the morning prayer and two laws in the evening prayer and does his work all day is considered as if he fulfilled all the Torah."

This brief review of the literature on the treatment of work according to Judaic sources reveals three approaches to the concept in Judaism. The most dominant approach sees work as the most important role in human life. This view is represented by the following precepts:

Work which honors its master is dignified. (Tractate Nedarim 49:2)

Rabbi Judeah says that a man does not die but from idleness. (Avot Derabi Natan 21)

If a man does not work on the Sabbath evening—what will he eat on the Sabbath? If a man does not plough, sow and harvest in the days of sun—what will he eat in the days of rain? (Tractate Avodah Zavah, 3:13)

A second approach, situated perhaps at the opposite extreme from the first, finds that the meaning of work lies solely in its being a daily prayer accompanied by study of the Holy Scriptures. This view is exemplified in such verses as the following: "This book of law shall not depart out of thy mouth but thou shalt meditate therein day and night, that thou mayest observe to do according to all that is written therein" (Joshua 1:8) "You must read and utter it day and night" (Beshelah: Vayisa B').

Finally, between the two extreme approaches exists a compromise view that suggests an integration of the practice of work and the study of Scripture. This approach is summed up in the epigram "If there is no flour, there is no Torah— If there is no Torah, there is no flour" (Avot 3:17).

WORK AND THE ZIONIST MOVEMENT

The Zionist movement evolved following the emancipation of various European nations in the mid-nineteenth century. The main purpose of Zionism was the return of the Jews from the Diaspora to their homeland in the Land of Israel and the establishment there of a Jewish state. Zionism was not simply an emancipation movement to counter enslavement, humiliation, discrimination, and estrangement. It was a movement of national redemption. The Jewish people wished to be redeemed from the Diaspora, or so went the premise, and Zionism would elevate the image of the Jew as well as the morality and spirituality of each Jewish individual.

Conditions in the Diaspora had distorted the economic structure of Jewish society. Because of governmental restrictions and prohibitions, the economic activities of the Jews focused on occupations somewhat removed from the primary stages of production, concentrating instead on arbitrage and finance, once considered risky vocations. One aim of Zionism was to "normalize" the Jewish situation through the establishment of a Jewish state. In supporting a national solution to the problem of the Jewish people, Zionism advocated Jewish self-fulfillment through a return to nature, to agriculture, and to creative work. The idea of fulfillment through work began to send out clear signals, as did some nonsocialist ideas. The main ideas forming the Zionist philosophy revolved around a return to the land, hard work, "real work," and "cultivating the land." Table 2.1 encapsulates the essence of these ideas as promulgated by the most outstanding personalities in the Zionist movement.

Especially in its relation to the soil, work was seen as a key to laying the human and social foundations of a new independent state. Indeed, one idealogue

Table 2.1

Major Zionist Leaders and the Essence of Their Ideas Concerning Work

Zionist Leader	Essential Idea Concerning Work
Moshe Hess (1812-1875)	"...work alone is the basis for every authorizing power in the state...." "Work is the essence without which the life of a society does not exist or develop." "The meaning of work is every exchange of materials for the sake of life of mankind....working, acting, creating, doing, employing - in short living, because... he who works lives." (Hess 1956)
Yehuda Alkalay (1798-1878)	"The people of Israel need to return to the Land of Israel in order to live there from agriculture and other types of work...." (Ackerman 1982)
Leo Pinsker (1821-1891)	"Only those who do not know the situation of the Jews... would dare say that they would refuse to work with their hands." (Pinsker 1967)
Peretz Smolenskin (1842-1885)	"Work in the Land of Israel will save [Jews] from idleness, which brings all evil." (Herzberg 1970)
Theodor Herzl (1860-1904)	"We should be given authority over a piece of land on earth... and all the rest we will do ourselves...." (Herzl 1960)
Nahman Sirkin (1864-1924)	"Work [in agriculture] should be measured not only by its duration but by the level of unsatisfactory feelings to be overcome...." (Sirkin 1986)
Aharon David Gordon (1856-1922)	"From now on, work needs to be our main ideal... We were stricken with work, and through work we shall recover." "We have to put work at the center of our aspirations to rear our children on it." "We must bring the Jew to pick up the spade and not with his mind but actually, with his hands." (Shechter 1957)
Dov Borochov (1881-1917)	"Only through a struggle with nature can a human being obtain the materials and means for existence." (Ackerman 1982)
Haim Arlosoroff (1899-1933)	"The Jewish problem derived from the almost absolute non-productivity of the Jewis economy." "As long as work in Israel is not Hebrew work, Israel is still a diaspora...." "The unworking human being is unsociable; a person who does not aspire to human gathering cannot make roots in society, because to live means to produce...." (Arlosoroff 1984)
Berl Katzenelson (1887-1944)	"The principle of Hebrew work must be physical labor, in all areas of the economy." "From a moral point: a man must work by himself...." (Katzenelson 1949)
Zeev Jabotinsky (1880-1940)	"The meaning of work is any exertion of effort by the body or the brain whose purpose is to earn a living for the worker himself, or as an aid to others. Any person engaged in such an effort belongs to the community of workers...." (Nedava 1980)
David Ben-Gurion (1886-1973)	"Building a state is - returning to work... we do not see work as a curse and as a bitter necessity or only a means of living...but as a social duty, a human duty, discovering the creative power of human beings and their domination of nature...." (Ben-Gurion 1949)

even preached a "religion of work," and groups of pioneers declared themselves for the "conquest of Hebrew work." The meaning of work, which played a remarkable role in the Jewish national rebirth, has travelled a long road as a value related to the development of the Zionist idea. Today, some 40 years after the establishment of the state of Israel, most of these same notions regarding the concept or meaning of work are still guiding ideals.

WORK VALUES IN MODERN ISRAEL

Studies on work values in modern Israel (that is, since 1948), which topic has greatly increased in interest and significance among researchers since the mid–1970s, can be grouped into four categories:

1. Work centrality and closely related topics, such as work involvement and commitment to work.
2. Attitudes and values of youth toward work.
3. Research on the "lottery question."
4. Importance of work goals or work outcomes.

Work Centrality

Relatively few studies have been published in Israel that directly address the topics of the meaning of work, work centrality, commitment to work, and work involvement. Several major projects carried out by a Technion–Israel Institute of Technology research team, headed by Bilha F. Mannheim, relate directly to the present study, although they focus on different aspects and groups.

In the first of these projects, Mannheim's data were collected by means of a closed interview with 778 males active in the labor force, aged 21–65 years, and living in the four largest cities of Israel. The respondents were categorized into seven groups according to their occupations. The authors argued that such occupational categorization reflected a differential educational and prestige structure and, in Israel, a different ethnic background as well (Mannheim, Chomsky & Cohen 1972). The independent variables employed in their study were job autonomy, role strains, significant-others' support, specific job rewards, and career stability. The dependent variable of "work role centrality" was measured by the following eight items:

1. the extent to which the respondent finds *interest* in his work relative to other activities;
2. the importance the respondent attaches to *success* in his work relative to other matters;
3. the extent to which matters related to work are of *concern* to the respondent relative to other matters;

4. the respondent's relative preoccupation with *matters not related* to work during work;

5. the respondent's relative preoccupation with *work-related matters* after working hours;

6. the respondent's concern with being *"in the know"* about what is going on in the workplace;

7. the respondent's beliefs about proper *time allocation* between work and other activities; and

8. the respondent's ego *identification* with the work role. (Mannheim, Chomsky & Cohen 1972)

The various groups of workers are ranked here according to their work centrality from high to low work centrality, as calculated by Mannheim and her team: (1) scientists and professionals; (2) technicians and high-level operatives; (3) administrative, executive, and higher clerical workers; (4) crafts, process, production, and construction workers; (5) traders, agents, and salesmen; (6) transportation and communications workers; and (7) services, sports, and recreation workers (Mannheim & Cohen 1978).

In an attempt to compare various occupational groups and demographic variables, Mannheim found the following:

- Israeli-born workers had the highest work centrality, while Israelis of Asian and Middle Eastern background had the lowest.

- Work centrality increases with an increase in level of education (differences among all groups were significant).

- The self-employed had significantly higher work centrality than employees and members of cooperatives.

- An overall positive relationship existed between work centrality and rewards obtained at work (that is, social, material, intrinsic, and hygienic); the same positive relationship existed between work centrality and a single item of a general satisfaction score (highest coefficient was $-.47$). Indeed, the rewards variable was later found to have the strongest effect on work centrality for most of the groups studied. The data suggested to Mannheim that "work centrality is not wholly consonant with satisfaction" (Mannheim 1975: 101).

Finally, B. Mannheim and A. Cohen (1978) employed a stepwise regression analysis to examine factors affecting the work centrality of the seven occupational categories sampled. Their major findings were as follows:

- Scientists and professionals. Most of the variance in work centrality was explained by the independent variable of *social rewards* (that is, high evaluation by co-workers, colleagues, and supervisors); the picture that emerged was that of a "highly satisfied and socially rewarded worker who experiences an intermediate level of person-role conflict."

- Technicians and allied workers. Most of the variance in work centrality was explained by intrinsic rewards; a work-oriented person in this category was also characterized by low person-role conflict.

- Administrative, executive, and clerical personnel. High general satisfaction contributed the most to an explanation of the variance in work centrality among this group; the profile of a work-centered individual in this category tends to be one who is achievement oriented, highly satisfied, and materially rewarded.

- Traders, agents, and salespeople. Here extrinsic rewards and high education were related most strongly with work centrality.

- Service, recreation, and allied workers. Work centrality was explained mostly by high general satisfaction and intrinsic rewards; it was also found that men with working wives in this category had lower work centrality.

- Construction, crafts, process, and production workers. In this category, which consisted of blue-collar workers, support at work and expectations of improvement in reward had the strongest effect on centrality.

In a second project on work centrality conducted by Mannheim and her associates some years later, 818 workers from 57 Israeli industrial enterprises were studied. Some of the major findings reported by B. Mannheim and R. Dubin (1986) were these: (1) workers in the private sector showed higher work centrality than did those in labor-owned (Histadrut) industries; (2) higher work centrality prevailed when production was organized in units rather than in batches; (3) work centrality was positively associated with task autonomy; and (4) a positive correlation existed between job satisfaction and work centrality.

In another study utilizing the same data, B. Mannheim and O. Angel (1986) studied the relationship between pay systems and work role centrality. They found that when *group incentives* were employed, work centrality was low, *individual incentives* made for high centrality, and a *fixed hourly* system led to an intermediate level. The relationship of task autonomy with work centrality was also found to be stronger under individual-incentive and fixed wages systems than for the group-incentive condition.

In investigating work role centrality from yet a third data base, this one consisting of 419 married academic professional women (lawyers, architects, and chemical engineers), B. Mannheim and M. Schiffrin (1984) reported relatively high levels of work centrality. Work centrality was not found to be affected by personal or family variables. Moreover, a positive relationship existed between ''intrinsic'' reasons for working and work centrality. Intrinsic rewards were the most significant contributors to the explanation of work centrality in this sample of professional females. Finally, an interesting finding was that despite their job demands, these women continued to hold the traditional home-making responsibilities even when their husbands were supportive.

A project dealing with preparation for retirement was conducted by J. Kremer and E. Weiner (1974), who interviewed 250 employees just before their retirement from five industrial and service organizations. Among other things, the employees were asked about two needs that work provides: (1) gives a feeling of being useful; (2) keeps one from being bored. The responses were distributed in the following manner:

	Gives Feeling of Being Useful %	Keeps One From Being Bored %
Definitely not important	5.3	11.5
Not so important	6.1	14.8
Slightly important	10.7	14.4
Important	28.7	28.8
Definitely important	49.2	30.5

Thus, with more than three quarters of the employees holding the opinion that work was important in giving them a feeling of being useful, and three out of every five of these older employees stating that a function of work was to keep them from being bored, the results indicate that work is central to preretired employees as much as it is to most other people.

J. Rein (1977) studied the influence of the social community on the work reality of production workers and compared, among other variables, the work values and work centrality of employees in metal-working plants in cities and development towns. In both samples, work was found to be of average centrality when compared with other life roles in the workers' role set. The total research population emphasized instrumental and diffuse values; however, city workers expressed more idealistic values than did development town workers, who inclined more toward instrumental values.

In a comparative study, S. Ronen (1978) contrasted kibbutz members and urban industrial workers who were employed in 11 kibbutzim. Based on kibbutz ideology, it was hypothesized—and the results confirmed—that kibbutz industrial workers would place significantly more importance on self-realization values (that is egalitarian, humanitarian, aesthetic, and intellectual values) than on aggrandizement values (that is, prestige, power, and wealth). On the other hand, Ronen found that the urban workers valued aggrandizement factors significantly more than did the kibbutz members.

In a comparative study involving commitment to work in six industrialized countries, E. Yuchtman-Yaar (1984) found that Israeli workers were highly committed to work and actually attained the highest scores. The order of work commitment in the rest of the countries was, going from high to low, as follows: United States, United Kingdom, Sweden, and West Germany. (Japan, the sixth country in this project, did not have data for this item.) No differences were found between men and women regarding commitment to work. Differences were recorded between white-collar and blue-collar workers, with the former expressing higher commitment. Finally, Yuchtman-Yaar noted that younger workers were less committed to work than were the older cohorts.

E. Krau (1984), who also studied commitment, compared the work commitment of new immigrants (resident in the country about one year) with that of "old-time" white-collar employees and a group of executives. He argued that one of the ways in which immigrants cope with the crisis of immigration is through their high work commitment. This commitment is apparent in their high work centrality, high work values, job involvement, and in their demonstrating a positive attitude toward figures of authority in the workplace. For Krau, obtaining a good socio-economic status is linked to high work commitment, and "the importance of work is capital and immediate."

High work centrality was found by N. Shefi (1986) in a study of the meaning of work among registered nurses employed in hospitals. The principal meaning of their work pattern was that of high work centrality related to extrinsic orientation, including societal norms of obligations and entitlements and an identification with work through both the organization and the profession. The nurses' twofold identification with their work was a kind of Cosmo/Local orientation (that is simultaneously being both cosmopolitan and local), which enabled the professionalization process to take place in the hospital setting.

B. Shamir (1986a) studied the consequences of employment commitment on the psychological impact of unemployment. Commitment to work was measured by the Protestant work ethic (Mirels & Garrett 1971) and the Work Involvement Scale (Kanungo 1982b). The Protestant work ethic was not found to moderate the relationship between employment status and psychological state. However, individuals with high work involvement tended to be more troubled by unemployment than were those less involved with work. The relative importance of work in the life space of the individual was also examined. A sample representing the adult Israeli population was asked to rank in importance three domains: work, leisure, and family (Shamir 1986b). Family was selected first, overwhelmingly by women (84 percent) and, to a lesser extent, by men (66 percent). Work ranked second (11 percent by women, 24 percent by men), and leisure third.

The Attitudes and Values of Youth

In a study of social/education factors and work values of high school students (in academic tracks only), V. Anavi (1982) found that students preferred intrinsic over extrinsic work values. Boys and girls rated work values significantly different, however, with the former favoring extrinsic values and the latter intrinsic values.

In a study on factors related to intergenerational agreement on work values, the younger generation (17-year-olds) was shown to be less committed to traditional work values than were their parents (Enav 1984). In addition, in the process of socialization, young people hold work values more similar to those of their peers than those of their parents. D. Enav (1984) concluded that the home atmosphere does not seem to generate an agreement on work values.

Finally Mannheim (1988) attempted to evaluate the extent to which adolescents' work values are affected by parental work values. She found that parental values and work attitudes, in addition to several demographic variables, explain only a small amount of the variance in adolescents' work values. On the whole, the attitudes and work values of parents have almost no effect on the attitudes of their children, except for attitudes toward earnings.

Research Findings on the Lottery Question

One of the first studies in Israel on attitudes to work was conducted by L. Adar and C. Adler (1965). They investigated the values given to various aspects of life (for example, family, education, social, work) by 533 eighth-grade students, mainly new immigrants from Islamic countries in North Africa and the Middle East. The fathers of these students were mostly unskilled laborers (only 1 percent were professionals). Six other eighth-grade classes, consisting of students who were Israeli-born and of Western origin, comprised a control group. Twenty percent of the fathers of the control-group students were professionals. One of the questions in this investigation was the classic "lottery question": "A young man has won a lottery and now has a considerable sum of money, sufficient for the rest of his life. Should he stop working? Why?" The possible answers and the distribution of responses follow:

Lottery Question Answer:		Students of:		
		Islamic Origin	Israeli & Western Origin	Control Group
1)	He should continue to work because -			
	a. His money will be exhausted	34.9	34.4	27.7
	b. Idleness breeds degeneration or crime	21.9	34.3	42.6
	c. Idleness and sin weaken the body	17.2	11.2	8.4
	d. Work is more interesting, idleness is dull	7.5	8.4	15.3
	e. Miscellaneous	12.3	10.3	5.7
2)	There is nothing wrong in his stopping work	6.2	1.4	0.4

It can clearly be seen from these data that very few students (and these mostly of Middle Eastern and North African origin) think that the young man should stop working altogether. In their responses, the majority of the research group suggested that he should go back to work because the money won in the lottery will be exhausted, whereas the control group pointed mostly to the fact that "idleness breeds degeneration or crime." It should be noted that a similar distribution of answers was also received from the parents of these students.

Using a sample of males employed in the four largest cities of the country, B. Mannheim and J. Rein (1981) employed the lottery question on different age groups to examine relationships between work centrality and the desire to quit working. Their main findings were as follows:

- Of the total sample, 85.2 percent would continue to work even after winning a substantial sum in the lottery.
- Age did not influence work centrality.
- A linear relationship existed between age and the desire to retire from work: in the total sample, 6 percent wanted to stop in the youngest (20–29 years) age group, but 26 percent in the oldest (60+ years) age group.

The same type of analysis, but by occupational categories (Mannheim & Rein 1975), revealed that this age-retire relationship appeared to be statistically significant only in the blue-collar category (that is, among construction workers, quarriers, miners, artisans, and production workers). In other findings, work centrality and the wish to stop working were negatively related for all but the 50–60 age group. In the younger group (ages 30–40) the significant factors affecting work centrality were high general job satisfaction and expected improvement of reward ($R^2 = .18$); whereas for the oldest group (ages 60+), intrinsic reward, low role ambiguity, high education, and career stability were the main factors influencing work centrality ($R^2 = .31$).

In Shefi's (1986) sample of registered nurses, mostly females, 96.5 percent indicated a wish to continue working.

Finally, Shamir (1986b) examined responses to a lottery question presented to various samples in Israeli society. He noted a consistent reply, ranging between 83 and 88 percent of all respondents, of wanting to continue working regardless of economic need.

Importance of Work Goals/Work Outcomes

In a study of the work motivation of engineers and scientists in industry ($n = 144$), M. Erez and Y. Rim (1975) asked respondents to rank-order work incentives (outcomes). The most important outcomes of work were ordered as follows: participation in decision making, responsibility, and accomplishment of professional knowledge. An examination of the local versus cosmopolitan orientation of this population (Erez 1974) showed that a professional worker with a high commitment to work prefers work outcomes supporting both orientations. Results also showed that work commitment is related negatively to expressive work outcomes.

Rim (1977) investigated the importance of work functions in relation to a Protestant ethic orientation (measured through Blood's [1969] Protestant Ethic Scale). He found that men with a high Protestant ethic propensity mostly preferred self-realization and intrinsic work satisfaction work functions. Men low on the Protestant work ethic scale also preferred self-realization, but they ranked as second the social contact work function. The latter was also selected by women who were high on the Protestant work ethic scale. Women with low Protestant work ethic values assigned equal importance to self-realization and security.

Z. Shapira (1983) examined the determinants of work values among industrial workers employed in electronics and military industries. The S. Wollack et al. (1971) Survey of Work Values was employed to measure general work values. Although Shapira reported differences between groups, these were not significant in a practical sense, and all workers responded basically in a similar fashion, emphasizing the intrinsic more than the extrinsic aspects of work. Out of six, the three work values selected most were (1) "pride in work" from doing a job well; (2) "activity preference" or a preference for keeping oneself busy and active on a job; and (3) "job involvement," or the degree to which one takes an active interest in co-workers and company.

D. Elizur (1984) conducted a study of two independent samples of the adult urban Israeli population. The ranking of work outcomes (work goals) revealed that in 1979 ($n = 489$) pay, security, and advancement were deemed the most important; in other words, mainly instrumental items. The 1980 ($n = 546$) sample results showed a different emphasis, mainly on expressive facets, in the following order: interesting work, responsibility, and recognition for doing a good job.

Lastly, in an attempt to discover the work goals that Israelis seek from working, Yuchtman-Yaar (1984) presented three alternative goals to a sample of Israeli workers and asked them to select only one. A majority, 54 percent, chose the option of having to "work to make a living and survive" (an economic goal). A further 26 percent selected "work to improve their standard of living and advance" (an economic/instrumental goal). Finally, only 17 percent replied that their most important work goal was "to develop themselves as persons." Men clearly differed from women with regard to their work goals: 65 percent of the men selected "make a living," whereas only 36 percent of the women did so, although they, too, gave this alternative the highest percentage. Similarly, the "make a living" goal was significantly more important for the blue-collar occupations than for white-collar employees. A trend was observed regarding age. "Make a living," which was selected first by all age categories, became more important with advancing age. A reverse trend was noted for the self-development alternative, which was selected as the least important work goal by all ages but was relatively more important among the younger workers.

MEANING OF WORK IN THE KIBBUTZ

The essence of work in the kibbutz is similar to what is found in other societies in that people exert physical and mental effort in order to obtain the means to satisfy their needs; however, the social organization of work is unique in kibbutz society. It is based on democratic foundations, with equal say for all members on work planning and the division of labor within their agricultural or industrial branch (Rosner 1960). The main role of the branch leader or coordinator (who is selected on a rotational basis) is to carry out decisions reached democratically. Kibbutz members do not receive differential economic compensation for their work. Hence, it was found that the most important rewards in the kibbutz motivational system were relational rewards, that is, identification with the work itself or with the values of the kibbutz (Cohen 1963, Rosner 1963, Shepher 1968).

M. Rosner (1980) found the value of work to be a central element in the kibbutz. As in the Zionist movement in general, the founders of the kibbutz had placed priority on physical, agricultural, and productive work. This spirit is still alive in most kibbutzim. According to Rosner, the concept of work draws from humanist and socialist values, which have to do with "equality of labor, aspirations toward a rounded individual and resistance to narrow professionalism."

In examining the centrality of work in the life of older kibbutz members, U. Leviatan (1980) conducted a secondary analysis of data collected from various studies of the kibbutz movement, mainly studies of the industrialization process in the kibbutz and of the "second generation" in the kibbutz. The data revealed that older kibbutz members were occupied in jobs similar to those of young people (for example, production and services), that they worked voluntarily more hours than were required of them, and that the role of work was the most important and most highly esteemed activity in their lives.

Leviatan's 1975 study demonstrated, in addition, the importance of work to older kibbutz members. The official policy of the kibbutz movement states that working hours are to be reduced with advancing age (thus, seven hours a day for men 50 years of age, six hours for those 55, five hours for those 60 years, four hours for those 65; and from age 70, work is optional). Data from one kibbutz showed that 119 members aged 60 and over worked more than the recommended norm, in fact contributing 65 percent more than the norm for their respective ages.

Another study (Rosner et al. 1978) showed that when older kibbutz members were asked to select from a list of statements about work- and nonwork-related activities, the most favored choice was that of the "devoted worker." Work, it was also reported, is a source of more enjoyment for the older members than is any other activity. Leviatan (1980), also, found that the role of work is more central in affecting the well-being of the older kibbutz member than that of the younger. One further example of the centrality of work comes from a study (Leviatan, Am-Ad & Adar 1982) in which 89 percent of the respondents viewed the domain of work as important or very important in their lives. This percentage was higher than that for any of the other life domains (79 percent for family, 73 percent for leisure activities, 54 percent for social relations). In addition, 42 percent opposed the possibility of making work optional at any age. When "general satisfaction with life" was regressed on measures of "satisfaction" with different life domains, the work domain explained about 10 percent of the total variance, and so the work domain was stronger in its explanatory power than was the family domain (9 percent), social status (9 percent), or social relations (3 percent).

Based on studies of work centrality for the older members of the Kibbutz movement, Leviatan (1975) concluded that work was the most important aspect of life for older male members, but not for older females. In fact, work was found to be less important for kibbutz women of all ages than for kibbutz men. Additional support for this finding came in a study of work and education in the kibbutz, in which Y. Ben-David (1975) asked a sample representing two generations in the kibbutz society ("parents," $n = 405$; and "children," $n = 917$) to rank six central roles/activities in their lives. For both samples, work and family were the most important roles; learning, public activities, hobbies, and sports were ranked much lower. In both groups, too, men thought that work was the most important role, whereas women valued the family more than any other activity (work was ranked second by women). Ben-David thought that the importance of work in the kibbutz was probably affected by the existence of competing alternatives and also by the extent to which work can provide needs, goals, and aspirations in relation to other roles.

Finally, differences between men and women regarding work were also found by U. Leviatan's 1976 study of the work sphere in the lives of women in the kibbutz. In comparing the sexes, he concluded that the domain of work was of relatively low centrality for both old and young women alike (Leviatan 1980).

The role of work in the kibbutz is not stable, and it seems to take on different meanings at different transition periods in the development of the kibbutz movement. Ben-David (1975) examined kibbutz work retrospectively and defined four stages in relation to its role:

1. Work as a way to achieve national reformation and social and economic revolution. This role held a key place in the value system of the founders of the kibbutz movement. Emphasis was placed on manual work, which contributed a great deal to the subsequent economic development of the kibbutzim (Rosner 1982).

2. Work as a moral concern in one's existence and in the interrelationships of people. This role originated in such humanist and socialist values as the equal value of all forms of labor (manual, skilled, services, and so on), equality of human skills, and opposition to narrow professionalism (Rosner 1982).

3. Work as a source of economic resources for the well-being and quality of life of kibbutz members.

4. Work as an individual's profession and as a means of self-actualization and personal development. Rosner (1982) argued that the aspirations of individual kibbutz members to be engaged in work, which enables them to self-actualize and develop their abilities, are strengthened through the collective ideology of the kibbutz economic system.

Ben-David (1975) posited that, regardless of the changes that have occurred in the emphasis given to each of these roles, all four have continued to exist and have always served as the value basis for determining the type of work for kibbutz members.

This chapter has examined the meaning of work in Israel through the ages. The portrayal of the role of work that has emerged from this review is generally one of high importance and centrality. At different periods in time, work seems to have been a central focus of attention for Jews/Israelis, a norm that has had an effect on other important life values and attitudes and has shaped generations of workers in Israel. In light of this historical perspective, it would be of particular interest to examine the work values and attitudes of Israelis in the 1980s.

3

Macro Socio-Economic Environment

Before we can discuss work attitudes in modern Israel, background information is needed concerning the status of social and economic conditions as well as the country's system of industrial relations. This chapter will familiarize the reader with the general situation in Israel during the early 1980s, the period during which the data for this book were collected. This will enable the reader to put in perspective the issues and findings to be discussed in later chapters, thereby understanding better the phenomena portrayed.

ISRAELI SOCIETY, POLITICS, AND ECONOMY

Social Issues

Israel is a new state. The horror of World War II, in which 6 million Jews perished in the Nazi Holocaust, was a catalyst of its creation in 1948. Many of its features, with no parallel in other nations, serve to make Israel a distinct society. An examination of these features will reveal some of the characteristics of Israeli society as well as put in perspective some of its principal concerns.

One phenomenon in the history of Israel is its absorption within a relatively short period of a mass immigration, with migrants coming from almost every country in the world. As a result, the country's population grew from over 650,000 Jews in 1948 to more than 4 million today. Between 1948 and 1968 alone, the population quadrupled, creating tremendous difficulties for the state. It had to provide its new citizens with shelter and jobs, overcome language and social differences, and absorb and integrate the migrants into a newly created society.

The mass immigration of individuals from extremely diverse ethnic and cultural backgrounds led to a situation still considered to be the most central internal problem of Israeli society (Eisenstadt 1986): "Oriental" immigrants (Sephardic Jews), hailing mainly from Moslem countries in Asia and Africa, have seemingly not become fully integrated into Israeli society. Ashkenazic Jews, who are of European and American descent, comprised the vast bulk of settlers who arrived prior to the establishment of the Israeli state; they also formed the majority of newcomers in the first years of the new state. The dominant ideology of these immigrants was pluralistic and egalitarian, and they became the elite of the country. Oriental Jews, on the other hand, arrived in the 1950s from societies that were basically feudalistic, patriarchal traditional, and underdeveloped technologically. This background may account substantially for their failure, and for that of their Israeli-born children, to do as well as Jews originating from Europe or America (Weller 1974). E. Yuchtman-Yaar and M. Semyonov (1979) clearly demonstrated that the social, economic, and political conditions of Afro-Asian Jews in Israel are inferior to those of the European-American Jews. As for the work situation, Ashkenazic Jews are also greatly overrepresented in the more prestigious occupations and in the better-paid job categories (*Statistical Abstract of Israel* 1982).

If the disparities between Jews of European-American origin and Jews of Afro-Asian origin may be considered Israel's foremost internal problem, the conflict between religious and secular elements within society may be regarded as its second most difficult issue (Weller 1974). The Jewish population of Israel may be divided roughly into two groups, religious (Orthodox) and secular (non-religious). Although the religious population is in a minority, with only about 17 percent of the population identifying itself as Orthodox (Ben-Meir & Kedem 1978), its influence in society is far greater than this percentage suggests. Religious political parties have taken part as a junior partner in every coalition government since 1948. As a result, many of their demands have been met by the various governments (for example, the banning of public transportation and most kinds of work on the Sabbath, the exemption of religious women and yeshiva [seminary] students from military service, the imposition of the strictures of *kashrut* [religious dietary laws] in public affairs). The Chief Rabbinate has been legally invested with complete authority over personal and family issues, such as marriage and divorce. Religious legislation based on *halacha* (biblical/talmudic law, or the Orthodox legal interpretation of it) affects all Israeli Jewish citizens, regardless of their religious orientation. Needless to say, many in the secular majority see themselves as being forced to behave in a manner that may conflict with their consciences or civil liberties. Hence, there is a constant tension between the two camps that sometimes prompts militant behavior on either side.

Finally, there is the basic problem of the physical survival of the state. Since 1948, Israel has been faced with external threats of annihilation by the Arab world in general, which has a combined population of over 100 million, compared to Israel's 4.5 million. (Only in the past decade has Egypt stepped out of this cycle of antagonism.) Since its establishment, Israel has fought five major wars and two long wars of attrition, and it has been involved in a ceaseless chain of hostilities and "small wars." As a consequence, the continuous state of war with their Arab neighbors is a primary concern of Israelis. In addition, terrorist activity inside the country adds to the sense of insecurity. The possibility of another holocaust is seen by many to hover as a constant threat. The cost of the wars—in human as well as economic terms—and the maintenance of a strong, well-equipped military put a tremendous burden upon Israeli society.

Compulsory military service (three years for men and two for women between the ages of 18 and 21), an average of one month a year of reserve duty for men until age 55, and long periods of tension exert an emotional, often stressful impact on Israeli citizens (Greenberg 1979) as well as disrupt economic activities.

Political Situation

Israel is a parliamentary democracy consisting of legislative, executive, and judicial branches. The Knesset, Israel's legislature, is elected every four years on a proportional representation basis. Because no single political party has ever obtained a robust majority in any election, Israel has always been ruled by coalition governments. The two major political blocs are the Labor Alignment and the Likud. An important political event occurred in the 1977 elections when, for the first time, Labor and its allies failed to form the largest bloc and thus found themselves out of the government for the first time since the establishment of the state. In the 1984 elections, neither of the two major blocs could muster a majority, which led to a grand coalition, or so-called unity government, that included both major parties.

The Economy

From 1948 to 1973 Israel's economy grew at the rapid rate of 10 percent a year. After 1973, as a result of the Yom Kippur War and the world economic recession of the 1970s, the country's economic growth slowed down. In 1978–79, it was 5 percent, falling to 3.2 percent in 1980–81 and 1.2 percent in 1982–83 (*Facts* 1985).

Israel's gross domestic product (GDP) consists, in round terms, of the business sector (70 percent), ownership of dwellings (10 percent), and the services of general government and private nonprofit-making institutions (20 percent). The private sector's share of the GDP is 50 percent, that of the cooperative Histadrut (General Federation of Labor) 20 percent, and that of the public sector 30 percent. These figures include both business activities and general services (*Facts* 1985). Business activities are carried out by large companies (by Israeli standards), by groups controlled by investment holding companies, and by a multitude of small firms.

The private sector is active mainly in industry, commerce, and construction. In such branches as textiles and diamond polishing, firms are almost exclusively privately owned; whereas in agriculture, the private sector has only a 15 percent share of overall production in this area. The cooperative sector, amalgamated within the framework of the Hevrat Ha-Ovdim holding company (the industrial and economic sector of the Histadrut), consists of various types of companies and cooperative organizations that are active in industry, agriculture, construction, banking, insurance, trade (wholesale and retail), transportation, and publishing.

The public sector includes enterprises owned by the state, local authorities, and national institutions. Traditional industrial branches include food processing, textiles and fashion, furniture, fertilizers, pesticides, pharmaceuticals, chemicals, rubber, plastics, metal products, and military industries. The highest growth rates are in those sectors that are capital intensive and require sophisticated production techniques as well as considerable investment in research and development (*Facts* 1985).

Industry

Since 1967 Israel's economy has been rapidly transformed into a modern industrial system whose output employs some of the more sophisticated production processes in the world today. In the main, industry has concentrated on manufactured products with high added values, in view of the country's lack of most basic raw materials. Almost 25 percent of the labor force is employed in industry, and manufacturing accounts for 20 percent of the GNP (*Statistical Abstract of Israel* 1985). Table 3.1 contains details of the GNP for the years 1950 through 1983.

The industrial sector is dynamic and widely diversified, producing for both domestic consumption and export. Israel has developed high-technology products based on its own scientific creativity and technical innovation and is currently a leader in the fields of medical electronics, agrotechnology, telecommunications, chemicals products, solar energy, and computer hardware. Industrial enterprises controlled by the public sector account for about 15 percent of the total industrial output. Government-owned enterprises are particularly prominent in such areas

Table 3.1
Gross National Product in Israel for the Years 1950–1983

Year	GNP at constant prices: ($ billion)	GNP per capita constant prices
1950	2.2	$1,710
1960	6.0	$2,850
1970	13.6	$4,580
1980	22.6	$5,570
1983	23.8	$5,824
Annual Compounded Real Growth Rate	7.5%	3.8%

Source: Statistical Abstract of Israel, 1985.

Table 3.2
Index of Industrial Production in Israel for the Years 1970 and 1982
(1968 = 100)

Industries	Industrial Production		Average Yearly Growth Rate
	1970	1982	
Total	126.8	226.2	7.6
Electrical &			
Electronics Equipment	159.0	387.6	12.9
Transport Equipment	164.0	355.0	12.0
Chemical & Oil Products	129.0	260.0	9.3
Rubber & Plastics Products	138.0	226.0	8.5
Clothing and Fashion	126.0	252.0	8.2
Metal Products	139.0	238.7	8.0
Food, Beverages, Tobacco	114.0	235.2	7.0
Textiles	116.0	201.8	5.9
Diamonds	102.0	171.4	5.3
Non-Metallic Minerals	126.0	156.1	4.3

Source: Facts about Israel, 1985.

as mining, heavy chemicals, transportation (including airlines), utilities, and military and aircraft industries (*Facts* 1985). For an index of industrial production, see Table 3.2.

Domestic Consumption

Domestic consumption in Israel has increased over the years and is reflected in the rise in the country's overall standard of living. (Table 3.3 shows households' possession of durable goods.) Government expenditures on defense and essential social services have also grown, but attempts to reduce such expenditures are limited by three requirements of crucial importance: maintaining na-

Table 3.3
Percentage of All Households Possessing Durable Goods

Selected Items	1970	1981
Refrigerators	89%	99%
Food Mixers	28%	56%
Washing Machines	16%	43%
Telephones	35%	66%
Air Conditioners	5%	15%
T.V. Sets	50%	91%
Private Cars	15%	33%

Source: Statistical Abstract of Israel, 1982.

tional security, encouraging immigration, and avoiding unemployment in a society based on the principles of a welfare state. Prior to the 1973 Yom Kippur War, inflation was relatively low. Thereafter increased fuel prices and heavier defense costs (some 25 percent of the GNP) led to a rapidly spiraling inflation, which reached over 100 percent in 1979 and about 139 percent in 1981 (*Statistical Abstract of Israel* 1982). Israel's system of linking wages and salaries to the consumer price index, as well as other economic factors, helped alleviate a good part of the impact of this inflation on the individual.

Labor Force Characteristics

Israel's civilian labor force numbered 1,348,500 workers in 1981 (*Statistical Abstract of Israel* 1982). The relatively young age of the country's population (one third are under the age of 14) (*Facts* 1985) ensures the continued growth of the labor force, even as the population both increases and matures (the percentage of workers has experienced an annual growth of about 7 percent since 1949; see Rosenstein 1981). The participation of women in most capacities throughout the economy has been rising steadily, reaching 36.1 percent of all workers in 1981 (*Statistical Abstract of Israel* 1982). Since 1973 the number of men and women in academic, professional, and technical occupations has grown in percentage as well as absolutely, as have those in sales, clerical, and managerial positions. At the same time there has been a decrease in such occupations as service workers and both skilled and unskilled workers in industry, building, and agriculture. A relatively high percentage of the workers in most occupations tend to remain employed in the same job for ten years or more (*Statistical Abstract of Israel* 1982). In the mid–1980s approximately 23 percent of the labor force was employed in industry, 5.5 percent in agriculture, and the rest in various public and private services and utilities (*Statistical Abstract of Israel* 1985). Unemployment levels held steady, being around 4 percent a year from 1974 to 1983.

INDUSTRIAL RELATIONS SYSTEM

Israeli labor relations are based on a system of collective agreements embodied in labor contracts and given legal recognition by the Collective Agreement Law (1957). These agreements, which are signed by members of the Employers' Association, on the one hand, and representatives of the Histadrut trade union, on the other, lay down the employee's working conditions: salaries, social benefits, working hours, shifts, and labor relations. In addition, they cover rules of conduct and discipline, engagement of staff, termination of employment, negotiation procedures, the settlement of disputes, and the rights and obligations of the two parties. Collective agreements may be "special," applying to a particular enterprise, or "general," applying to the whole or part of the country or to a specific type of work. Collective agreements are registered by the chief labor relations officer at the Ministry of Labor. The minister is empowered to order extending the application of the general collective agreement to employees or employers who are not organized in a trade union or the Employers' Association.

The industrial relations system is, therefore, tripartite, consisting of workers and their unions, employers and their association, and the government.

The Histadrut

The Histadrut (General Federation of Labor) represents more than 80 percent of the salaried workers in Israel (Rosenstein 1984). One important characteristic of this federation is its wide organizational basis, as workers without any professional or sectoral common denominator may be included under its umbrella. This wide basis enables the Histadrut to unite most of the country's workers and to create a unified central body that includes nearly every trade union. The achievements of the Histadrut and its constituent trade unions also affect workers who are not members of the union because of an extension order, which enables the minister of labor to extend the rights of workers to those not included in the agreement. Another characteristic of the Histadrut is that it is an alliance of political parties and is run according to interpartisan agreements. Representatives are elected to the Histadrut Central Committee on the basis of a proportional political system. In 1984 over 70 percent of valid votes cast were given to the Labor bloc in the Histadrut. The membership itself is rather weak, since a member of the Histadrut does not have to belong to any specific trade union. It is also possible to be a member of several unions simultaneously.

Apart from labor federation, being a large-scale trade union, the Histadrut undertakes various national tasks, such as settlement, housing, education, and productivity. Membership in the Histadrut provides the worker with comprehensive health insurance through its health fund and with mutual aid. The Histadrut operates a large network of social and cultural services, including day-care centers, rest and recreation facilities, and old-age homes. From this brief sketch, it may be surmised that the Histadrut is very powerful economically and politically, this power enabling it to participate in major national economic decisions.

The Trade Union Department of the Histadrut, consisting of approximately 40 national unions, both of blue- and of white-collar employees (Bartal 1978), is the organizational arm of the labor federation. Usually the Trade Union Department and the Employers' Association conclude the agreements negotiated by any individual national union and the corresponding section of the employers' organization.

In addition to being very powerful on the labor front, the Histadrut is itself also a major entrepreneur and owner of industry. Hevrat Ha-Ovdim is the central organization for all economic enterprises owned by or affiliated with the Histadrut. This holding company is at present made up of five components, whose contribution to the net product of the economy is as follows, in descending scale: (1) collective and cooperative settlements—kibbutzim and moshavim; (2) wholly

and partially owned enterprises (known as the Institutional Economy); (3) manufacturing, transportation, and service cooperatives; (4) marketing and consumer
associations; (5) Histadrut nonprofit-making organizations. The main influence
of Hevrat Ha-Ovdim is evident in the Institutional Economy, which is directly
under its control. The various forms of worker participation adopted by the
Histadrut have been introduced into enterprises belonging to the Institutional
Economy (Rosenstein 1981).

Employers

Three sectors exist in the Israeli economy: private, state, and labor (Histadrut).
The private sector, organized through a roof organization, the Coordinative
Chamber of Economic Organizations, encompasses about 80 percent of Israel's
industry and employs about 70 percent of all factory workers. The chamber,
which was founded in 1966, includes industrialists and merchants in most of the
main sectors in the economy, but not all of them. This weakens it somewhat.
As the representative of the private sector, it negotiates framework skeleton
agreements with the Trade Union Department of the Histadrut (Shirom 1983).

Another major employer in the Israeli economy is the Histadrut itself, working
through Hevrat Ha-Ovdim, the central organization for all economic undertakings
owned by or affiliated with the labor federation. In the early 1980s it employed
about 22 percent of the labor force in Israel (Shirom 1983).

The government is the third major employer, with about 40 percent of the
salaried labor force (Shirom 1983). Its interests are expressed through its representatives on the boards of directors of state-owned companies. Since the
creation of the state, the government has tried to give priority to increasing
productivity and advancing industrialization. Until 1977 the Labor party dominated both the government and the Histadrut. At the same time successive Labor
governments promoted the private sector and enhanced a strong Employers'
Association (Shirom 1983).

The Government

The participation and influence of the government in Israeli labor relations
are intensive and pervasive. Sixty percent of the capital in the Israeli economy
comes from the government and is directed through the budget. The government
is responsible for creating economic management, the capital market, preventing
unemployment, increasing productivity levels, creating a transportation base,
and providing professional education and national security. As an employer, the
government negotiates with representatives of the public sector. Government
influence is also exerted through extensive labor legislation as well as the use
of arbitration and mediation procedures and labor courts for settling labor disputes. Perhaps the most important way the government makes its influence felt
is through its economic policy and the economic actions it takes. The need for

capital and the deficit in the country's balance of payments, along with constant levels of high inflation, have required the government to try to prevent wages from rising, on the one hand, and to increase taxation, on the other. This situation naturally creates unrest in industrial relations both on the part of employees and on the part of the employers (Galin & Harel 1978).

Labor Disputes

Unrestful industrial relations and tense work relationships are usually fomented at the plant level; however, labor disputes also have their origin in a country's socio-political and economic systems. The cause of most strikes is economic in nature, related to the economic cycle, the level of economic prosperity, changes in the levels of employment, and the gap between the workers' desires for benefits and the actual benefits they receive (Shirom 1983).

Statistics relating to labor disputes and strike activities in Israel should be compared with similar figures for other countries. However, since it is impractical to compare raw statistical data from various countries because of differences in their size and in other socio-economic factors, two relative measures have been utilized to effect the comparison (see Bar-Tzuri & Batzri 1985). The first is a measure of tendency to strike. This consists of (1) the number of strike days lost per 1,000 salaried employees $\left(\dfrac{\text{working days}}{\text{per 1000 employees}}\right)$, (2) the number of strikers relative to 1,000 salaried employees $\left(\dfrac{\text{strikers}}{\text{per 1000 employees}}\right)$, and (3) the number of strikes relative to 100,000 salaried employees $\left(\dfrac{\text{strikes}}{\text{per 100,000 employees}}\right)$. A second general measure is that of "strike intensity." This involves (1) the number of strike days lost relative to the number of employees taking part in strikes $\left(\dfrac{\text{work days}}{\text{strikers}}\right)$, (2) strike days lost relative to the number of strikes $\left(\dfrac{\text{work days}}{\text{strikes}}\right)$, and (3) the mean participation rate of strikers in a single strike $\left(\dfrac{\text{strikers}}{\text{strikes}}\right)$.

Table 3.4 presents data on "tendency to strike" in the major industrial countries, based on the ILO *Year Book of Labor Statistics* (1983) for the year 1981. All three components of the "tendency to strike" measure and a composite of the three place Israel relatively high on this measure. As for "strike intensity," data on this measure is given in Table 3.5. Again, Israel ranks relatively high in comparison to other industrialized countries. The pattern of strikes in Israel shows that the work stoppages tend to be relatively short but include relatively large numbers of participants.

Table 3.4
Tendency to Strike According to Various Criteria and Its Rankings in Various Countries in 1981

Country	Work days per 1000 employees	Ranking	Strikers per 1000 employees	Ranking	Strikes per 100,000 employees	Ranking
Australia	776.6	4	231.9	4	54.0	2
Canada	844.0	2	32.0	8	9.9	6
Denmark	287.7	6	23.6	10	4.1	9
Finland	356.7	5	265.0	3	86.0	1
France	84.4	10	18.6	11	13.8	5
Germany (W)	2.5	14	216.0	5	--	--
Israel	782.7	3	315.4	2	9.0	7
Italy	1,690.6	1	539.7	1	14.4	4
Japan	13.7	13	6.1	13	2.4	11
New Zealand	226.0	8	72.5	6	26.7	3
Norway	17.0	12	2.6	14	1.0	13
Sweden	53.8	11	25.5	9	1.7	12
Switzerland	--	--	--	--	--	--
UK	189.5	9	67.0	7	5.9	8
USA	247.0	7	10.8	12	2.6	10

Source: Bar-Tzuri, R., and Batzri, T. *Strikes in Israel for the Years 1974 -1984*, 1985.

Table 3.5
Strike Intensity and Its Ranking in Various Countries in 1981

Country	Work days Strikers	Rank	Work days Strikes	Rank	Strikers Strikes	Rank
Australia	3.349	6	1.438	9	0.429	6
Canada	26.225	1	8.471	3	0.323	8
Denmark	17.799	3	6.930	4	0.568	5
Finland	1.348	13	0.414	13	0.307	9
France	4.546	5	0.612	11	0.134	13
Germany (W)	0.230	15	na	na	na	na
Israel	2.481	10	8.692	2	3.503	2
Italy	3.263	7	4.776	5	3.732	1
Japan	2.240	11	0.579	12	0.258	11
New Zealand	3.123	8	0.848	10	0.271	10
Norway	6.580	4	1.662	8	0.252	12
Sweden	2.108	12	3.075	7	1.458	3
Switzerland	1.000	14	0.015	14	0.015	14
UK	2.820	9	3.188	6	1.094	4
USA	22.881	2	9.630	1	0.420	7

Source: Bar-Tzuri, R., and Batzri, T. *Strikes in Israel for the Years 1974-1984*, 1985.

Space limitations preclude presentation of additional issues or a more thorough discussion of the socio-economic factors that have been included. Nonetheless, the issues raised here provide a framework for placing the findings that are recorded and analyzed in the succeeding chapters of this book.

4

Model and Concepts of the Meaning of Work

A review of the literature reveals that a well-articulated theory of the meaning of work, that is, one with transsituational validity, including a multilevel perspective and the capability of yielding clearcut policy implications, is not yet available. Based on a conceptually sound understanding of the meaning of work itself, such a model would be able to specify the critical antecedents of consequences of the central domains. In the absence of any such generally accepted theory, it would seem unwise to allow any one theoretical position to specify all the variables measured. Within these limits the model presented in this chapter is basically heuristic in nature. It is based on the conception that the meaning of work is determined by the choices and experiences of individuals and by the organizational and environmental contexts in which they work and live.

The model presented in Figure 4.1 shows the major variable sets and the most direct and straightforward relationships initially considered to be of primary importance in the study of the meaning of work. The arrows in the model indicate that an attempt will be made to determine the extent to which variables of one set explain in a statistical sense variables of another set. A causal interpretation of such findings would, of course, have to take into account the probable development sequence of those variables studied in the lives of individuals as well as the likely possibility that variable complexes may be interlinked in a complex manner.

The heuristic model specifies those levels at which variables are chosen and

This study uses a model and conceptual framework identical to that employed in the International Meaning of Work project (developed jointly by the international research team, of which the present author was a member). Therefore, this chapter was adopted from MOW-International Research Team, *The Meaning of Working* (1987).

Figure 4.1
Heuristic Research Model of the Meaning of Working

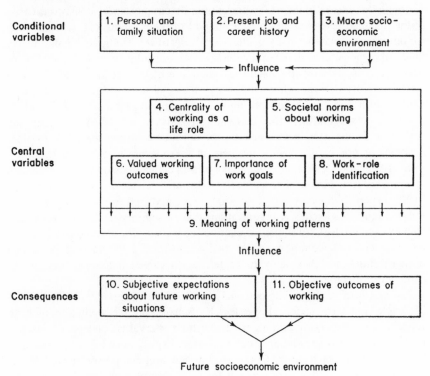

operationalized: conditional variables (antecedents); central domains (meaning of work); and consequences.

The chapter focuses on the conceptualization of these three levels, and the discussion follows the organization of the model as presented in Figure 4.1.

CONDITIONAL VARIABLES (ANTECEDENTS OF THE MEANING OF WORK)

Conditional or antecedent variables are all those background variables that may influence the central MOW variables. These may be divided into three broad categories:

1. Personal circumstances, including family situation, age and birth cohort, sex, and education.
2. Present job and career state, including job characteristics, work schedule, aggravated work conditions, turbulent careers and unemployment, and career progress.
3. Macro socio-economic environment.

Personal Circumstances

Family Situation. In this study current family circumstances consist primarily of the financial responsibility for the support of others. Financial responsibility for others may relate to many of the MOW constructs. On the one hand, heavy financial responsibility may require that a person substitute (that is, choose) work over family as a major life sphere and therefore may correlate negatively with work centrality. On the other hand, heavy financial responsibility may increase work identification and valuation, thus contributing to perceptions of the self as a worthy person and therefore correlating positively with work centrality and obligation norms. (Obligation denotes the norm of contributions made to organizations and/or society, while entitlement norm refers to one's opportunities from organization and/or society. Both are fully elaborated on in the next section of this chapter.) Financial responsibility can also relate to entitlement norms. These responsibilities are a type of need frequently used to justify and to legitimate claims on societies or organizations that provide for financial support and employment security for modes of distributive justice. These responsibilities are also one criterion commonly used to determine need for support. Financial responsibilities are also likely to be related to valued outcomes from work, particularly income.

Age and Birth Cohort. The personal characteristic of age includes individual life cycle and birth cohort properties. K. Schaie's (1965) definition of birth cohort as members born within a particular time interval is conceptually useful. Both chronological age and birth cohort suggest explanations for work meanings that complement each other. Chronological age suggests person-related developmental processes that may account for relationships with MOW constructs. Birth order cohorts recognize contextual or ecological events such as wars, major economic conditions, or major legal and social trends. These events related to birth order cohorts can affect work socialization and learning, or they can influence societal dialectic and, as a result, social policy affecting work.

Typically, influences related to chronological age and birth order cohort are intermingled in explanations of age differences in the meaning of work. As an example, C. Hayashi, and others (1977) use maturational explanations to account for age differences in work centrality and societal norms among the Japanese. But they also "explain" these differences by contrasting the meaning of work between people born prior to World War II, during the postwar reconstruction period, and subsequent to the economic boom of the early 1960s. Similarly, G. Trommsdorff (1983) uses both types of explanation in her comparison of value changes in Japan, the United States, and Europe. In the present research we recognize that age-related processes and cohort birth order–related events that shape or modify socialization and dialectical processes may clarify an observed relationship between age and MOW constructs.

Sex. Societally shaped socialization and dialectical processes (including those that differ for successive birth order cohorts) that operate prior to and during work experiences may help explain observed sex differences in the meaning of work. These processes include the general cultural values of a society (Psathas 1968; Trommsdorff 1983), the values of the family (Hall 1976; Foreign Press Center Japan 1977; Trommsdorff 1981), feminine role perceptions (Crawford 1978; Pharr 1977), and lack of self-confidence among women (Maccoby & Jacklin 1974). These processes and societal differences are reflected in the beliefs of adolescents that men should work while women should stay at home. In a survey conducted in Japan, approximately one third of adolescents rejected this belief, while in West Germany and the United States the respective figures for adolescents rejecting this belief were 58.7 percent and 71.4 percent (Youth Bureau 1978).

In Israel more than 36 percent of the labor force in the early 1980s consisted of women. The trend is for the proportion of women in the labor force to grow. It is expected that some differences between the sexes will be found regarding MOW constructs. These differences will likely vary in magnitude among different groups and in different birth order cohorts.

Education. Most well-designed national surveys regularly find a relationship between education and the values or beliefs of individuals irrespective of country. This is true even when other influences such as maturation, cohort, socio-economic background, and work experience are statistically controlled (Hayashi et al. 1977; Kohn & Schooler 1983; Youth Bureau 1978). Educational attainment, apart from providing high levels of technical competence, may relate to the meaning of work because it provides the opportunity for people to examine their beliefs and values more thoroughly and systematically. In addition, education encourages people to engage in such a process of enquiry and reinforces their efforts when they do. The process of learning that produces the greatest change appears to be both dialectical and experiential, where one's cognitive development and experiences confront one's values, beliefs, and norms (Murphy & Gilligan 1980; Rest 1979). Two consequences of this process of cognitive development are an increase in self-directedness orientation and an increased valuation of self-direction for self (Kohn & Schooler 1983). The self-directedness orientation is a latent belief that one has the personal capacity to take responsibility for one's actions and that society is so constituted as to make self-direction possible.

The opportunities for systematic reasoning provided by education may increase the capacity for self-directedness and lead to a higher valuation of self-directedness beliefs. These beliefs are, in turn, a central part of a person's cognitive restructuring, including the formation of different evaluative norms of fairness and social order. Similarly, the development of self-directedness beliefs during education may be one reason why education has been found to relate to preferences for task-dependent outcomes rather than to environmentally dependent outcomes, and for internal standards rather than externally mediated standards in national labor force studies (Lacy, Bokemeier & Shepard 1983). Thus, it may be concluded that the educationally evoked development of self-directedness changes valued working outcome preferences. The general increase in self-directedness resulting from education may also influence work centrality.

Present Job and Career State

Job Characteristics. From Marx (1932) and Weber (Gerth & Mills 1946) to
the present day, sociologists and psychologists have developed theories and have
sought to account for the influence of task characteristics and conditions on the
meaning of work. M. Kohn and C. Schooler's (1983) lengthy research on a
national sample in the United States provides one demonstration of the relationship between properties of jobs or occupations and the meaning of work. A
central concept in their research is occupational self-direction. This occurs when
people are relatively free from close supervision (that is, when they have some
autonomy and control over major task decisions), when they engage in complex
work requiring higher-order mental and interpersonal processes, and when they
work on nonrepetitive tasks that form a complete, integrated unit.

The theoretical guidance drawn from Kohn and Schooler's study is based on
the idea of reciprocal causation. Without occupational self-control (including
autonomy and decision making, variety and some freedom from routine, acquisition of new skills or knowledge), it may be increasingly difficult to develop
the higher levels of work identification and commitment that make work more
central to one's life. Similarly, an increasing presence of occupational self-control
is likely to increase the valuation of expressive task or occupation characteristics
and to decrease the valuation (at least relatively) of pay and comfort. Finally,
one would expect to find a relationship between increased personal control
through occupational self-direction and the societal norms of obligation and
norms of entitlement, although the magnitude of the relationship between these
job characteristics may be culture specific. It is possible that this relationship
will vary depending on whether individuals in a society view their inputs as
placing a demand on the organization or society to provide opportunities for
self-direction equally, or whether the individuals in a society view outcomes as
being distributed to everyone under a parity rule regardless of input.

In addition, individuals select themselves for jobs with particular levels of
self-direction partially because of their values, beliefs, and norms. Similarly, J.
Thompson (1968) suggested that organizations select individuals for jobs on a
continuum of their capacity and motivation for self-direction. While not examined
in the present study, this causal explanation is plausible and is widely documented
in research on work and organization socialization. Many of the findings of Kohn
and Schooler regarding reciprocal relationships between job properties and psychological properties or people may be generalized to countries other than the
United States (Hoff & Gruneisen 1978; Naoi & Schooler 1981).

Work Schedule. Between 20 and 30 percent of the workforce in industrial
societies work on shifts other than day shifts (Evans 1975). Further, people
working shifts other than the day shift tend to have certain characteristics in
common. They are employed primarily in blue-collar, lower white-collar, or
service occupations; they are younger, usually male, and less educated (Hedges
& Sekscenski 1979). Ethnic minorities tend to be overrepresented on the night
shift (typically 11 P.M. to 7 A.M.). Research indicates that shift work can have

widespread negative effects on the physical, psychological, and social well-being of individuals. It also indicates that these consequences may vary from community to community and from country to country. For instance, large metropolitan areas in the United States often have a lower percentage of shift workers than many European countries (Dunham 1977). The negative effects of shiftwork are also typically greater among urban workers in the United States than in Europe. However, national differences in relationships between work schedules and meaning of work do not appear to be as great in small towns, particularly those in which there is a higher percentage of shift workers.

In general, community characteristics in relationships between shift work and the meaning of work seem to depend on two considerations. The first comprises social sanctions (for example, the scheduling of work and nonwork social activities), so that the various roles individuals adopt are more in balance. In the second, individual values, beliefs, and norms are at least partly determined socially. Community and country differences in these work meanings may reflect broader cultural values, beliefs, and norms concerning shift work.

Aggravated Work Conditions. By aggravated work conditions we mean the physical and psychological demands of the job or work situation. In this concept are included work load demands (physical, mental), unsafe conditions, and unhealthy conditions. The demands arising from the load and threats to safety place the individual in a motivated or energized state of stress. When experienced over long periods of time, the person must constantly adapt and readjust to the work load demands and threats to personal well-being. H. Selye (1974) terms this lengthy adaptation process to work load demands and unsafe or unhealthy conditions ''distress.''

Poor safety or health conditions existing for long time periods in work situations are likely to influence several MOW variables. The stress from these conditions is likely to result in lower levels of work centrality and norms of obligation. Additionally, entitlement norms are likely to increase with increased stress conditions. Lastly, stress conditions are likely to increase relative preferences for money and comfort as valued working outcomes.

Finally, work load demands of jobs (physical, mental, consequences of mistakes) must be considered in conjunction with job self-direction (autonomy, variety, decision making) to discern their influence on the meaning of work. Following R. Karasek (1979), one would expect that jobs matched at high levels in self-direction and demands would be positively related to work centrality—a balance between obligation and entitlement norms and importance of intrinsic valued working outcomes. This expectation may be due to selection factors (self-organization, for instance) that place individuals in jobs based on their competence to exercise self-control over decisions, as well as to the rewards commensurate with these demands.

Turbulent Careers and Unemployment. Three career sources that influence the meaning of work are included in the present study: unemployment history, career turbulence, and career progress. Turbulence refers to a career characterized by a mixture of progress and decline or progressive decline. It is worth noting at this juncture that a significant history of unemployment and career turbulence are correlated notions (Hepworth 1980; Parnes & King 1977). P. Warr (1984) concluded that the career pattern for the unemployed person, therefore, may be one of further unemployment and movement down the occupational ladder. H. Wilensky (1961) suggested that careers characterized by unemployment and decline reflect a lack of functional relatedness between jobs or hierarchical status progression; he termed these "disorderly" careers.

Careers characterized by unemployment and turbulence can have several influences on the meaning of work. The material and psychological outcomes valued by people and derived from work—such as personal identity, money, task variety and use of skills and social contacts—are either removed through unemployment or obtained in diminished amounts through career turbulence. Theories of motivation suggest that economic factors such as pay would become more important, and that task variety and use of skills and social contact become less important with prolonged unemployment or career turbulence. Studies have indicated decreased social contacts by blue-collar workers who experience unemployment and turbulence (see Warr's 1984 review; Wilensky 1961).

Prolonged unemployment can reduce feelings and beliefs concerned with personal control, a notion that underlies both obligation and entitlement norms. Some evidence indicates that the unemployed endorse norms of entitlement, for example, that the government guarantee jobs for everybody (Rundquist & Sletto 1936). This endorsement is likely to be more acute when the causal attributes for unemployment are economic conditions including levels of unemployment, inadequate management, or other environmental factors beyond the individual's control. The endorsement of norms of obligation to society are also likely to be lower among those who experience unemployment for any prolonged period or who have turbulent careers.

Work centrality seems to act more as a mediator variable in the relationship between unemployment or career turbulence and societal norms or valued working outcomes. Several researchers (Stafford, Jackson & Banks 1980; Warr 1978) have found that the negative psychological effects of unemployment are greater for people with high work involvement. Some evidence indicates that for at least fairly prolonged periods of unemployment, work centrality does not decline (Warr & Jackson 1983). Studies also suggest that blue-collar workers, more than white-collar workers, and older workers are likely to experience more frequent and prolonged periods of unemployment and turbulence. Thus the levels of certain valued working outcomes, work goals, and societal norms for older workers or blue-collar workers with high work centrality may be particularly affected by unemployment.

Career Progress. Work careers characterized by progress are likely to be positively correlated with work centrality levels. Wilensky (1961) labeled these as "orderly careers," with the sequence of jobs being functionally related. This allowed for the acquisition of higher levels of skill, knowledge, and abilities, leading to increased status or prestige. Building on ideas like this, D. T. Hall

(1971) proposed a model of career subidentity development. In this model, identity refers to an individual's perception of self in relation to the environment, a view similar to properties of work centrality. Growth in career subidentity occurs as a result of socialization processes and features of tasks such as those included in Kohn and Schooler's (1983) concept of self-direction. Earlier jobs with these task properties are related to later jobs with higher levels of these properties, as well as to work values, beliefs, and norms. It is these features of careers that lead to an increase in the centrality of working as a part of the total identity (Hall 1971).

In summary, career theory suggests that there are important influences on work centrality. Individuals perceive that their careers have been marked by progress; there is an absence of unemployment; and work tasks are characterized by autonomy, variety, and a good match with skills. These career features are likely to relate positively to a valuation of intrinsic outcomes and negatively to a valuation of comfort. Finally, these career features are likely to relate positively to an increased balance between various societal norms.

Macro Socio-Economic Environment

Each of the variables concerning the social and economic environment may be distinctly related to the meaning of work. In addition, other societal factors not mentioned previously probably have an influence on the meaning of work. These include laws, the industrial relations system, labor force participation rates, the educational system and levels of education, unemployment rates, and the general levels of affluence.

For the reader unfamiliar with the Israeli socio-economic environment, Chapter 3 is designed to shed light on the peculiarities of the society and economy of Israel. No further discussion of social and economic factors is carried out here. In summary, there are environmental conditions and trends that can influence the meaning of work. However, so widespread are some of these trends and conditions that the cross-sectional design may operate to prevent one from discerning their effects.

Several potential relationships between conditional or antecedent variables and variables relating to the meaning of work have been discussed here. Not all these relationships are examined, however, for to do so would require a monograph devoted solely to that task.

The preceding discussion has at several points touched upon the topic of societal influences on the meaning of work, for example, when the age cohort explanation for differences in work meanings was examined. The societal frame of reference may thus be a serious consideration in the assignment of meaning. Moreover, when considered in conjunction with norms of obligation and from the perspective of distributive justice, individuals may well demand from society more than they contribute. Societies, too, may demand from individuals more than they distribute in terms of obligations; or the outcome of the exchange process between persons and institutions can be balanced. Finally, the discussion of work schedules has drawn on differences in societal support as a mediator of the relationship between shift work and the meaning of work. Conversely, the meaning of work may be an important variable alongside societal characteristics. Work centrality may affect involvement in work as measured by labor force participation and hours of work.

CENTRAL MEANING OF WORK DOMAINS

In the ensuing section attention will be turned to the nomological network of the MOW constructs or domains.

The heuristic model presented in Figure 4.1 includes five major and distinct constructs/domains that related individuals to the phenomenon of work. These five domains are (1) centrality of work, (2) societal norms, (3) valued work outcomes, (4) work goals (their importance), and (5) work role identification. All five of these MOW constructs function theoretically to describe different bases for attaching individuals to the phenomenon of working. Initially, the discussion examines the conceptual representation of each work meaning construct in terms of the properties of the construct. The relationship between construct definition and construct measurement, termed ''the epistemic correlation'' by F. Northrop (1959) or ''operationism'' by P. Bridgman (1927), is a critical connection for two reasons. First, there is frequently a tendency to assume isomorphism between a construct and measures of the construct when the two are less than isomorphic. This tendency is due to deficiency (variability in the construct not captured by the measure) or contamination (variability in the measure not found in the construct). Second, theoretical predictions and explanations about a construct are derived from the conceptual representation, whereas testing of theoretical propositions about a construct come from measurement of the construct.

The discussion will also examine the conceptual relationship between each of the MOW constructs and other constructs of theoretical and practical importance. Included here will be some expectations regarding relationships between measures of the particular work meaning and measures of the antecedent variables or consequences.

In presenting the domains of valued work outcomes, work goals, and work role identification we acknowledge the frequent criticism that the preferred outcomes included in research are usually selected without guidance from a theoretical framework that hypothesizes dimensions of work outcomes (Hulin & Triandis 1981). However, our conclusion based on a review of proposed taxonomies of work outcomes (i.e., Dubin, Headley & Taveggia 1976; Hulin & Triandis 1981; Vroom 1964) was that they are not particularly helpful. The classifications proposed do not yield mutually exclusive types of rewards or goals and often generate confusion rather than understanding. Based on these taxonomies, the valued working outcomes or work goals included may or may not depend on considerations such as task performance and mediation by the person or external agents. These outcomes and goals can also have symbolic or concrete properties and may be particularistic (that is, depend on the person receiving them) or universalistic. Little more than this can be said about the classification of outcomes, goals, and work role identifications included in this study.

Centrality of Work

At the outset it is important to remember that the referent in this study is work in general as distinct from working on the current job. In addition, our concern is with the psychological meaning of work to individuals. Involvement with work is conceptually distinct from involvement with the present job (Kanungo 1979; 1982b). Work centrality is defined as a general belief about the value of working in one's life. There are two major theoretical components of the work centrality construct, each with specific properties. The first component involves a belief or value orientation toward work as a life role. The second component involves a decision orientation about preferred life spheres for behavior. Both of these will be analyzed and conceptually integrated.

Belief-Value Component of Work Centrality. Two important properties of this component of work centrality are identification with work and involvement or commitment to work. Identification with work has been a major property in several previous discussions of work values (Lawler & Hall 1970; Lodahl & Kejner 1965; Maurer 1968). Work identification is the outcome of a cognitive consistency process based on a comparison between work as an activity and perceptions of self. The outcome of this comparison is the development of a distinct identification of work as either central or peripheral to one's self-image. Identification with work emerges from this process as part of self-identification.

The second property of this component of work centrality is involvement or commitment. Work involvement is an affective response to working as a part of one's life. Involvement with working may also include behavioral elements such as the amount of time spent participating in work activities. .Commitment to work is partially free of short-run experiences. Thus the belief-value component of work centrality has a future intentional element as well as a present behavioral involvement element. Work identification and involvement commitment are thus mutually reinforcing.

Given this representation of work centrality, the measurement issues are also clear. Individuals should use themselves as the referent. The task for the individual is to make an evaluation involving both work and self as referents. Finally, the measurement procedure should capture the involvement-commitment property. The process examined by the general measurement task consists of the attachment of an affective element of involvement-commitment to a cognitive consistency comparison of work in relation to self-identification.

Decision Orientation Component of Work Centrality. The decision orientation view of work centrality parallels R. Dubin's (1956) central life interests, R.

Barker's (1968) theory of behavioral settings, and F. Heider's (1958) theory of interpersonal relations. This view begins with the premise that an individual's experiences are segmented into different subspheres and that people differ in their preferences for particular life spheres. One may participate in a less preferred life sphere because it provides rewards for calculative or instrumental behavior but one may nevertheless attach greater significance to those behaviors that take place in more highly preferred life spheres.

This representation of work centrality contains two principal elements. First, there are the life sphere–behavior segments. The work segment can occupy a peripheral or less preferred position in one's life. This property implies a notion of identification based on a person's relative preferences for different life spheres.

The second element in the decision orientation representation of work centrality is choice or the extent to which a person chooses a preferred life sphere and the behaviors associated with it. This choice of life sphere implies a notion of involvement and provides the conditions whereby a person establishes affective and behavioral attachments to the environment. Since one need not become equally involved or committed to all segments of one's life (some behaviors may be prescribed rather than voluntarily chosen), commitment or involvement is a selective process. In other words, this second component of work centrality represents the process of identification as a consequence of interactions between individuals and their segmented behavioral environments. Involvement or commitment depends on the choice of settings and the potential range of preferred behaviors available while in a particular setting.

The measurement issues posed by this second view of work centrality are clear. First, the measure must include major segments of the person's life, only one of which is work, as choice alternatives. Second, the person must be allowed to choose between the various life spheres and order them so as to provide an indication of the degree of involvement or commitment.

By way of a general summary, the value orientation and decision orientation representations of work centrality do have some conceptual similarities. Both include properties of involvement, both have relational properties, and both are concerned with a person's identification with working in general. However, there are differences in the content of the two representations. The relational component in the belief-value orientation view is work in relation to self, while in the decision orientation view it is the work segment in relation to other life segments. Identification in the belief-value approach is a product of a cognitive consistency process between work as a life activity and the self as a referent. In the decision representation, identification is based on the preferences for working among multiple life spheres. Because of these differences in representation, measures of these two components of the work centrality construct are likely to be only moderately correlated. The combination of these two representations provides a more complete conceptualization of the work centrality construct as a general belief of the value of work in one's life. Work centrality is a measure based on cognitions and effects that reflect the degree of general importance that working has in the life of an individual at any specific time.

Societal Norms

One relatively unexamined aspect of the meaning of work concerns the standards people employ when making normative evaluations about work. Potentially there exist a large variety of norms or standards to draw upon, two of which capture much of the historical and contemporary discussion relevant to the meaning of work. In the ensuing discussion it is useful to begin with the developmental antecedents of the norms included in Figure 4.1. An antecedent of these norms is the development of normative reasoning in individuals. Initial concern is thus with the development of normative reasoning and its relevance for norms of social exchange and distributive justice in work. This is followed by a conceptual representation of the two norms included in the study: obligation and entitlement orientations.

Various approaches expressed by political writers, legal scholars, social philosophers, and social scientists have relied on some form of social contract in examining the nature of the individual's relationship with society. A central theme in developmental psychology is adults' use of principles in their normative reasoning (Kohlberg 1963; Olafson 1961; Piaget 1965). From this perspective, a critical issue is the abstract principles of social justice and fairness that people use at work in order to achieve cooperation or to distribute the benefits of cooperation. In the following discussion of norms and principles an attempt is made to remain neutral on this issue, thus not claiming the superiority of any particular normative orientation.

Two contrasting reference points appear in much of the discussion of this view of normative principles based on a social contract. One reference point begins with the individual and concentrates on social standards or norms concerned with an obligation to society. Within psychology, D. McClelland's idea of obligation to society includes such a notion (McClelland et al. 1958). This notion is also prominent in L. Kohlberg's (1963) discussion of evaluative standards based on principles of social order and an obligation to duty; in J. Piaget's (1965) operational/concrete cognitive stage; in E. Durkheim's moral philosophy (1893), in Confucian values (giri) (Mae 1981), and in the Protestant ethic (Weber 1930). In these sources normative behavior consists of fulfilling one's duty or obligation to society, having respect for delegated authority as a social obligation, and upholding norms that support social order.

The second reference point also concentrates on the individual but highlights the social standards or norms underlying the rights (or entitlements) of the person and the obligation of society to the individual. For example, there are discussions of obligation to self (McClelland et al. 1958). Such discussions are frequently linked to explicit or implicit assumptions about the equitable exchange relations between an individual's contributions and the social system's recompense. The social theoretical concept of the social contract (Rousseau 1916) might be considered a guiding model of such approaches. In this context it might be interesting to explore the conceptual similarities and differences between our own representation and those proposed in developmental psychology, which often imply differential stages of development and maturation (Kohlberg 1963; 1971; Piaget 1965). However, such an attempt is beyond the scope of this chapter.

In summary, normative reasoning in this view consists of individual rights or entitlements that have been agreed upon as society's obligation to its citizens. It is on these obligations to society and entitlements from society as central social norms in the meaning of work that we now focus our attention.

The Entitlement Work Norm as an Evaluative Standard. The entitlement or opportunity norm, as it is sometimes referred to in the literature, is one component of the meaning of work which has received extensive attention from such diverse sources as public opinion polls (Yankelovich 1979), organization behaviorists (Locke & Schweiger 1979), and institutional economic theories of unionization (Perlman 1976). Although the level of analysis differs among these sources, each tends to couch discussions of opportunity entitlement in terms that relate to rights and the psychological contract. As an example, "I would like to have a steady job" may be transformed into the imperative statement "We all have a right to a steady job." In theory, any motive or belief can be transformed into a right or entitlement through social or legal processes that establish its legitimacy. Aspects of this process in the development of normative reasoning have been discussed by Kohlberg (1971). The integral relationship between the social and legal process as they affect *externally* established standards and principles governing work relationships and exchange has been discussed by J. Ledvinka (1982). The relationship between the social and quasi-legal processes as they affect *internally* established standards and principles governing work relationships and exchange has been addressed in theories of internal labor markets (Doeringer & Piore 1971).

Two special discussions of the entitlement view of work norms can be found in M. Perlman (1976) and E. Locke and D. Schweiger (1979). Perlman concludes that "social welfare" and "social institution" theories offer the best explanations of unionization in the United States. In "social welfare" theories property claims or opportunities are restricted to economic issues. "Social institution" theories extend property claims (entitlements) to include working conditions such as security and due process. Related to due process is decision participation as a form of property right. Locke and Schweiger (1979) examine decision participation as a worker right and compare the scope of claims, as well as the social-legal vehicles for legitimizing the claims in the United States and Europe. One notion common to both sources is that opportunity is concerned with rights or claims that regulate personal and collective action.

An example of an opportunity norm in this study is agreement with the statement "Every person in our society should be entitled to interesting and meaningful work."

The Obligation Work Norm as an Evaluative Standard. The question of the individual's obligation to an employer and to society through working has been of central concern in theories of organizational, political, and legal aspects of authority (Etzioni 1961; Simon 1947). Two aspects of this obligation are personal responsibility, or internalized norms of duty, and social or institutional commitment. As used here this orientation, following the view of T. Parsons and E. Shils (1952), has an ''ought to'' element: one *ought* to contribute to society through work or ought to save for one's future security. The obligation norm represents the belief that all people have a duty or responsibility to social units through working. Such reasoning is also conceptually similar to Kohlberg's (1963) type 4 social order and obligation to duty orientation, as well as to Piaget's (1965) operational/concrete cognitive stage discussed earlier.

Relation between Levels of Analysis of the Norm of Entitlement and Obligation. Throughout the discussion of societal norms an implicit view has been that entitlement and obligation are conceptualized on two levels. One is the societal level, the other the individual level. It is appropriate here to consider the relationship between these levels. In tracing this relationship and its implications for the meaning of work, we begin by drawing on the earlier discussions that sought to link the present conceptualization of these norms to different types of normative reasoning.

Social interaction can be conceptualized as an act of exchange in which each person invests certain inputs (time, effort, attention, expertise) in exchange for outcomes (money, growth, satisfaction). Therefore, the relative proportion of the total outcomes an individual can expect to receive from other members or institutions that control the group or society can be seen as a measure of how much the distributor values the individual's inputs to the group or to society. The modes of distribution reflect the distributor's attention to different kinds of inputs from members.

The causal relationship between the norms and the distribution of socially mediated work outcomes is not certain. One explanation suggests that the direction is from the individual level of a norm—entitlement, as an example—to organizational or societally mediated outcomes. An individual's claims based on entitlement orientation may lead to actions aimed at legitimizing these claims. Another explanation suggests that the direction of causation is from work outcomes mediated by organizations or societies to the development of entitlement or opportunity norms. In other words, people who are dissatisfied with the distribution of work outcomes attempt to close the gap between themselves and others by adopting norms that espouse fair or equal treatment irrespective of individual differences. Quite the opposite argument would be made for obligation norms.

Although the organizational or societal implications of these norms are not entirely clear, we can suggest some possible linkages to organizational and societal considerations. Social psychologists (Weick 1979), sociologists (Coleman 1966), and economists (Olson 1965) all address the issue of the formation of groups, including unions, social movements, pressure groups, and special interest groups. K. Weick, drawing from F. Allport (1962), argues that convergence of people with similar beliefs precedes and is a necessary condition for, the emergence of groups.

Thus an initial overlap among people in their beliefs—an overlap that looks like behavior controlled by norms—makes it possible for more enduring social relationships to emerge. . . . Having first converged on shared ideas of how a structure can form (i.e., on means), the persons then activate a repetitive series of interlocking behaviors—that is, they form a collective structure. The range of their behavior narrows before a group forms, not after; the group is made possible by this narrowing and convergence. (Weick 1979, p. 90)

To paraphrase Weick, the causal impact would run from the individual level of social norms or claims to a convergence with similar normative beliefs, and then to social or political pressures that legitimize these normative beliefs regarding the appropriate modes of distributive justice.

Valued Work Outcomes

In this study *value* means evaluations of importance so defined as to include what the person knows about each of the outcomes and the preference relationship among them. Thus it is assumed that those making the evaluation of importance sufficiently know or have experienced each outcome to be able to link them to each other in an ordered manner.

Our conception of importance evaluations of work outcomes has been influenced by J. Cragin's (1983) research. Specifically, we consider the importance or preference assigned to an outcome to be a function of its cognitive centrality, the dependence of other outcomes on the outcome in question, the criticality, and the salience of the outcome. Here, cognitive centrality means the degree to which an outcome is in the forefront of a person's consciousness rather than being remote; the term also refers to the extent to which other outcomes organize around that outcome. Dependence means the extent to which cognitions of an outcome influence the cognitions of other outcomes associated with it. Criticality means the degree to which the person perceives readily available substitutes for the outcome in question. Finally, salience means the extent to which immediate socio-economic and work conditions draw temporary but forceful and explicit attention to an outcome that would not otherwise be as dominant. In summary, the importance evaluations of the work outcomes included in this study are a function of how central the outcome is in the person's cognitive structure, the dependence of other outcomes on it, the criticality of the outcome, and its temporal salience. Evaluations of importance or preference imply choice. Choice is the implementation of values for work outcomes, and for the specific type of identification with working.

Work Goals

Another way of understanding what is important to individuals in their working life is to focus on a uniform set of work goals or facets of working and to ascertain how important each is to individuals in an absolute sense and in a relative (to each other) sense. The conception of work goals, their evaluation and importance, has also been influenced by Cragin's (1983) work. Hence, the importance or preference allotted to a work goal is considered a function of its centrality, prominence, and importance in relation to other work goals (in this sense it is similar to valued work outcomes).

The voluminous literature on work goals or work aspects covers topics such as job satisfaction, work values, work needs, and incentive preference. Most of these topics have identified elements or facets that are important to the individual, for example, expressive, economic, improvement, and comfort goals (Herzberg et al. 1957; Locke 1976; Quinn 1971; Weiss et al. 1964). In addition, the information on work goals sheds some light on the basic question of why people work, or why they exert more or less effort at work. Work goals may also be used to indicate why some work situations are attractive to individuals while others are less attractive.

Work Role Identification

Role theory (Turner 1956) and attribution theory (Kelley 1974) have provided the conceptual rationale for development of the work role identification in this MOW study. The extent to which one identifies personally with work in terms of its tasks, company or organization, product or service, occupation or profession, provides an important insight into the relationship of these roles and the meaning of work.

From literature on organizational commitment and job involvement it becomes clear that terms like *identification, commitment, attachment,* and *involvement* are used as synonyms (Cook & Wall 1980; Moch 1980; Mowday, Steers & Porter 1979; Rabinowitz & Hall 1977; Saal 1978; Steers 1977). It is further indicated that task identification (or task commitment), occupation identification (or job involvement), and company identification (or organizational commitment) are distinct work identifications. An exception is R. N. Kanungo (1982a), for whom work identification is the centrality of work in life. The product/service identification was not explicitly labeled as a specific work identification.

Four work identifications are classified in C. Hulin and H. Triandis's (1981) taxonomy as environmentally related and also as internally mediated using personal standards. The task identification and the product/service identification group together as particularistic and symbolic. The company identification and the occupation identification are classified as universalistic, the former as concrete, the latter as symbolic.

Two additional work roles were included in the present study—the role of people with whom one works and the role of the money one receives from work. It was thought that their inclusion would enable individuals to relate to a broader spectrum of work roles.

Relationship between Meaning of Work Concepts

The previous sections have treated the major MOW concepts separately. However, these concepts are related theoretically and empirically. As an example, a strong adherence to a norm of obligation may also be a statement of a personal sense of obligation. To the extent that this reasoning is correct, the expectation is that norms of obligation and work centrality beliefs will be positively related. Further, valued work outcomes and work goals can be inferred by examining what the worker is willing to give up in order to maintain employment. This idea is implicit in the choice representation of work centrality. Other choice tasks in the present study also recognize and assess this view of outcomes.

Another example of conceptual and empirical relatedness is found in a study of R. Dubin, R. A. Headly, and T. C. Taveggia (1976). They found that workers with high work centrality valued outcomes such as their superior's confidence in them, the job responsibility, the usefulness of the organization's products or services, and in particular the chances for advancement and promotion. In contrast, workers with low centrality scores particularly valued having time for personal needs, knowing tasks in advance, talking to others while working, the method of remuneration, and working in a modern plant.

Some common and fundamental reasons exist for these conceptual and empirical relationships of the MOW concepts. The primary reason may lie in the structure of labor markets and occupations, as well as in their influence on the salience and functional relationship of MOW concepts. Economists use the concept of dual-labor markets to distinguish between those segments in which workers would obtain high levels of several of the outcomes included in this study, and have steady or steadier employment, and those segments with the opposite conditions (Reynolds 1974). This second group often includes high proportions of women or minority groups. Observations about occupations yield similar conclusions. For example, ordering occupations by status appears to be overdetermined, since doing so depends on many, rather than on a single, underlying characteristics. Thus high-status occupations have better pay, more interesting content, better working conditions, greater responsibility for the welfare of others, greater autonomy in choosing tasks and the methods of accomplishing them, and greater control over one's time (Vroom 1964). These are also the occupations that Dubin and his colleagues found to contain relatively higher proportions of individuals with work reflecting a high central life interest.

Additionally, the salience and functional relationships between the MOW concepts may be a function of the uncertainty of attainment. If workers have high expectations for an outcome because of previous experience, family background, or reward history, then both frame-of-reference and cognitive consistency theories yield predictions of low salience (Hulin & Triandis 1981). A similar level of salience might be expected when workers' expectations are very low. For many workers their jobs do not provide for status or autonomy, but they do provide income with moderate certainty during periods of employment.

Finally, in some cultures or subcultures work as an abstract concept is highly valued, whereas in others it is considered a necessary evil (Triandis 1972). These differences may partially reflect an ideology valuing hard work (Weber 1930). Cultures also differ in the degree to which they foster needs for achievement (McClelland 1961). To the extent that work is perceived as a necessary evil, it is unlikely that the work itself or the outcomes from work will be as highly valued as is the case in which the culture views work more favorably.

Thus, moderately difficult and demanding cultural contexts may influence the salience and functional form of several MOW concepts. Industrial societies may allocate rewards with differential probabilities to a greater extent than do more traditional societies (Soliman 1970).

In conclusion, labor market characteristics, occupations, and cultural differences may be considered as existing potent influences on the salience and functional relationships between the meaning of work concepts.

Meaning of Work Patterns

The five MOW domains identified and discussed earlier in this chapter will be used to generate empirical work patterns. The study of dominating work patterns or profiles may provide us with a valuable outlook on those work-related values and norms prevailing among various target groups, as well as in Israeli society. An example of such a pattern may be individuals who view working as very central to their lives, favor instrumental outcomes from working, and identify strongly with their employing organization. This issue is elaborated upon in Chapter 12, which focuses on the MOW patterns that emerged empirically in this study.

Consequences of the Meaning of Work

The consequences of the meaning of work have been embedded in much of the discussion thus far. A more complete treatment of some theoretical issues relating to the consequences and relationships between MOW variables and selected consequences appears in Chapter 13. In brief, the model in Figure 4.1 recognizes two categories of consequences associated with the meaning of work: subjective expectations about future work situations and objective outcomes of working. Examples of the former category of consequences include the future importance of working, preferences for working fewer hours for less pay, and recommendations about work to one's children. Examples of the latter category include hours of work, training so that the worker can enhance present or future work opportunities, and choice of tasks regarding work continuation or cessation and types of jobs.

GENERAL SUMMARY

This chapter has had several aims. The model and concepts develop a set of major MOW variables, domains, and patterns. The central focus of the chapter has been on the meaning of work as conceptualized through five major domains. Work centrality includes identification with work, involvement and commitment to work, and choice of work as a major mode of self-expression. The societal norms of entitlements and obligations were viewed as having their origin in the development of individuals. Each norm incorporates key notions of distributive justice: the right to rewards or opportunities (entitlements), or duty and contribution to society (obligations). The valued work outcomes, work goals, and work role identifications include reward content and intensity as inducements to work and preferences for differential work situations.

In developing and measuring these major MOW domains, subsequent chapters treat each separately and in combination. The idea of patterns of work meanings is an empirical extension of the ideas discussed earlier regarding the relationship between MOW concepts. To examine individuals in terms of each of the separate meanings they assign to work is an important research task.

One weakness of this strategy is that it provides a rather segmented view of individuals. The idea of patterns of work meanings provides a somewhat more idiographic and holistic view of individuals in terms of the interrelated meanings they assign to work.

The measures of the MOW concepts are to be related to antecedents and consequences at the level of individuals, occupations, and societies, recognizing the possibility for reciprocal causation between concepts in the model. Common to all three categories of antecedents in Figure 4.1 is the view that identification with and valuation of working in one's life is a function of past cultural conditioning, personal development, and socialization. Additionally, socio-economic conditions influence meanings assigned to work. We view the consequences of work meanings to include some of the major choices individuals make in their lives. These choices include decisions to work or not to work, how much to work, and what kind of work to do. In later chapters, antecedents and consequences are considered not only separately but in combinations or patterns as they relate to the meaning of work.

5

Measurement of the Meaning of Work

This chapter focuses on various measurement issues associated with the study of the meaning of work. It presents an overview of the nature of this project, procedures, data collection, instruments, samples employed and their description, and decisions regarding data analysis.

FRAMEWORK OF THE STUDY

This study is a large-scale survey field research. In its design, consideration was given to various issues:

1. Questions were devised to examine specific perceptions of developmental aspects and subjective expectations with respect to future developments. Reference to the past and the future, therefore, was made through respondents' viewpoints. Such an approach may have some limitations; however, it has advantages as a source of information.
2. Several of the questions used in previous studies under different social, economic and political circumstances were employed. Comparison of answers in the present and previous studies may provide additional insights into the changes taking place over time.
3. An intentional selection of particular samples of respondents was made to assist in dealing with this issue. Several target groups were selected to reflect different and crucial stages in adult career development (beginning, midcareer, final stage, retirement), thus providing useful information for developmental explanations (MOW-International Research Team 1987: 43).

This chapter draws considerably on Chapter 3 in MOW-International Research Team, *The Meaning of Working* (1987), since its description, decisions, and procedures contain exactly those also carried out in Israel.

Measurement instruments were developed based on the following considerations:

- Width of applicability, that is, covering as many aspects of the sphere of the meaning of work as possible. Exclusive concentration on only one of the dimensions discussed in the literature was considered too limiting for such a complex and multifaceted phenomenon. The total scope of the meaning of work should be covered.

- Inclusion of both open-ended and closed questions, the latter with a view to comparability and standardization, the former with a view to the personal, often fruitful, account they provide. Data from open questions can be used for illustrative and interpretative purposes as well as for hypothesis generation.

- Multimethod measurement of various concepts wherever possible. This makes for greater confidence in the information acquired than in that provided by any single method; it also augments the information, which would be limited if measured by a single item or scale.

- Relevance to a wide range and to diverse groups of respondents. The questionnaires were to be used with respondents who differed substantially in professional and occupational levels, educational background, and age, and who resided and worked in different geographical locations. This called for careful wording and phrasing so as to generate comparable responses.

- Utmost comprehension and application. This criterion refers to the requirement of producing usable variance. Here, account was taken of past experience where Likert-type scales attempting to assess sensitive issues run a serious risk of producing highly socially desirable responses with very small variance. In view of this problem, a ranking or forced distribution procedure was selected where appropriate instead of or in addition to Likert-type items.

- Proliferation of interest and motivation. Much thought was devoted to the sequence of the questions and the type of questions, as well as to the total length of the questionnaire. (MOW-International Research Team 1987: 44–45).

SAMPLES

Two types of samples were employed in the study: a set of ten target groups and a representative sample of the labor force.

Target Groups Samples

Three central and overlapping factors in the intensive study of target groups guided this project:

1. Each target group should be homogeneous with respect to a number of characteristics considered particularly pertinent (age, sex, and education).

2. The target groups should include those segments critically important to policy concerns and policy making (for example, increasingly important groups in the labor force such as women and part-time employees; current and potential problem groups such as the unemployed or employees in declining industries).

3. The target groups together should reflect different degrees of integration into the workforce (for example, fully employed, unemployed, temporarily or partially employed, just prior to employment), different work settings and work histories (for example, occupational level, degrees of professionalization), and major differences in personal and social background. (MOW-International Research Team 1987: 45–46).

Although career development per se is not the primary variable of concern in this study, we have been influenced in our selection of target groups by stratification within groups so as to cover clearly the major adult career stages suggested by the research and theory of E. H. Erikson (1963), D. J. Levinson and others (1974), and D. E. Super (1957; 1978).

Characteristics of the Target Groups Samples

The ten target groups employed in the study are presented under three major categories: (A) not yet working, (B) working now, and (C) not working.

A. *Target Groups: Not yet working*
   1. Students
      Description: Males studying mechanical or machine trades or equivalent in vocational-technical schools, females studying for clerical-secretarial occupations in full-time schools. These individuals may be employed part time, but we primarily sought students who would enter employment immediately after their vocational training or after their military service.
      Sex distribution: 45 males, 45 females.
      Sampling method: Students were located in the four largest cities (Tel Aviv, Jerusalem, Haifa, Beersheva) in several schools in the most representative areas of each city so that we could get a heterogeneous population. Students in each school were randomly selected from the list of classes. Every student was individually interviewed.
      Location of interview: At school.

B. *Target Groups: Working now*
   1. Chemical Engineers
      Description: Graduates of university-level training and currently engaged in professional chemical work (not as managers) in companies employing 200 workers or more.
      Sex distribution: 90 males
      Sampling method: The chemical engineers were randomly sampled from a list of members of the engineering association supplied by the association. The interviews took place throughout the country.
      Location of interview: At work.
   2. Self-employed businesspersons
      Description: Only those employing less than eight people. The businesses were commercial service and crafts. They did not include professionals such as

lawyers, physicians, or dentists. The intention was to take "small shop-keepers."

Sex distribution: 79 males, 11 females.

Sampling method: Businesses were chosen in three streets in the most representative areas of the four largest cities. The interviewees were approached during the most convenient hours for an interview or to arrange an appointment with them at their homes.

Location of interview: At work or at home.

3. Teachers

Description: Teaching grades 4 and 5 (nine- and ten-year-olds) where the main assignment was to teach many subjects to a whole class as opposed to only one subject to many classes. Teachers were selected from state (public) schools only.

Sex distribution: 90 females.

Sampling method: Several schools in the four largest cities were selected in the same way as in the students' sampling method. School principals were asked to refer interviewers to suitable teachers.

Location of interview: At work.

4. Temporary workers

Description: Clerical workers, nonskilled to low-skill levels, who work for and are assigned to temporary work locations by private employment agencies only. Students were not included.

Sex distribution: 90 females.

Sampling method: Workers were sampled randomly from lists of present temporary workers provided by the two largest companies that supply temporary labor services in Israel.

Location of interview: At work.

5. Textile workers

Description: Low-level or semiskilled jobs such as weavers.

Sex distribution: 60 males, 30 females.

Sampling method: Workers were interviewed in two large textile plants in Qiryat Shemona (north) and in Qiryat Gat (south).

Location of interview: At work.

6. Tool and die makers

Description: A highly skilled group selected from the electrical appliance, metalwork, and related industries.

Sex distribution: 91 males.

Sampling method: Individuals were randomly sampled from a list of union members supplied by the relevant trade unions. They were chosen in Jerusalem and in northern and central parts of Israel.

Location of interview: At work.

7. White-collar employees

Description: The intention was to select low/semiskilled or lower service function employees whose occupations were being influenced by automation and technology. Employees were selected from the banking industry.

Sex distribution: 45 males, 45 females.

Sampling method: Interviews were held among bank officers of low-level po-

sitions such as cashiers. Three or four banks in different parts of each of the four largest cities were chosen. After an appeal to bank managers for cooperation, the relevant workers were interviewed in the bank itself, during their free time.
Location of interview: At work.

C. Target Groups: Not working

1. Retired

Description: Not presently working and of mandatory retirement age.
Sex distribution: 45 males, 45 females.
Sampling method: From a previous national opinion survey conducted by the surveying agency, a representative sample of retirees was located and interviewed again, now for the MOW project.
Location of interview: At home.

2. Unemployed

Description: Medium to low skill levels, all having been unemployed for at least the past six months.
Sex distribution: 48 males, 42 females.
Sampling method: The unemployed were randomly sampled by the employment service of the Ministry of Labor. Interviews took place in Jerusalem and in northern and central parts of Israel.
Location of interview: At home.

Each of the ten target groups selected for the study contained approximately 90 individuals. The total population of the target samples was 901, with a distribution of 503 males and 398 females.

National Sample

In addition to the target groups a national sample was included in the study. The rationale for this was that (1) it provided a national picture of MOW patterns for policy evaluation, for a comparison with past studies, and as a reference point for future studies; and (2) it serves as a national reference group for evaluating and understanding critical target-group data (MOW-International Research Team 1987: 45).

A representative sample of the labor force was drawn from a list of those among the Jewish population eligible to participate in the Israeli general elections. That is, the sample includes interviewees aged 18 and over. It does not include the kibbutz population or Arabs living in Israel because sampling and interviewing these groups is very costly and cumbersome. Sampling was carried out according to the ecological method. Hence, the country was divided into ten strata as defined by the Central Bureau of Statistics. Eight of these strata represent the urban areas and include 95 percent of those Israelis eligible to vote, and two strata represent the rural settlements and include 5 percent of those eligible to vote. This division accords with the distribution of population in Israel.

The stratification of the sample ensures a high level of representation and decreases sampling error. The final sample consisted of 973 individuals representing the national labor force. Table 5.1 presents the sample in relation to the stratum from which it was drawn. Some characteristics of the national MOW sample as compared with official statistics from the *Statistical Abstract of Israel* (1982) are presented in Table 5.2 (this includes the data for the year 1981, when MOW data were collected in Israel). The data suggest that our sample resembles quite closely the official Israeli statistics. Therefore, some of the conclusions from the findings presented later may be inferred for the general population. Data were collected via individual interviews. All interviews for both target and national samples were conducted by professional interviewers provided by a national surveying agency.

MEASUREMENT INSTRUMENTS DEVELOPMENT

Pilot Study

A pilot study was conducted to evaluate ease of understanding, applicability, reliability, and other properties of the questionnaires developed. On the basis of the data obtained in the pilot study in Israel ($n = 89$) and in the other countries participating in the MOW project, changes and adaptations were made (the size of the pilot samples in all countries combined was 669).

Table 5.1
Sample Representing the Labor Force in Relation to the Stratum from Which It Was Drawn

The stratum	Percentage of people eligible to vote	Number of interviews
Jerusalem	8.5	83
Tel Aviv	14.8	144
Haifa	8.4	82
Beersheva	3.0	29
"Old" cities[a]	35.3	344
New cities	12.4	121
Old urban settlements[b]	5.8	56
New urban settlements	6.6	64
Old rural settlements	1.5	15
New rural settlements	3.6	35
Total	100.0	973

Notes:
[a] A city founded before the state of Israel was established (May 14, 1948).
[b] An urban settlement — a town that is administrated by a local municipality.

Table 5.2
Comparison of MOW National Sample with Official Statistics Representing the Israeli Population (in percentages)

Variable	MOW Sample	Statistical Abstracts
Sex		
Male	63.8	58
Female	36.1	42
Age		
14-17	2.7	--
18-24	13.8	11.8
25-34	32.5	31.9
35-44	19.9	22.2
45-54	16.0	16.5
55-64	10.9	12.2
64+	4.1	4.3
Education		
Elementary school	23	19
High school	50.5	45.5
Some college	6.9	18.3
University graduate	12.7	16.1
Missing	--	1.1
Occupation		
Scientific & Academic	8.2	11
Technical	14.9	9
Administrative/Managerial	3.7	6
Clerical related	19	21
Sales related	7.6	6
Service related	11.2	14
Agricultural	5.5	3.6
Tool makers and operators, machine and production related	25.8	19.1
Unskilled in industry	4.2	2.0
Military	--	3.2
Others	--	5.1
Work Tenure		
Up to 1 year	15.6	14.2
Up to 2 years	8.1	8.7
Up to 3 years	9.7	8.3
Up to 4 years	6.6	6.8
Up to 5 years	4.7	4.8
Up to 6 years	6.0	5.8
6-10 years	17.9	18.0
10-15 years	13.0	10.1
15+ years	18.4	23.1

Questionnaires

The following decisions and suggestions based upon the pilot study were implemented in the final set of questionnaires and interview procedures.

- To maintain the interest and motivation of respondents the total length of the interview should not exceed one hour.
- The number of open questions, although providing interesting information with a "personal touch," should be kept to a minimum.
- Certain types of questions were deleted in the final questionnaire because they were difficult or time consuming (for example, Osgood's semantic differential and a sentence completion list).
- A number of questions were deleted because they lacked variance, too much time was required for explaining or answering them, or social desirability factors had too obvious an influence.
- Many questions were changed and improved on the basis of the reactions of the respondents, the distribution of the answers, and/or the postquestionnaire interviews held with a large number of respondents.
- The results of a number of factor analyses, item analyses, and interrater reliability were further used to select questions or scales from duplicating or parallel sets of questions or scales, which had been incorporated for comparative purposes.
- The instructions (general and for each question), the choice of the sequence of questions, interviewing modes, and procedural aspects, such as the introductory letter, anonymity, and feedback procedures, were all standardized.

Since not every question applies equally well to each target group, three versions of the final questionnaire had to be developed. The questions in each questionnaire are similar but whenever necessary were adapted for application to a particular category of respondents.

Form A was used with samples of employed persons included in the target groups of chemical engineers, teachers, self-employed, tool and die makers, white-collar employees, textile workers, and temporary workers (this questionnaire is presented in Appendix I). Form B was used for the unemployed and retired (not working), and form C for students (not yet working) (MOW-International Research Team 1987: 51).

Interview Procedures

The procedures followed in administering the target groups surveys and the national surveys are described generally here. The general introductory statement at the beginning of each interview was as follows:

This interview is about *working,* about what working means to you in general, about your specific working situation and about how you view working in the future.

The interview is anonymous. That is to say, no one will see or hear your answers except for the researchers who are conducting the study. Many different types of people will be interviewed. Therefore it is possible that some questions do not apply exactly to your situation. If a question is not clear to you, or if you have any comment, please feel free to ask or tell the interviewer.

Many different types of questions are covered in this study. There are no "right" or "wrong" answers but it is important that you give us your opinion. You will answer some questions directly on the forms provided and the interviewer will record your answers on other questions. These questions are being asked of about 2,000 individuals in each of ten countries throughout the world [actually, only eight countries finally participated in the MOW project] to find out what *working* really means to people. The Israeli portion of the study is being conducted by a research team from the University of Haifa. Your answers are important and we thank you in advance for helping us in this important study. (MOW-International Research Team 1987: 55)

SUMMARY OF ITEMS AND SCALES

The underlying model in the present study is based on the conception that the meaning of work is determined by the individual's choices and experiences and by the organizational and environmental contexts in which he or she works and lives. For an illustration of this conceptual model see Figure 4.1 in Chapter 4. This model represents the major variable sets and the most straightforward relationships that can be studied.

As indicated in the model, the variables have been chosen and operationalized at three different levels.

1. *Conditional variables.* This level includes the following:

A. *Personal and family circumstances* such as age, sex, family status, spouse's work situation, education, religious orientation, urban-rural upbringing, parents' education, similarity or difference in the education of parents to that of the respondents, individual and family income (questions 69–77 in the questionnaire, Appendix I).

B. *Present job and career history* such as present job situation, job level, frequency and direction of career changes, unemployment (frequency and duration), factors that prompted job changes (questions 1–27 in the questionnaire).

2. *Central Domains.* In this category, the core variables in the MOW study are operationalized. The meaning attributes refer not just to the present job or work, but rather to the interest in the importance, value, significance, and meaning of having work and performing work per se. Meaning of work was defined conceptually in terms of the following five domains:

A. *Work centrality* (as a life role) (questions 29, 30). The issue is, how central is the role of working in one's life in absolute terms and as compared with other life roles?

B. *Societal norms* (about working) (question 47). This scale contains a set of questions about work and working in terms of what should be expected from working (entitlements) and what society should expect from all individuals in terms of working (obligations).

C. *Valued work outcomes* (question 28). In this question, the respondent is asked to indicate what outcomes he or she seeks from working and the relative importance of each. The major expressive and instrumental meanings identified in the literature are incorporated.

D. *Work goals* (question 32). Respondents are asked about the relative importance of various aspects of working, such as variety, autonomy, skill utilization, pay security, promotional opportunities, and physical working conditions. In addition, a great number of hypothetical choices are presented to the respondent. A pattern of responses indicates a particular priority or work-aspect preference.

E. *Work role identification* (question 31). This question concerns the extent to which one personally defines and identifies working in terms of various roles such as task role, organizational role, product or service role, and occupational/professional role.

3. *Consequences*. A third set of variables deals with the expectations, plans, aspirations, and future intentions regarding working (questions 56–68). These questions refer to expected future mobility, expected types of work, and changes in work. Most of them are subjective. Some questions, however, are objective or behavioral in nature, such as those referring to concrete steps currently being taken to achieve expected or aspired-to work situations in the future.

Finally, some additional questions were incorporated in the questionnaire to provide information on a number of other aspects of the work situation or work attitudes felt to be relevant for the present research topic. These include the following:

1. The classic "lottery question" (question 48), which has been used in a number of previous studies and would therefore enable us to make relevant comparisons across time and national borders (Jakubowski 1968; Kaplan & Tausky 1974; Mannheim & Rein 1981; Morse & Weiss 1955; Parker 1965; Parker & Smith 1976; Tausky 1969; Warr 1984).

2. Definition of work—a question that tries to identify aspects considered essential in the definition of working (question 49). It provides a basis for comparisons between groups and organizational levels regarding their perception of work.

3. Three questions on job or occupational satisfaction (question 50A, B, C), a question on expected attitudinal change toward working (question 52), and three questions on the relationship between work and leisure time (questions 53–55) (see also Jakubowski 1968; Kaplan & Tausky 1974; Morse & Weiss 1955; Parker 1965; Parker & Smith 1976; Tausky 1969; Warr 1984).

In view of the large number of questions in the study, not all could be analyzed to the same depth in this volume.

This chapter has presented an overview of the different instruments and questions used in the study and of the various procedures followed in the analysis and interpretation of the data. The overview has been made on a level considered necessary to understand how the data have been collected, analyzed, and interpreted. A full description of the analysis procedures and the development of the scales, indices, and patterns is available (Holvoet 1984). Further insight may be obtained from the following chapters, where the results of these analyses are discussed in detail.

6

The Structure of the Meaning of Work

Acceptance of the view that work is important to individuals, organizations, and societies highlights the conceptual value of identifying and understanding the variety of common meanings attached to work by individuals. While it is possible to approach this task from various levels of analysis (individual, organizational, societal), this chapter starts at the level of the individual. The primary concern here is the identification and understanding of a common structure of what working means to individuals. Subsequent chapters will explore, develop, and modify these common work meanings at different levels of aggregation and for different purposes. Here the aim is to answer two broad questions about individual work meanings:

1. What empirical structuring of work meanings is revealed when the data are viewed as a whole, across all participants from various occupational groups?

2. How consistent is this general structure of work meanings when the data are viewed separately for each target group as well as in a national sample of the labor force?

MEASUREMENT OF THE MEANING OF WORK

The basic data utilized in this chapter for identifying the empirical structure of work meanings come from the major measurement domains shown in the heuristic research model (Figure 4.1 in Chapter 4). The meaning of work was defined conceptually in terms of five major domains: work centrality, societal norms, valued work outcomes, work goals, and work role identification. It should be noted that meanings attributed to a person's current work are not the only ones of interest; we are concerned with the importance, value, and meaning of

Portions of this chapter are derived from Itzhak Harpaz, "The Factorial Structure of the Meaning of Working," *Human Relations*, 39, (1986):595–614.

work in general. The core notion addressed in each MOW domain and the resulting measurement scales are described below. Although primary theoretical development of the MOW domains has been addressed in Chapter 4 and will be treated in more detail in subsequent chapters, it is useful to highlight the core notion addressed in each central MOW item domain and the related measurement scales. (Original item numbers are retained for reference to the data collection instrument and to the factor-loading tables shown in this chapter.)

Work Centrality. How significant is one's work role compared with other life roles and in absolute terms? The series of "central life interest" studies by R. Dubin and others was most helpful in developing this concept (see Dubin, Champoux & Porter 1975; Dubin, Headley & Taveggia 1976; Mannheim & Cohen 1978; Orzack 1959; Parker 1971). Two measures of work centrality were utilized. The first is an absolute (scaled) measure:

29.   How important and significant is working in your <u>total</u> life?

One of the least important things in my life	1	2	3	4	5	6	7	One of the most important things in my life
				of medium importance in my life				

The second is a relative measure comparing work with other activities or roles in life. It was obtained from the number of points assigned to "my work":

30.   Assign a total of 100 points to indicate how important the following areas are in your life at the present time.

30A   _ _ My leisure (like hobbies, sports, recreation and contacts with friends)

30B   _ _ My community (like voluntary organizations, union and political organizations)

30C   _ _ My work

30D   _ _ My religion (like religious activities and beliefs)

30E   _ _ My family

Societal Norms. What should one expect from work (entitlements or opportunities) and, in turn, what should one expect to contribute through working (obligations)? The definition used in developing the normative statements comes from the work of H. Triandis (1972) on subjective culture: "Norms involve relationships between a person category and a behavioral category and they usually specify whether the behavior is appropriate" (p. 15). An example of such a norm dealing with work-related obligations is "It is the duty of every able-bodied citizen to contribute to society by working." "Every able-bodied citizen" is the person category, and "contribute to society by working" is the behavior category. A set of 42 societal norm statements about working was reduced through international pilot-testing to the present ten items:

47. On this page are some work-related statements that people might make. We would like you to decide whether you agree or disagree with each of these statements depending on your personal opinions. If you strongly agree with a statement, please circle the number 4; if you agree somewhat with the statement, circle the number 3; and so on.

		Strongly Disagree	Disagree	Agree	Strongly Agree
47A	If a worker's skills become outdated, his employer should be responsible for retraining and reemployment.	1	2	3	4
47B	It is the duty of every able-bodied citizen to contribute to society by working.	1	2	3	4
47C	The educational system in our society should prepare every person for a good job if they exert a reasonable amount of effort.	1	2	3	4
47D	Persons in our society should allocate a large portion of their regular income toward savings for their future.	1	2	3	4
47E	When a change in work methods must be made, a supervisor should be required to ask workers for their suggestions before deciding what to do.	1	2	3	4
47F	A worker should be expected to think up better ways to do his or her job.	1	2	3	4
47G	Every person in our society should be entitled to interesting and meaningful work.	1	2	3	4

		Strongly Disagree	Disagree	Agree	Strongly Agree
47H	Monotonous, simplistic work is acceptable as long as the pay compensates fairly for it.	1	2	3	4
47I	A job should be provided to every individual who desires to work.	1	2	3	4
47J	A worker should value the work he or she does even if it is boring, dirty or unskilled.	1	2	3	4

Statements A, C, E, G, and I represent entitlement norms, while statements B, D, F, H, and J represent obligation norms.

Valued Work Outcomes. What are the general outcomes one wishes to obtain through working, and what is their relative importance? The valued work outcome measure draws on the typology of six general meanings of working, as developed by H. R. Kaplan and C. Tausky (1974) from a review of several studies of the functions and meanings of working:

28.   To help explain what <u>working means to you</u>, please assign a total of 100 points, in any combination you desire, to the following six statements. The more a statement expresses your thinking, the more points you should assign to it. Please read all the statements before assigning points.

28A1 __ __ Working gives you status and prestige.
28A2 __ __ Working provides you with an income that is needed.
28A3 __ __ Working keeps you occupied.
28A4 __: __ Working permits you to have interesting contacts with other people.
28A5 __ __ Working is a useful way for you to serve society.
28A6 __ __ Working itself is basically interesting and satisfying to you.

Work Goals. What is the relative importance to the individual of various goals or aspects of working, for example, good interpersonal relations, considerable autonomy, convenient working hours, and good pay? The relevant literature on work goals is voluminous and covers the areas of job satisfaction, work values, and work needs. The Minnesota Importance Questionnaire (Weiss et al. 1964) and the review of job satisfaction by E. Locke (1976) were employed, as well as items from studies by F. Herzberg and others (1957), L. W. Porter (1964),

R. P. Quinn (1971), and R. P. Quinn and W. Cobb (1971). The combined ranking-rating procedure attempts to standardize the degree of importance assigned to the various goals by the respondent and was adopted after pilot experimentation with several formats:

32. What about the nature of your working life? How important to you is it that your work life contains the following:

32A —A lot of opportunity to LEARN new things
32B —Good INTERPERSONAL relations (supervisors, co-workers)
32C —Good opportunity for upgrading or PROMOTION
32D —CONVENIENT work hours
32E —A lot of VARIETY
32F —INTERESTING work (work that you really like)
32G —Good job SECURITY
32H —A good MATCH between your job requirements and your abilities and experience
32I —Good PAY
32J —Good physical working CONDITIONS (such as light, temperature, cleanliness, low noise level)
32K —A lot of AUTONOMY (you decide how to do your work)

Respondents were asked to rank these items by first selecting the most important item, then the least important, until all 11 work goals were finally ranked.

Work Role Identification. Which work roles, for example, task roles, company or organizational roles, product or service roles, occupational or professional roles, are most important? Role theory (Turner 1956) and attribution theory (Kelley 1967) provided the conceptual rationale for the work role identification items:

31. When you think of your working life, which of the following aspects of working seem most significant and important to you? Please rank these items from 6 = most significant to 1 = least significant.
31A __ The tasks I do while working
31B __ My company or organization
31C __ The product or service I provide
31D . __ The type of people with whom I work
31E __ The type of occupation or profession I am in
31F __ The money I receive from my work

Analytic Procedure

The analytic method for identifying and interpreting the individual structure or work meanings consisted of a principal components factor analysis of the 39 scores of the work-meaning items that emerged from the five MOW domains described above. Factors with eigenvalues exceeding 1.0 were rotated to simple structure by the varimax procedure. Factor loadings with an absolute value greater than or equal to 0.35 were used in defining and interpreting the factors. Relevant information from the initial item intercorrelation matrix was used to verify interpretation decisions.

The first analysis of structure combined all target groups into one total sample of individuals who had provided complete data on the 39 work-meaning items ($n = 901$). This analysis is regarded as presenting the most general but systematic view of individual work-meaning structures across occupational groups. A second set of analyses examined responses within a given target sample ($n = 90$) as a representation of individual work structure within that occupational group. In addition, target groups were compared with the national sample ($n = 973$) to gain further insight into the representativeness of the factorial structure obtained.

GENERAL STRUCTURE OF WORK MEANINGS

Table 6.1 displays the factor matrix for all target-group samples combined. Item loadings with an absolute value of less than .35 are omitted from the table. Fifteen factors with eigenvalues greater than 1.0 accounted for 62.2 percent of the common variance among the 39 MOW items, but only 13 factors were clearly interpretable.

The first factor consists of five entitlement/opportunity statements (items 47A, C, E, G, I) and three obligation norms (items 47B, D, F). This was an unexpected finding because these two sets of items were designed a priori to tap two distinct features. Respondents appear to believe that working should provide both a high level of entitlements (opportunities) and obligations to all. Attribution theory suggests that although there is an egalitarian quality to this belief, respondents may express such a view primarily as a way of indicating that the entitlements are due to them as individuals. This factor was labeled *obligations and opportunities*.

Factor 2 shows significant loadings on items dealing with income (item 28A2), money (item 31F), and pay (item 32I). As a result, it was labeled the *income* factor. It clearly indicates the preeminence of economic rewards as a valued work outcome. It should be noted, however, that this may have emerged as the second factor partly because income or money features in three of the MOW domains. On items 32A–K, where good pay is only one of 11 work goals, a broader economic factor, closely associated with a comfort factor, emerged (factor 6, described below).

Factor 3 loads significantly on such work aspects as opportunity to learn (item 32A), good interpersonal relations (item 32B), variety (item 32E), and interesting

Table 6.1

Significant Factor Loadings of Meaning of Work Questionnaire Items for the Combination Sample of Target Groups

MOW item no.	Item description[a]	1. Obligations and opportunities	2. Income	3. Expressive	4. Work centrality	5. Family and leisure	6. Economic and comfort	8. Organizational identification	9. Product service identification	10. Religion	11. Task identification	12. Co-worker identification	13. Community	14. Contacts
28A1	Status-prestige													
28A2	Income		.82											
28A3	Time absorbing													
28A4	Interpersonal contact													.73
28A5	Serve society													
28A6	Intrinsically interesting													
29	Work importance (in life)				(.26)*									
30A	Leisure role importance					-.89								
30B	Community role importance												.80	
30C	Work role				.91									
30D	Religious role importance									.90				
30E	Family role importance					.63								
31A	Task identification										.70			
31B	Organizational identification							.82						
31C	Product identification								.87					
31D	Interpersonal Identification											.84		
31E	Occupational Identification										-.46			
31F	Income identification		.56											
32A	Learning opportunity			.54										

Table 6.1 (continued)

		Factor and loadings												
MOW item no.	Item description[a]	1. Obligations and opportunities	2. Income	3. Expressive	4. Work centrality	5. Family and leisure	6. Economic and comfort	8. Organizational identification	9. Product service identification	10. Religion	11. Task identification	12. Co-worker identification	13. Community	14. Contacts
32B	Interpersonal contact			.40										
32C	Promotion opportunity													
32D	Convenient hours						(.34)*							
32E	Variety			.51										
32F	Interesting work			.51										
32G	Job security						.47							
32H	Ability-job match													
32I	Good pay		.35				.45							
32J	Good working conditions						.57							
32K	Autonomy													
47A	Retraining responsibility	.36												
47B	Duty to work	.53												
47C	Educational preparation	.53												
47D	Saving responsibility	.45												
47E	Employee participation	.38												
47F	Worker contribution	.46												
47G	Meaningful work entitlement	.45												
47H	Monotony pay acceptance													
47I	Job providing responsibility	.36												
47J	Value work													

[a] Item belongs in factor but lower than the .35 factor loadings.

work (item 32F). The substance of significant scores on factor 3 is the desirability of a work setting that permits personal involvement or self-expression. Accordingly, this was designated the *expression* factor.

Factor 4 shows high loading on the importance of work compared with other life roles (item 30C). The absolute measure of work centrality (item 29), although relatively low, was the second highest item in this factor and correlated 0.26 (p <.0001) with item 30C; it is therefore shown in Table 6.1 in parentheses. These measures differ chiefly in that item 30C specifies the comparative standards against which working is evaluated (namely, other nonwork life roles), involving a cognitive and decision-making framework for response. No framework was provided in item 29, which is thus likely to be more idiosyncratically interpreted by respondents. This is the *work centrality* factor.

Factors 5, 10, and 13 refer to highly valued nonwork areas of life. *Family and leisure* (factor 5) is bipolar with positive and negative loadings; *religion* (factor 10) loaded significantly only on item 30D; *community* (factor 13) received a high loading on item 30B.

Factor 6, the *economic and comfort* factor, concerns working conditions and economic benefits. These include convenient work hours (item 32D), job security (item 32G), good pay (item 32I), and good physical working conditions (item 32J).

Factors 8, 9, 11, and 12 all relate to work role identification. Factor 8, with a significant loading on item 31B, is *organizational identification*; Factor 9 (item 31C) is *product/service identification*. Factor 11 loads highly on "the task I do while working" (item 31A) ; it also loads negatively on "the type of occupation or profession I am in" (item 31E). This might be viewed as a result of the ipsativity between items 31A and 31E. (These two items are also negatively correlated: -0.23, p < .001.) Factor 11 is therefore named *task identification*. Factor 12 shows a high loading on "the type of people with whom I work" and was labeled *co-worker identification*. Finally, Factor 14 exhibited significant loadings on "working permits you to have interesting contacts with other people" (item 28A4) and was designated *contacts*.

These empirical findings from the sample of ten target groups led us to modify the original heuristic model. The 13 dimensions of individual work meanings are presented in Figure 6.1, together with the MOW domains from the heuristic model and the MOW domains that are supported by the factor analysis results.

Of particular interest is the emergence of a new domain, which is based on dimensions that proved significant in the factorial design but not directly related to work. These nonwork spheres were initially intended to provide an indication of the relative importance of work (item 30). However, their emergence as independent factors points to their significance in Israeli society.

Family plays a central role in Israel. The stability and centrality of the Israeli family, and the predominance of the family-centered lifestyle, have been documented by Y. Peres and R. Katz (1981). On item 30 of the MOW questionnaire respondents assigned the highest number of points (out of 100) to family: 38 in the total target groups sample and 43 in the national sample. Work, which was

Figure 6.1
Meaning of Work Domains and Their Corresponding Empirical Dimensions

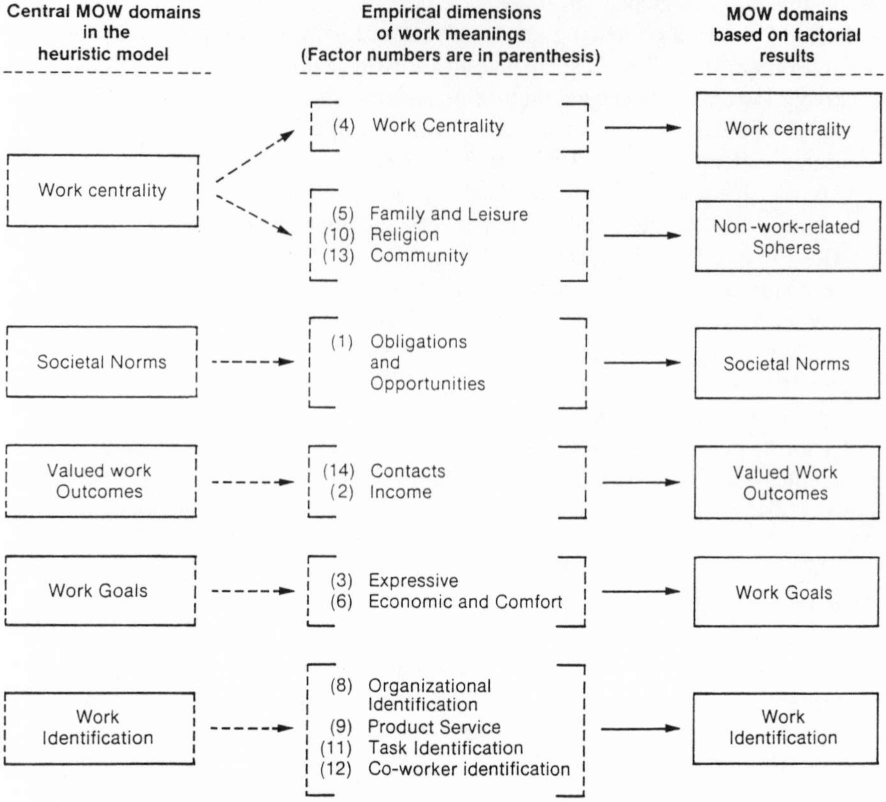

Central MOW domains in the heuristic model	Empirical dimensions of work meanings (Factor numbers are in parenthesis)	MOW domains based on factorial results
Work centrality	(4) Work Centrality	Work centrality
	(5) Family and Leisure (10) Religion (13) Community	Non-work-related Spheres
Societal Norms	(1) Obligations and Opportunities	Societal Norms
Valued work Outcomes	(14) Contacts (2) Income	Valued Work Outcomes
Work Goals	(3) Expressive (6) Economic and Comfort	Work Goals
Work Identification	(8) Organizational Identification (9) Product Service (11) Task Identification (12) Co-worker identification	Work Identification

ranked second in importance to family, received about 28 points in both samples. Leisure, which forms part of the same factor as family, may be interpreted as having additional time to spend with one's family. This interpretation gains support from findings that indicate that spending time with family is one of the most important personal needs in Israeli society (Katz & Gurevitch 1973). A later study reports that among nonworking Israeli women, as well as in a representative sample of females in the Israeli labor force, joint family activities were rated as the major leisure pursuit (Peres & Katz 1984).

In many areas of Israeli life, state and religion overlap. The existence of religious political parties and a state-religious educational system are just two examples. The emergence of religion as an exclusive factor in the present study may reflect the influence of religion and tradition on the Israeli lifestyle. In response to the questionnaire item on the extent of their religious affiliation, a majority of the respondents acknowledged the importance of religion in their lives: 12.3 percent defined themselves as religious, 42.6 percent as traditional, and 45 percent as secular.

To sum up, the central MOW domains in the heuristic model are supported empirically by the factor analysis results. The latter yielded an additional new domain, nonwork-related spheres.

STRUCTURE OF WORK MEANINGS IN THE NATIONAL SAMPLE AND IN INDIVIDUAL TARGET GROUPS

Table 6.2 compares the factorial structure of work meanings found in the combined sample of target groups, in the national sample, and in individual target groups. Numbers denote the factors in which the MOW dimension was observed.

The factorial structure of the national sample overlaps with that of the total target groups sample in about 80 percent of the dimensions.

Target groups that deviate sharply from the general structure are the temporary workers and the self-employed. Both groups represent specific attitudinal sets. While it is not surprising to find that temporary workers lack a work centrality factor, this was unexpectedly found to be lacking among the self-employed as well. The income factor was also absent from the factorial structure of temporary workers, whereas the economic and comfort dimension was divided among four factors for this group. This implies that the latter dimension, as opposed to income alone, was valued by temporary employees. This may be one reason why these individuals do not seek full-time employment.

Another characteristic of the self-employed was the absence of a family and leisure factor from their MOW structure. Instead, a work versus family factor emerged only in this group and among the tool and die makers, suggesting a conflict between work and family roles in both groups.

Target groups most closely resembling the general factorial structure were chemical engineers, teachers, and the unemployed. The MOW dimensions that appeared to be dominant and most consistent across all samples were economic and comfort, obligations and opportunities, work centrality, expressive, income, and family and leisure. In addition to the lack of a work centrality factor among the temporary workers and self-employed, other major omissions were the absence of an expressive factor for chemical engineers and the retired, and of an income factor for temporary workers, tool and die makers, and in the national sample. Finally, family and leisure dimensions were not observed in the self-employed, white-collar, and student groups.

Unlike the factorial structure of the total target groups sample, where each dimension consisted of only one factor, some dimensions contained two or more factors in several target groups, notably the teachers, unemployed, and students. Some factors emerged along new dimensions not found in the combined sample of target groups. These were observed mainly in the valued work outcomes and the nonwork-related domains, but this phenomenon was not significant and occurred only in some groups. The principal new MOW factors were societal service and learning. Both were found in the national sample and among the teachers and tool and die makers. The societal service factor was also observed

Table 6.2

Qualitative Comparison of Factorial Structure in Combined Target Groups Sample, National Sample, and Individual Target Groups (numbers denote original factor number)

Meaning of working dimensions	Total target groups	National sample	Chemical engineers	Teachers	Self-employed	Tool and die makers	White collar	Textile workers	Temporary workers	Unemployed	Retired	Students
Centrality of work as a life role												
Work centrality	4	4	4,14	8	—	9	5	2	—	3	11	5
Societal norms about working												
Obligations and opportunities	1	1	2,8	4,5	2,8	2,10	—	5	3,5,11	1,8	4,9,1	2,12
Valued work outcomes												
Income	2	—	12	1,14	7	—	14	13	—	9	1	3,4
Contacts	14	14	7	—	—	—	—	13	—	—	—	—
Status and prestige (28A1)	—	—	—	—	—	—	—	13	13	—	14	—
Societal service (28A5)ª	—	8	—	11	—	15	—	—	—	4	8	8
Interesting and satisfying	—	—	—	—	—	—	—	6	—	—	—	—
Importance of work goals												
Expressive	3	2	—	12	3	11,12	3	3	9	5,14	—	1,10

76

	13	2, 10	12,10	1,6,10,12	8,9,14	9,15	13	1	3,15	3	3,7	6
Economic and comfort Learning (32A)*	—	—	—	14	—	4	3	—	13	—	13	—
Nonwork-related spheres Family and leisure	—	7	7	4	4	—	4	—	6	10	5	5
Religion	—	12	—	—	—	12	14	—	—	11	9	10
Community	—	—	—	—	—	6	—	—	—	9	11	13
Family (30E)*	—	—	—	—	—	—	—	—	—	—	—	—
Work(30C) vs. family(30E)*	—	—	—	—	—	—	6	5	—	—	—	—
Work role identification Organizational identification	9	—	—	—	—	—	—	10	9	6	—	8
Product service identification	—	—	13	—	—	—	—	—	—	—	—	9
Task identification	—	—	—	—	12	10	—	9	10	—	—	11
Co-worker identification	11	6	6	—	10	11	8	—	12	—	—	12
Occupational identification (31E)*	6	5	—	—	11	8	—	—	—	—	10	—

*Items which did not emerge in the original factorial structure of the total sample of combined target groups.

77

in the unemployed, retired, and student groups; and the learning factor appeared among the white-collar and temporary workers.

SUMMARY OF WORK-MEANING STRUCTURES

The results show similarities and differences in MOW structures between target groups and the national sample when treated at the level of the individual. There is a qualitative similarity of about 80 percent between the total sample of target groups and the national sample. The factorial structures of individual target groups varied from only 38 percent (temporary workers) to about 70 percent (chemical engineers, teachers, and unemployed) overlap with the total factorial structure.

On a general level, 13 dimensions of individual work meanings were identified by analyzing data across all target groups. By modifying the heuristic research model presented in Figure 4.1, these dimensions were organized into six domains: (1) centrality to work as a life role, (2) societal norms about working, (3) valued work outcomes, (4) importance of work goals, (5) nonwork-related spheres, and (6) work role identification.

One dimension, work centrality, was interpreted as representing the importance of working as a life role. It emerged as the factor with the highest loadings. It seems reasonable that attitudes concerning work should differ between target groups and be related to measures of general work involvement, such as the investment of time and effort.

The domain of societal norms about working consists of statements about what one should expect to gain from working (entitlements/opportunities), and, in turn, what one should expect to contribute through working (obligations). Contrary to what was expected, both emerged in a single factor. In this sample it is suggested that workers do not actually distinguish opportunities and obligations as separate entities.

In the domain of valued work outcomes, two such dimensions were identified as income and contacts. One would expect to find behavioral intentions and actual behavior logically consistent with the work outcome preference. For example, individuals who highly value the income function of working would be expected to make job choices that might promote this preferred outcome.

Two dimensions emerged in the domain of importance of work goals, indicating what is significant to individuals in their working life. The first, an expressive dimension, included such aspects as the opportunity to learn, good interpersonal relations with supervisors and co-workers, variety, and interesting work. The second was an economic and comfort dimension, including convenient working hours, job security, good pay, and good physical working conditions.

Life aspects not directly related to work, but which interact with working life, are family and leisure, religion, and community. The data show that in Israeli society these nonwork-related spheres are of particular importance, and they should be included in an MOW model.

The major work role identifications that emerged indicate the various frameworks within which individuals view the processes, activities, and outcomes of work. These are (1) the company or organization of which one is a member, (2) the product or service provided, (3) the tasks performed while working, and (4) the people with whom one works. These may reflect the relationship individuals perceive between their own activities and the broader work context.

The data elicited from a variety of target groups and from a representative sample of the labor force may contribute to a better understanding of the values and norms about work currently prevailing in the Israeli labor force. These insights may assist organizations and policy makers in improving, redesigning, or planning work settings. Empirical dimensions identified here may be useful for a future study of NOW patterns or profiles, and also for comparisons across subgroups of workers at the level of occupations, age groups, organizations, industries, and nations.

7

Work Centrality

Concern for decline in the commitment to work and the work ethic along with growth in alienation from work have been voiced in Western societies since the mid–1960s (Sheppard & Herrick 1972). A. Etzioni (1979) cites several social observers and researchers who have detected a weakening in the traditional work and business ethic, along with a growing preoccupation with leisure, quality of working life, comfort, and the avoidance of risk. Others have concluded that the traditional work ethic is no longer adequate in motivating today's workers (Myers & Myers 1974; Rosow 1974; Special Task Force 1973). J. Juzanek (1978) contends that many employers complain about deterioration in the quality of work and levels of skill among workers, lack of achievement and motivation, and unwillingness to accept responsibility. Other researchers (Cherrington 1980; Yankelovich 1979) argue that for younger workers in particular work is becoming less important and that the importance of leisure is increasing.

All this has resulted in a persistent interest and a spate of empirical research in this phenomenon. Consequently, research dealing with the concept of work involvement and other similar or related concepts is relatively recent.

Nevertheless, some researchers (Kanungo 1982b; Morrow 1983) have claimed that no systematic conceptualization or theorizing has resulted from these studies. On the contrary, researchers have used different terms, culminating in the formation of 30 forms of concepts or measures related to work commitment (Morrow 1983).

For example, R. B. Dunham (1984) reviewed the writings of the major job involvement theorists and researchers. He identified three elements of work and job involvement. One element is a conscious wish and determination to partake in work or a job. The second is the degree to which a person considers work as a central life interest. Third, there is the degree to which individuals consider work/job to be central to their self-perception.

S. Rabinowitz and D. T. Hall (1977) recorded terms such as R. Dubin's (1956) central life interest, T. Lodahl and M. Kejner's (1965) job involvement and others such as work role involvements, ego-involved performance, occupational involvement, and even concepts not directly related such as moral, intrinsic motivation and job satisfaction. B. Mannheim (1975) introduced an additional concept termed work role centrality. She defined it as "the relative dominance of work-related contents in the individual's mental processes, as reflected in responses to questions concerning the degree of concern, knowledge, and interest invested in the work role relative to other activities and in the individual's emphasis on work-related subidentities "(p. 81).

P. C. Morrow (1983) classified the 30 work commitment concepts described in the literature in five categories according to the focus of the concepts:

1. *Values*. The intrinsic value of work as an end in itself.

2. *Career*. The importance of work and career in the individual's total life.

3. *Job*. Degree of psychological identification with job/work.

4. *Organization*. Devotion and loyalty to the individual's employing organization.

5. *Union*. Devotion and loyalty to the individual's union.

P. C. Morrow (1983) views the degree of redundancy among these forms of work commitment as a methodological problem. However, the MOW-International Research Team (1987) argues that a more serious conceptual problem could have been identified if the various approaches to work commitment did not display some degree of overlap. This reasoning, however, assumes that all researchers in the area are engaged in the study of one overarching, genotypical view of work importance and that the different foci primarily reflect different approaches to the same thing. Such an assumption is confusing (MOW-International Research Team 1987).

Rabinowitz and Hall (1977) reviewed 83 studies in relation to job involvement. They summarized some of the conclusions about job involvement:

1. Job involvement is related to three classes of working variables: personal characteristics, situational characteristics, and work outcomes.

2. Job involvement is quite stable.

3. Much of the variance in job involvement remains unexplained.

4. The data are more consistent with the "importance of work" definition of job involvement than with the "extent to which performance affects self-esteem" definition.

5. Job involvement seems to be a "feed-back variable," both a cause and an effect of job behavior.

6. Personal and situational variables have independent effects on involvement.

7. Situational variables seem to have more effect on the attitudes of low job-involved persons than on highly job-involved persons. (pp. 284–85)

THE CONCEPT OF WORK CENTRALITY

In the MOW project we have attempted to develop a useful concept that focuses on the generalized importance of work. Termed "work centrality," it is a concept dealing with the life of a human being as the focal unit of analysis and the "relative importance of work in the individual's life" at a given period as the area of concern. We do not first single out an a priori reason why work should be important in life, or in what way it is important, and then attempt to have work centrality represent that particular explanation for work importance. Rather, we choose to remain neutral toward various rationales for work importance. Work may be important principally because of what one extracts from it, or primarily because of what one invests in the process of work, or because of some combination of these and other reasons. To these differing explanations for work importance the general concept of work centrality must remain neutral, as should our measurement procedures. R. N. Kanungo's (1982a) conceptual distinction between work involvement and job involvement, and his argument for separating measurement of the state of involvement (centrality, in our terms) from its antecedents or from its consequences, is in accord with this project's conceptualization. Work centrality is thus defined as the degree of general importance that work has in the life of an individual at any given time (see Dubin 1956; Dubin, Champoux & Porter 1975; and Dubin, Headley & Taveggia 1976 for a similar concept).

THE MEASUREMENT OF WORK CENTRALITY

While several measurement procedures may be used to assess the general importance of work in life (see Kanungo 1982a for three related measurement devices), two measurement procedures were chosen. In the first, the importance of work is directly compared with the importance of other major life areas or roles. The evaluative frame of reference for this procedure is complex but structured, involving self and working versus self and other major life areas. The primary intended features of this measurement procedure are comparative in nature and involve cognitive and decision-making elements. The question utilizing the comparative item that was used to assess work centrality (question 30) is as follows:

30.   Assign a total of 100 points to indicate how important the following areas are in your life at the present time.

30A   __ __ My leisure (like hobbies, sports, recreation and contacts with friends)

30B   __ __ My community (like voluntary organizations, union and political organizations)

30C   __ __ My work

30D   __ __ My religion (like religious activities and beliefs)

30E   __ __ My family

For any individual, the degree of importance of work as a life area (based on the number of points allotted) may range from first to fifth.

The second measurement procedure consisted of a seven-point scaled response to the question "How important and significant is working in your *total* life?" The anchor statement at the low end of the scale was "one of the least important things in my life" while the anchor statement at the high end was "one of the most important things in my life" (question 29). Here the frame of reference is self in working and no comparative standards are specified, as in the case of question 30; hence this is an absolute or scaled measure of work centrality.

The two indicators of work centrality are moderately related ($r = .26, p < .0001$). Although the two are not highly correlated, they are combined to provide a general index of work centrality at the level of the individual.

The work centrality index was constructed by combining the two measures (questions 29 and 30c) for all responses. This was done through the simple addition of the number of points (out of 100) assigned to "my work" (question 30c) and the mean score on the scaled measure (question 29) of work centrality. To eliminate scaling differences in the aggregated variables, the index was standardized (z score). Setting the mean equal to 50 and the standard deviation equal to 10 is a convenient measure to eliminate the problems of dealing with negative z scores.

WORK CENTRALITY AND OTHER IMPORTANT LIFE AREAS

Table 7.1 presents various results concerning work centrality. An examination of the relative importance of major life areas reveals beyond question the significance of the family role in the Israeli population. In every target group (except for the self-employed) as well as in the national sample, significantly more points were allotted to family than to any other life area, amounting to about 38 percent in the target samples population and over 43 percent in the national sample. It seems that the mental and physical effort, along with the time commitment required by the self-employed to "invest" in their privately run businesses, probably makes work for this group more important than their family (the self-employed work an average of 52.5 hours per week—more than any other target group; this compares with an average of 42 hours per week in the national sample). However, as noted, this is the exception. The importance of the family, its role, and family relations are highly valued in the Jewish tradition and in Israeli society (Peres & Katz 1981).

The function and role of the family incontestably demonstrates every other life area. The family is the core element in the individual's life and provides, among other things, basic needs, warmth, support, and security.

After family, the role of work is next in importance in the life of Israelis. With one exception, every sample participating in this study selected work as its second most important sphere. The exception was tool and die makers, who awarded leisure one point more than work, dropping work into third place.

Table 7.1
Points Assigned to Various Life Areas (out of 100), Absolute Work Centrality Scores, and Scores on Work Centrality Index

Variable	National Sample	Students	Chemical Engineers	Self-Employed	Teachers	Temporary Workers	Textile Workers	Tool & Die	White Collar	Retired	Unem-ployed
a. Leisure	18[a]	24	17	19	15	24	14	21	23	19	22
b. Community	4	13	4	3	5	4	5	5	5	13	7
c. Work	28	25	36	37	31	26	32	20	28	12	24
d. Religion	5	11	4	8	5	2	8	6	9	5	7
e. Family	43	28	39	30	43	44	40	43	36	48	34
Importance of Work in Life[b]											
Mean	5.53	5.64	5.85	5.52	5.53	4.93	5.97	5.54	5.08	5.96	5.22
S.D.	1.32	1.21	1.07	1.65	1.19	1.42	1.62	1.64	1.26	1.19	1.42
Work Centrality Index[c]											
Mean	50.25	49.58	53.40	52.57	50.91	46.98	52.83	49.31	48.52	47.47	47.85
S.D.	7.77	5.64	6.33	10.39	6.01	6.76	6.43	7.88	7.37	6.40	8.15

Notes:
[a] Scores are rounded.
[b] Ranges from 1 = least to 7 = most.
[c] Work Centrality Index statistics for the national sample: distribution of score range 25.42 to 74.32; mode 56.16; median 50.12; variance 60.39.

The role of leisure is third in importance for the Israeli population. It should be noted that objectively the opportunities for leisure time and leisure activities are relatively limited. In Israel there is a six-day working week, Saturday is an official rest day, and most people work about six hours on Friday. There has been a slowly developing trend in recent years toward a five-day week. Along with this an awareness of the role of leisure in modern society has begun to develop. However, it is true to say that at present leisure is still less advanced and is considered less important than it is in other industrialized nations. Nevertheless, leisure seems to be more central for some groups than for others. Particularly noticeable are tool and die makers, who assigned one point more to leisure than to work; temporary workers and the unemployed, who assigned only two more points to work than to leisure; and finally white-collar workers, who assigned five more points to work than to leisure. For the rest of the working groups as well as the national sample the gap between work and leisure was significant and wide.

In this population the importance of the remaining two roles, religion and community, is markedly low. Figure 7.1 displays how important work is in the individual's total life (question 29): it is very important. In every group it received over five points out of seven, with the exception of textile workers (4.93 points).

Work centrality index scores among the ten target groups and the national sample are presented in Table 7.1. The pattern of the work centrality index seems best indicated by the clustering in Figure 7.2. Three groups are distinctly higher than the rest regarding work centrality: chemical engineers, textile workers, and the self-employed. Temporary workers are placed at the other extreme, with the lowest work centrality, the remaining groups are distributed in between. Work

Figure 7.1
Relative Importance of Various Life Roles in the National Sample (points assigned out of 100)

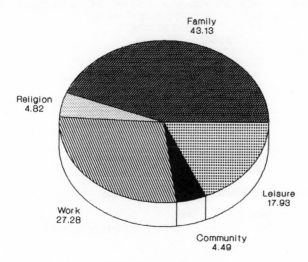

Figure 7.2
Cluster of Target Groups and National Sample of Work Centrality index

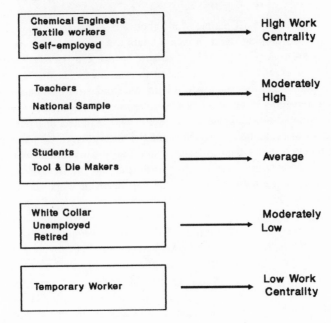

Chemical Engineers Textile workers Self-employed	→ High Work Centrality
Teachers National Sample	→ Moderately High
Students Tool & Die Makers	→ Average
White Collar Unemployed Retired	→ Moderately Low
Temporary Worker	→ Low Work Centrality

Figure 7.3
Comparison of Work Centrality among the Target Groups Samples, and by Sex and Age

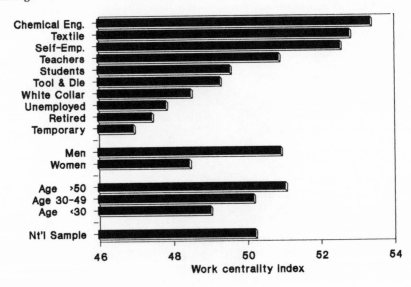

centrality scores for target groups, the sexes, three age categories, and the national sample are presented in Figure 7.3.

The analysis of differences between men and women is presented in Table 7.2. Of the various life areas, two received most attention. In the first place, family was awarded most points by both sexes, but significantly (p = .003) more by women (over 45 points). Work was ranked second in importance by both sexes but was significantly (p = .001) more important for men than for women. These distinctions may also be observed in Figure 7.4. No significant differences were found between men and women in the remaining life areas. A similar trend was also reported by B. Shamir (1986b) in his study of Israeli data in 1983. There the differences were even more pronounced. Respondents were asked to allocate 100 points to three life areas. Family received 84 points from women and 66 from men, while work was assigned 24 points by men and only 11 by women. In the third category of leisure no significant difference was observed. It is possible that had Shamir utilized five life areas instead of three, less points would have been awarded to family. Nevertheless, Shamir's data strongly support the present finding, which points to the differences in the emphasis that men and women place on family and work. This is also supported by findings concerning differences between men and women regarding family

Table 7.2
Differences between Men and Women Regarding Importance of Various Life Areas and Measures of Work Centrality (out of 100 points)

Variable	Men	Women	t value	P value
Life Areas				
a. Leisure	17.57	18.36		
	(15.94)	(15.34)		
b. Community	4.54	4.41		
	(8.29)	(9.84)		
c. Work	29.56	25.54	3.38	.001
	(19.92)	(16.80)		
d. Religion	5.06	4.49		
	(11.62)	(11.41)		
e. Family	41.34	45.41	-2.94	.003
	(21.21)	(21.17)		
Importance of Work in Life	5.65	5.37	3.08	.002
	(1.32)	(1.31)		
Work Centrality Index	50.95	48.84	4.10	.0001
	(7.88)	(7.46)		

Notes:
Standard deviations are given in parenthesis.
Owing to some missing responses, scores do not sum up to 100 points.

Figure 7.4
Relative Importance of Life Roles in the National Sample

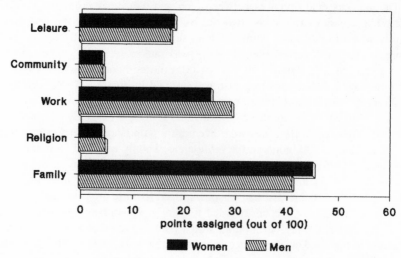

and work in Y. Ben-David's (1975) kibbutz study. Further evidence of the importance of work in the life of men as compared with women is shown in Table 7.2. Men score significantly ($p = .002$) higher than women on the absolute work centrality scale (question 29), as well as on the work centrality index ($p < .0001$). Men were also found to work significantly more hours per week than women (48.03 versus 34.11). These results clearly show that the role of work is significantly more central for men than for women.

Some of the explanations for the principal differences between men and women regarding work can be related to a distinction in the orientations of the sexes to work as a life role. It has been suggested that the socialization of women to sex roles causes them to regard work as being less central to their lives (Ritzer 1972; Saal 1978). S. D. Saleh and M. Lalljee (1969) found that men perceived their occupation to be more central to their lives than did women. H. B. Presser and W. Baldwin (1980) claimed that working women experienced a conflict between their expected role as a homemaker and their role as a full-time career- oriented worker . D. N. Izraeli (1982) contends that working women have a heightened awareness to their children and the well-being of their family members. This recognition leads women to give priority to family functions over work.

An analysis of the relationship between work centrality and some other variables revealed no association between educational level and work centrality. However, a trend could be observed in the relationship between the rate of monthly pay and work centrality (see Table 7.3). The higher the pay, the more central the work to the individual. Regarding the relationship between age and work centrality, the latter is significantly higher with each successive age group ($p = .01$).

Table 7.3
Relationship between Work Centrality and Level of Pay in National Sample

Pay Level	Work Centrality Score	Standard Deviation	F Value
Low	46.40	7.23	
Average income in labor force	48.50	8.10	19.65 [a]
Moderately high	50.64	7.52	
High	52.23	7.24	

Note: [a] $p < .0001$.

NONFINANCIAL EMPLOYMENT COMMITMENT*

In considering the issue of work centrality and the commitment to work, a distinction should be made between instrumental and noninstrumental reasons for working and being involved with the job (Warr 1982). Instrumental motivations for working are economic, whereas noninstrumental motivations are mostly socio-psychological. P. Warr (1982) termed the latter "non-financial employment commitment." A useful indicator of the non-financial employment commitment of individuals is the so-called lottery question. This question, considered as an inferred measure of work centrality (England & Harpaz 1983), served as an additional approach for gathering work centrality data in this study. It asks if a person would continue working if he or she won a lottery or inherited a large sum of money. The question thus posits a situation where the economic rationale for, or the necessity of, working has been removed, thereby setting the stage for assessing a person's nonfinancial and socio-psychological commitment to work.

The lottery question was first posed by N. C. Morse and R. C. Weiss (1955) in their classic study of the function and meaning of work. In a national sample of employed men in the United States, 80 percent of the respondents indicated that they would continue working even in the absence of any further need to earn a living. This question, generally in the same form, was presented to workers in various countries (e.g., Campbell, Converse & Rodgers 1976; Kaplan & Tausky 1974; MOW-International Research Team 1987; Quinn & Staines 1979; Takeuchi 1975; Tausky 1969; Vecchio 1980; Warr 1982) in addition to Israel (e.g., Mannheim & Rein 1981; Shamir 1986b; Shefi 1986). All these studies revealed a similar relative inferred importance of work, namely, that between 70 and 95 percent of the respondents would continue to work.

The lottery question in this study (question 48A) took the following form:

*This section is derived from Itzhak Harpaz, "Variables Affecting Non-financial Employment Commitment," *Applied Psychology: An International Review* 37 (1988): 235–48.

48A Imagine that you won a lottery or inherited a large sum of money and could live comfortably for the rest of your life without working. What would you do concerning working?
    1 I would stop working.
    2 I would continue to work in the same job.
    3 I would continue to work but with changed conditions.

Answers 2 and 3 were considered to express a desire to continue working.

Since a comparison with earlier data will be made in this paper, a methodological problem may arise because a choice of only two possible responses was offered in previous studies (e.g., Morse & Weiss 1955; Mannheim & Rein 1981; Vecchio 1980). These consisted of (1) "I would continue to work" and (2) "I would stop working." Firstly, respondents who selected answers 2 and 3 of the lottery question also assigned the highest number of points to work on the life spheres measure: 30.8 and 30.61 (out of 100 total) respectively (question 30, described earlier), (t value $= -0.29, p = .769$). Thus there were no significant differences in this regard between respondents in these two groups. Moreover, both groups differed significantly from respondents who chose answer 1 ("I would stop working"). The latter assigned only 21.8 points to work (t value $= 3.23, p = .002$) and awarded their highest number of points to leisure (29.8). Respondents who selected answers 2 and 3 gave leisure 22.3 and 21.8 points respectively. Since work appears to be of considerable importance to those in our sample who chose answers 2 and 3, it is likely that they would continue to work regardless of their financial circumstances.

Further, we tested empirically the proposition that those who expressed a preference to continue working would do so in any circumstances, whether at the same job or under different conditions (that is, alternatives 2 and 3 are equivalent). Two versions of the lottery question, one of them offering a choice of two answers and the other a choice of three, were administered to 313 adult students in 15 classes of the Extension Division of the University of Haifa, Israel. Each class was split randomly into two groups, each of which was presented with one version of the lottery question. All respondents were full-time workers in a variety of occupations (for example, production, services, teaching, clerical, finance, sales, engineering, management, self-employed). The distribution of age and educational background, which resembled the national sample, were similar in both groups.

The results showed that among the group that was offered two response alternatives ($n = 161$), 11.8 percent indicated that they would stop working and 88.2 percent that they would continue working. In the second group ($n = 152$), 9.3 percent indicated that they would stop working, 49.7 percent that they would continue at the same job, and 41 percent that they would continue, but under different conditions. Thus only a small proportion of either group indicated they would choose to stop working. The majority preferred to continue, regardless of the specific conditions. The availability of a third choice does not appear to have affected the overall pattern of the expressed intentions to continue or stop working.

A degree of caution is in order before we analyze and interpret our findings. The lottery question proposes a hypothetical situation. It is unlikely that respondents would really be faced with the opportunity to quit work because they had come into an unexpected fortune. We are therefore left to ponder how the expressed attitudes toward commitment to work may be linked to actual behavior. Moreover, as in the case of other attitudes, the attitudes toward work elicited by the lottery question may reflect socially desirable judgments. Nevertheless, the data presented by Warr (1982) from his research and from others suggests that this sort of measure of employment commitment is in fact indicative of actual behavior at the workplace (Sheppard & Belitsky 1966; Stafford, Jackson & Banks 1980; Warr 1978; Warr & Lovatt 1977). To the extent that this is so, the lottery question may be regarded as a fairly good determinant of nonfinancial employment commitment.

The analysis of the lottery question revealed that 87.5 percent of the respondents in the national sample indicated they would choose to continue working even if they no longer had any financial reason for doing so (50.3 percent at the same job, and 37.2 percent under different conditions). Only 12.5 percent indicated they would prefer to stop working. Results with similar and even higher proportions of willingness to continue working were reported in all Israeli studies so far published (Mannheim 1981; Shamir 1986b; Shefi 1986).

Figure 7.5 displays the results of the response to the lottery question among target groups and in relation to the national sample. Significant differences were

Figure 7.5
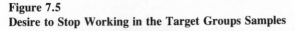
Desire to Stop Working in the Target Groups Samples

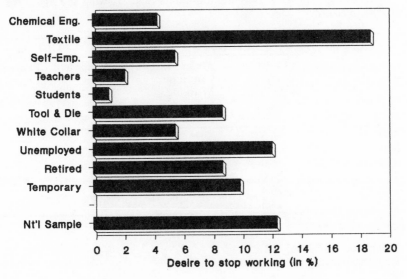

noted between different groups in relation to their expressed desire to continue or stop working (Chi-square 31.75, $p = .0001$). Textile workers, probably the group of blue-collar workers with the lowest levels of skills, desired more than the others to stop working (18.9 percent). At the other extreme, students, most of whom had not yet worked, expressed a somewhat idealistic portrayal of the world of work; a mere 1.1 percent expressed a desire to stop working. A very high desire to continue working was also indicated by teachers and chemical engineers. Finally, concerning the results presented in Figure 7.4, it is evident that the desire to stop working is lower for all target groups (with the exception of textile workers) than for the national sample.

For purposes of comparison, the results obtained by B. Mannheim and J. Rein (1981) in their analysis of Israeli data are examined alongside the present data. However, the Mannheim and Rein data referred only to a sample of men in the labor force. Consequently, this comparison includes only men ($n = 552$). As can be discerned in Table 7.4, the current response distributions are similar to those obtained ten years earlier. In both samples a significant majority of workers preferred to continue working rather than stop.

Although more people than before indicated a desire to continue working, these similarities change markedly when a comparison is made by age groups in the same two populations. A breakdown according to age cohorts revealed some important changes in the response structure between 1971 and 1981. The proportions of respondents who preferred to continue working are presented according to the different age cohorts in Table 7.4 and in Figure 7.6.

In the 1971 data, the relation between the preference to stop working and age

Table 7.4
The Relationship between Preference to Continue/Stop Working and Age, 1971 and 1981 (men only)

Age Categories	1971 Data[a]				1981 Data		
	Prefer to Stop Working		Prefer to Continue Working		Prefer to Stop Working		Prefer to Continue Working
	n	%	%	n	%	%
20-29	142	6.3	93.7	110	15.4	84.6
30-39	143	8.2	91.8	143	10.7	89.3
40-49	141	16.0	89.0	110	12.6	87.4
50-59	155	20.0	80.0	106	12.1	87.9
60 & over	91	26.4	73.6	75	12.9	87.1
Total	672	14.8	85.2	544[b]	11.1	88.9

Notes:
[a] Mannheim and Rein, 1981.
[b] Reduced n owing to missing data.

Figure 7.6
Comparison of Desire to Stop Working of Different Age Groups in 1971 and 1981

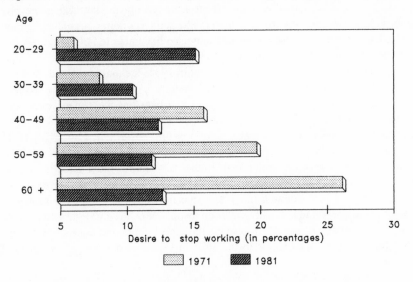

Note: 1971 data besed on Mannheim and Rein, 1981.

increases linearly, with a minimum in the youngest cohort and a maximum in the oldest. On the other hand, our 1981 data show almost a straight line, with a tendency toward an increase in the preference to stop working in the youngest and oldest age groups. A Chi-square test yielded nonsignificant results, suggesting that in the current sample the preference to continue or to stop work does not depend on age. Major changes occurred mainly among the youngest and oldest age categories. An increase approaching 150 percent was noted in the expressed desire of young people to stop working (6.3 percent to 15.4 percent); yet a decline of over 100 percent was observed among the oldest respondents in their desire to stop working (26.5 percent to 12.9 percent). Young people in Israel appear to have a somewhat different attitude to work in the 1980s from that of their counterparts of a decade ago. The noted trend of changes in work values observed in affluent Western societies is apparently evident in Israel too (e.g., Cherrington 1980; Etzioni 1979; Juzanek 1978; Yankelovich 1979). This is particularly noticeable among the respondents in the youngest age cohort (20–29),a circumstance that has been reported elsewhere (e.g., Cherrington 1980; Levitan & Johnson 1982; Vecchio 1980; Yankelovich 1979).

At the other end of the age continuum, we clearly observe a different phenomenon. Figure 7.6 shows a stronger preference among the older members in our sample to continue working than was expressed by their counterparts ten years earlier. Thus, something seems to have affected the attitudes of older

Israelis too. The main influences on the decision to retire earlier or later may be related to economic factors. R. E. Barfield (1970) found that the better the economic conditions workers can expect after retirement, the higher the probability they will choose early retirement. The acute economic problems that have beset Israeli society in the last decade may also have affected older Israelis more than their juniors. Inflation in Israel soared from annual rates of 10–15 percent in the early 1970s to more than 130 percent in 1981. It should be noted, however, that Israel has one of the most advanced systems of indexation in the world. In 1981, cost-of-living adjustments to wages and pensions were made every three months, at a rate of about 80 percent of the inflation level. As a consequence the nation's middle-income earners were not seriously affected by inflation. The case has been rather different for retired persons relying on pensions, which are lower than their income from work. Rather than retire, older Israelis therefore prefer to remain fully or partially employed, and probably more so today than a decade ago. Thus although the lottery question was intended to neutralize the effect of the economic necessity factor on respondents, the environmental realities cannot be totally eliminated from their thoughts. Economic considerations may therefore be a primary factor in the shift in the older age group's response to the lottery question.

A stepwise discriminant analysis method was used to classify the characteristics of workers expressing their wish to continue/stop working. A unique feature of this procedure is that it allows us to infer the likely response of other workers with similar characteristics (Klecka 1975). The independent variables studied here were selected because their relevance to work-related values had previously been demonstrated (Vecchio 1980). These were education, religious affiliation (question 72), place of residence (urban verses rural), level of income, ethnic origin, and sex.

Table 7.5 presents the results of the stepwise discriminant analysis, in which the preference to continue or to stop working is the dependent variable. It shows the order in which significant variables were entered into the model, as well as their discriminant function coefficients.

Ethnic origin emerged as the most significant discriminating variable. Afro-Asian Jews immigrated to Israel from underdeveloped countries. This may substantially account for their failure, and that of their Israeli-born children, to do as well as European-American Jews (Weller 1974). Other studies (e.g., Yuchtman-Yaar & Semyonov 1979) clearly indicate that the social, economic, and political conditions of Afro-Asian Jews in Israel are inferior to those of European-American Jews. The latter are also greatly overrepresented in the most prestigious occupations and in the better-paid job categories (Statistical Abstract of Israel 1982). In a study with aims similar to ours, B. Mannheim (1975) also found that work had the least centrality among workers of Afro-Asian origin. Ethnic origin therefore appears to be the most important variable differentiating between Israeli males who would prefer to continue working and those who would prefer to stop working.

Table 7.5
Stepwise Discriminant Analysis of the Preference to Continue/Stop Working in the Labor Force (significant variables only)

Independent Variable	Discriminant Function Coefficients			
Ethnic Origin	.526			
Occupational Satisfaction	.481			
Sex	− .393			
Religious Affiliation	− .381			
Education	.353			

Canonical Correlation	Wilk's Lambda	Eigenvalue	χ^2	df	p
.251	.937	.0669	49.795	5	.00001

Group	Centroid
Would continue working	.098
Would stop working	−.678

Occupational satisfaction was the second most significant discriminating variable. This finding is in line with the large quantity of data available on the relationship between dissatisfaction with work and worker absenteeism and worker turnover. The prevalent explanation of this relationship is that an unpleasant or dissatisfying work situation will influence a person to withdraw from work by either absence or changing jobs (e.g., Arnold & Feldman 1982). S. E. Seashore (1973) points to an ultimate form of withdrawal from work—opting out of the labor force completely without trying to secure other gainful employment. A similar process may be at work among our sample. Given the hypothetical opportunity of stopping work, those among the sample of this study who were experiencing low job satisfaction were more likely to choose this option.

A third important discriminating variable in the present study is *sex*. There are significant differences between responses of males and females on the lottery question. Of the men, 89.9 percent indicated their desire to continue working, while only 83.8 percent of women did so. Although work is important to both groups, as indicated by their relatively high response, it is clear that if women had the opportunity to quit working, they would more probably do so than men. This is in accord with other findings presented earlier in the chapter concerning the place of work in women's lives.

The next variable to emerge was *religious affiliation*. Only 10.3 percent of the secular respondents expressed a desire to stop working, while 21 percent of those with close religious attachments demonstrated such a tendency. When the latter were asked, "Why would you stop working," their overwhelming reply was "To practice and study the Torah." Religious workers assigned only 20.24 points out of 100 to work as compared with 30.11 points given by nonreligious, a clearly significant difference ($t = 5.67, p = .0001$). In a similar vein, workers who are religious and who also received a religious education scored significantly lower than nonreligious respondents on the work centrality index (47.41 religious verses 50.33 nonreligious; $t = 3.66$, $p = .0001$). These findings can reflect that religious Jews may see work as less important in comparison with their practice of religion.

The final variable to emerge in our analysis was that of *educational level*. C. Tausky (1969) found education to be the single most important variable related to the meaning of work. Men who had not completed high school were found to have an instrumental attitude toward work, while those with some advanced technical or vocational education placed a higher value on the prestige associated with work. In a survey of working conditions conducted in 1969–70, it was found that respondents with higher educational levels were closely associated with intrinsic values (for example, interesting work, opportunity to develop abilities); whereas among those with low educational levels, financial considerations were of greatest importance (Katzell 1979). In this connection R. A. Katzell (1979) notes that in a survey of college students reported by Daniel Yankelovich, job challenge and the ability to make meaningful contributions were the factors that ranked the highest in students' career choices, while financial and comfort factors (for example, working hours, work load) were low on the list of priorities. Similarly, B. Mannheim (1975) reports in her Israeli study that work centrality increased as the level of respondents' education rose.

In sum, the utilization of a stepwise discriminant analysis enabled us to determine which variables may distinguish between those who desire to continue or to stop working in the present Israeli labor force. Five variables emerged from a list of work-related independent variables: ethnic origin, occupational satisfaction, sex, religious affiliation, and education. Based on the analysis, it may be possible to draw a profile of those who are likely to continue or stop working in the event of winning a lottery or inheriting a large sum of money or, alternatively, those who show a higher commitment to work. Those who would continue to work are more likely to be men of European or American origin, to be satisfied with their work, to be nonreligious, and to have attained higher levels of education. The extent of nonfinancial commitment to work, as measured by the lottery question, does not appear to have changed in Israel over the last decade. The lottery question has been considered as an inferred measure of work centrality (England & Harpaz 1983), so that the results obtained here may be taken to indicate that work is highly central for the population involved in the present study. This attitude is in keeping with the role that work and the work ethic have traditionally played in Jewish history and culture. These figures remained constant in spite of current labor unrest and the changes in work values and the attitudes toward work that have occurred in the industrialized world over the past two decades (Yankelovich 1979; Levitan et al. 1981).

CONCLUSION

Various analyses were conducted in this chapter to assess the centrality of work. The message conveyed through the data is quite clear. Work is one of the most central elements in the life of Israelis. There is no doubt that the institution of the family has been and remains the most basic constituent in the Israeli reality. It is considerably more important than work or any other role or domain in life. However, next to family, work occupies the most important position.

The data reveal some trends as well as providing support for the expected findings concerning work, of which the most salient are the following:

- The centrality of work is relatively high in this population.
- Work is significantly more important to men than to women.
- Work is less central for younger than for older workers.
- The nonfinancial employment commitment for young workers is significantly lower than in the early 1970s.
- The occupational groups (target groups) of chemical engineers and the self-employed exhibit relatively higher work centrality orientations.
- Occupational groups loosely attached to the labor force (temporary workers, the retired and unemployed) seem to have lower work centrality levels.

In sum, the present chapter suggests that the constituent element of the work ethic represented by various work centrality measures, that is, the value of desiring to work and to hold a job, is still very much in evidence among Israeli workers today. Although younger Israelis show changes in attitudes to work, as a group, they nevertheless remain highly committed to work. The majority (about 85 percent) of the respondents in the younger age cohort and even a higher proportion in the rest of the population continue to hold a positive attitude to work.

The data reinforce our view that work centrality is one important work meaning that probably has a significant impact on individuals, organizations, and society in general. It may be argued that work centrality for the individual human being is a fundamental concept almost universal within industrial societies (MOW-International Research Team 1987). Work centrality is a useful scientific concept that probably has important practical and policy implications for those concerned with the present and the future of work, and working lives.

8

Societal Norms
Concerning Work

Social norms and normative viewpoints about work are of current interest just as they have been in the past. This interest has been brought on by changes taking place in the world of work. Salient are the changes taking place in the composition of the labor force, namely, expansion in the participation rates of women, a delay in the entry into the labor force, and higher educational levels of the new entrants. Transformations have occurred in the content and structure of the workplace, including changes in the context of work, in demands on competence, and in the degree of worker control and autonomy. Another visible trend in the nature of work is the overall shift toward white-collar and service employment. Technological changes and innovations contribute not only to higher productivity and efficiency but also to a potential loss of skills, displacement of workers, and insecurity. All of these, along with other phenomena, affect and shape normative views toward work and may change prevailing societal norms about work.

An important issue is the extent to which changes in work and working situations are accompanied by changes in what work means to individuals and, consequently, by changes in the standards people use for reasoning about work.

Here, a brief clarification is in order about the nature of norms. G. C. Homans (1950) defined *norm* as "an idea in the minds of the members of a group . . . specifying what the members or other men should do, ought to do, are expected to do, under given circumstances" (p. 123). Norms are social phenomena expressing social beliefs and values that refer to unwritten rules and mores of a society (Yankelovich 1981). The concept of norm holds two elements. First, there is some agreement on the behaviors that group members should (or should not) adopt; and, second, nonconformity with these agreed norms will be followed by sanctions (Homans 1950). Norms are not generated in a vacuum but are part of a culture and the value system maintained by its members. Social norms emerge from the expectations held by the population. The expectations held by the majority of the community carry much moral weight as to what is considered right or wrong behavior. Nevertheless, Homans (1950) contends that norms are only ideas; they are not actual behaviors but what people think that behavior ought to be.

Two central work-related norms discussed and analyzed here focus on "rights" and "duties" related to work; hence, they are viewed as important to contemporary discussion about the nature of work and its future development. The first is an *entitlement* norm, an outgrowth of prosperity and a rise in standards of living and the expectation that they will continue, as has been the experience in the Western world and in Israel in the last few decades. Moreover, workers become increasingly better educated and eventually more highly informed about the nature of jobs. These changes make workers more aware of matters of direct concern to them, and they are thus more inclined to attend to their interests. Such anticipations and awareness are, in turn, gradually perceived as entitlements, or social rights. This process is termed "psychology of entitlement" (Davis 1980). Through it, wishes or needs are transformed into a set of assumed rights (Yankelovich 1974).

The entitlement norm as developed and used here represents the underlying work rights of individuals and the work related responsibility of organizations and society toward all individuals. In the present study this norm includes the following notions:

1. Employing organizations should retrain and reemploy workers if their skills become obsolete.
2. It is the responsibility of the educational system to prepare people for good jobs.
3. Workers have the right to participate in decisions affecting work methods.
4. Every person is entitled to meaningful and interesting work.
5. Every person who wishes to work is entitled to a job.

In contrast to the entitlement norm is a norm that emphasizes one's *obligation(s)* to a prospective employer or society. This norm is generally in concert with the traditional work ethic. Under this ethic personal success is attributed to an individual's efforts in accomplishing various obligations. It encourages hard work for the benefit of self as well as society at large.

The obligation norm developed and used here represents the underlying duties of all individuals to organizations and society with respect to working. This norm includes the notions that everyone

1. has a duty to contribute to society by working;
2. is obliged to save for the future;
3. contributes through improving job procedures;
4. accepts any type of work as long as there is fair compensation; and
5. values work whatever its nature.

The measurement of these two societal norms comes from the extent of agreement with the ten normative statements about working entitlements and obligations in question 47 (see questionnaire in Appendix I). It should again be noted that we have utilized an evaluative rather than a descriptive meaning of norms; in other words, norms tell us what should be, not what is. The ten statements involve general expectations about approximate behavior concerning working.

Two indices (an entitlement index and an obligation index) have been derived from subsets of the ten statements as described in Chapter 5. After a principal components factor analysis, it was found that statements in items 47A, E, G, and I (entitlement items) and 47B, D, and J (obligation items) generally form the appropriate dimension for the national sample but not for the combined samples of target groups. As may be observed in Chapter 6, in the combined sample of all ten target groups only one factor emerges, without distinguishing entitlement and obligation norms.

LOCATION OF SAMPLES IN THE WORK NORM SPACE

Since we consider these two work norms as primarily societal or group representations as opposed to individual representations, it is most appropriate to focus on the comparisons of the target groups as well as the national sample to gain a better perspective on outcomes. It also seems appropriate to explore the extent to which the two norms might be considered balanced within a target group or the national sample in terms of relative agreement with the items defining entitlement and those defining obligation. Since we lack an adequate standard for transforming the degree of agreement with statements comprising each norm into "balanced" terms for each one of our samples (that is, equivalence on the two norm indices), we have chosen to report a crude measure of balance obtained from the total societal norm space as defined by the two norms in every sample studied. It should be recognized that this crude indicator of balance between the norms in a given sample is a relative indicator. It is relative to differences in norm agreement levels within a target group as referenced against such differences in all target groups or the national sample.

Figure 8.1 presents the location of the target groups and national sample in societal norms space as defined by the entitlement and obligation indices. The entitlement index was created by adding the scores on entitlement items—questions 47A, G, I, and E—standardizing their scores (z scores), setting the mean equal to 50 and the standard deviation equal to 10. Similarly, the obligation index was obtained by adding obligation items—questions, 47B, D, and J—transforming them into z scores with a mean of 50 and a standard deviation of 10. Results of this analysis are displayed in Figure 8.1, in which the t-scores with a mean of 50 and an SD of 10 are displayed.

Figure 8.1 portrays two major features of societal norms space: (1) relative levels of agreement with each norm among the ten target groups and the national sample and (2) relative levels of balance between the two norms in each target

Figure 8.1
Location of Target Groups and National Sample in Societal Norms

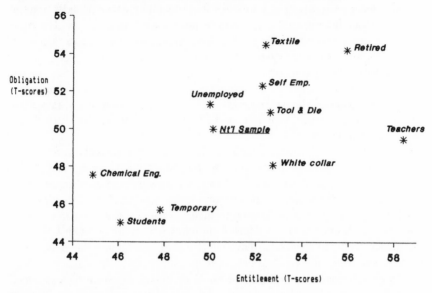

Note:
Differences of 1-2 T-scores points between samples comparedhere can be considered significantly different in a statistical sense.

group as well as for the national sample. There is a general tendency toward the entitlement norm in this population rather than toward the obligation norm. Retired persons, textile workers, and the self-employed as well as the national sample show the highest agreement with the obligation norm; unemployed, tool and die makers, and teachers are in the middle category in this respect; and chemical engineers, white-collar workers, temporary workers, and students show the lowest agreement with the obligation norm. Regarding the entitlement norm, retired persons, teachers, and tool and die makers show the most concern; textile workers, the self-employed, the national sample, and white-collar workers are in the middle group; whereas the unemployed, temporary workers, students, and chemical engineers are distinctly lowest on the entitlement norm.

Concerning the relative equilibrium between the two norms, the self-employed and students show close to a perfectly balanced level of agreement with the two norms; the self-employed are balanced at a rather high level of agreement with both norms, while students are at the lowest level of agreement with both norms. In the national sample, retired persons, tool and die makers, and unemployed groups show a relatively balanced level of agreement with both norms. White-collar and temporary workers display a moderate degree of imbalance in scopes of agreement with the two norms. The remaining target groups of teachers, chemical engineers, and textile workers show a relatively large imbalance in levels of agreement with the two norms.

The implications of the differences for each of the two norms and of the different balance configurations within the samples are far from clear. Naturally, it would seem desirable at any time for a reasonable balance to exist between the entitlement and obligation orientations toward work in a society. Nevertheless, a general overview of Figure 8.1 projects a picture of relative degrees of balanced norms with a tendency toward an entitlement predilection.

What these data suggest about societal norms concerning work in Israeli society is more appropriate to reasonable hypothesis generation than to hypothesis testing. Later chapters in which these work norms are related to various work patterns and work outcomes (see Chapters 12 and 13) provide material for the formulation of several hypotheses.

Important changes are occurring in the labor market, especially in relation to demographic variables. For example, the number of roles that women play in the labor force is steadily increasing. There is a growth in the numbers of retired people (partially due to life extension), on the one hand, and the difficulties that young people experience in relation to their entry into the labor force, on the other. Levels of education and educational requirements are constantly rising in accordance with job demands. Thus, it is useful to examine the relationship between sex, age, and educational level in relation to societal norms. These demographic variables have been shown to be important, since they delineate differentiating standards toward work (Buchholz 1978; Iso-Ahola & Buttimer 1981).

Table 8.1 displays the societal norms scores on the demographic variables for the national sample. No differences were found between men and women in terms of agreement with entitlement items as reflected through the entitlement index. However, men are significantly more obligation oriented than women.

Table 8.1
Entitlement and Obligation Scores per Various Demographic Variables in the National Sample (mean _t_ scores)

Demographic Variable	Societal	Norms					
	Entitlement				Obligation		
Sex	males		females		males		females
	52		52		54		52
Age Category	young (under 30)	middle (30-50)	old (over 50)		young (under 30)	middle (30-50)	old (over 50)
	51	52	52		52	53	55
Education Level	Primary Secondary	Some College	University		Primary Secondary	Some College	University
	52 52	53	51		55 53	53	51

The effect of sex is distinctly larger on obligation orientation in comparison with entitlement orientation. The disclosure that men have higher obligation scores than women may be associated with the long socialization histories that men have had as the principal wage earners in the family. There is a possibility that this distinction has changed and that the gap between the sexes will narrow as the number of women in the labor force continues to increase and as they accumulate longer tenure and more equal opportunity in employment.

The relationship between age and entitlement norm is not substantial. These data obviously do not support the commonly expressed notion that young people in general and particularly younger workers are more entitlement oriented then their older associates. Notwithstanding, concurrence with the obligation norm clearly increases with every age category. This can probably be explained by a different value system held by the older generation.

Education levels are related significantly to obligation orientation. The lower the educational level, the higher the agreement with the obligation norm. However, education shows no consonance or actual relationship with the entitlement norm.

CONCLUSION

The findings presented in this chapter shed light on work-related norms prevailing in Israeli society. Two fundamental norms have been identified, resulting in two indices. One taps a significant share of the normative "rights" or *entitlement* perspective about work, and the other concentrates on the normative *obligation* or "duty" individuals "owe" to their employing organization and society at large.

The picture that emerges from the data is one of general equilibrium in terms of relative agreement with the entitlement and the obligation norms. This balance occurs at various levels of agreement with both norms. There is no clear-cut interpretation of this.

Nevertheless, the phenomenon may be explained in two ways. First, it can be speculated that this observation is due, at least in part, to an "agreement" response-set bias operating in the samples studied; however, no data are available to support such an assumption. Therefore, it appears sensible to accept tentatively the equilibrium designation but to be cautious about interpretation. Another rationale for the relatively balanced state of the two norms is that in the combined target groups sample no distinction is made between the two indices of question 47. This might be explained by the prevailing collectivist norm in Israeli/Jewish culture, where there is no distinction between entitlement and obligation, which are interwoven and viewed as interrelated. (Their correlation of .30, $p < .0001$, was among the highest of all the indices utilized in the MOW project.) A similar finding was reported by N. Shefi (1986). In a study on the meaning of work of an entirely different and independent sample (378 registered nurses in Israel), Shefi found no distinction between the entitlement and obligation norms. Both were clustered in a single factor. Nevertheless, when the unbalanced results are examined, the group of retired persons stands out in its tendency toward an obligation norm.

By contrast, a strong tendency toward the entitlement norm in relation to the obligation norm is demonstrated by the teachers and chemical engineers.

The major finding concerning the relation of sex, age, and educational levels to the entitlement and obligation norms is that they are hardly related to entitlement but rather consistently and strongly related to the obligation norm. The emerging pattern is that of a high obligation orientation among men, among older members of the workforce, and among the less-educated members of the labor force. However, it is this particular segment of the labor force that may shrink during the last part of the twentieth century. Will this loss of obligation orientation to work actually occur? If so, what will its influence be? Will it be generally advantageous or detrimental to society? These questions pose weighty challenges for the future.

9

Work Attributes

Two closely related work attributes important in understanding the meaning of work will be analyzed in this chapter: first, the outcomes most valued by individuals; second, the work roles with which the individual most identifies. The ability to identify work roles or the outcomes or functions provided through work is essential for organizations. With this ability, employers will be able to attend better to the needs of employees for their mutual benefit. Also, work organizations will be able to make more effective decisions concerning the designing or redesigning of organizational structure, reward systems, and other human resource functions.

The most useful data in this study for assessing the relative importance of the broad functions fulfilled by working is provided through the domain entitled "valued work outcomes" (question 28). As shown in Chapter 4, this domain is based on a typology of various meanings of work, including a range of both expressive and instrumental meanings attached to working (see Kaplan & Tausky 1974; Tausky & Piedmont 1967). Question 28 asks respondents to assign a total of 100 points to six broad functions or outcomes of working to indicate their relative importance in explaining what working means to each of them. The six functions of work are those that provide or foster

1. status and prestige
2. income
3. occupation of time
3. interpersonal contact
4. societal service
5. intrinsic value or opportunity for self-expression

The second domain, designated "work role identification," (question 31) was approached in a slightly different manner. As noted in Chapter 4, the theoretical conceptual background for this domain is based on role theory (Turner 1956) and attribution theory (Kelley 1967). Six major work-related roles were presented to the participants in the study, who were asked to rank them from most to least important. These roles were (1) tasks one identifies with, (2) company or organizational identification, (3) product or service identification, (4) identification with people with whom one works, (5) occupation or profession identification, and (6) identification with money one receives.

The principal studies dealing with the elements of these two major work attributes—valued working outcomes and work role identification—will briefly be reviewed here.

Status and Prestige. L. Braude (1963) has argued that insofar as persons relate to each other through a reciprocal system of statuses, work becomes that "central life interest" through which they make their generalized position in the system known to themselves and to others (p. 347).

All the groups in the study by E. Friedman and R. Havighurst (1954) discovered self-respect and secured respect or recognition from others by means of their work. Indeed, in other studies work has also been found to be a source of status and self-respect (Donald & Havighurst 1959; Jahoda 1979; Kaplan & Tausky 1974; Shimmin 1966; Steers & Porter 1975; Warr 1981).

Income/Money. Work is viewed as a means of survival and basic maintenance. Thus it has an instrumental meaning (Kaplan & Tausky 1974). This concept is shared by Friedman and Havighurst (1954), C. Tausky (1969), M. Jahoda (1979), and P. Warr (1981).

Time Occupying. Work is viewed as a scheduled or routinized activity that keeps the individual occupied. It consumes time and energy, and it may be viewed as a vehicle for avoiding negative consequences associated with laziness and idleness, for example, hustling and illegal activities (Kaplan & Tausky 1974). Other studies expressing similar views are those of Friedman and Havighurst (1954), N. C. Morse and R. C. Weiss (1955), Jahoda (1979), and Warr (1981).

Interpersonal Contacts. Work fulfills social functions. The workplace provides opportunities for meeting new people and developing friendships. This is an argument advanced by M. Donald and R. Havighurst (1959), Friedman and Havighurst (1954), Jahoda (1979) H. R. Kaplan and C. Tausky (1974), R. Steers and L. Porter (1975), and Warr (1981).

Societal Service. Work as an activity providing a prescribed role in society is the view of Friedman and Havighurst (1954), Donald and Havighurst (1959), Kaplan and Tausky (1974), and Jahoda (1979). Early Jewish philosophers saw work as having a contributory role in the construction of a society. In their opinion, lack of working will lead to social dysfunction (Alon 1967).

Interest and Satisfaction. Work is important as a source of interesting purposeful activity and as a source of self-actualization. Self-actualization means the possible presence of a desire for new experience and to learn more, and the possible need for responsibility and autonomy. Friedman and Havighurst (1954), Donald and Havighurst (1959), Kaplan and Tausky (1974), and Steers and Porter (1975) are among those who share this view.

Two contrasting perspectives have emerged from studies on patterns of work identification. The first differentiates persons committed to or identifying with their *occupation* or *profession* (cosmopolitan). The stronger the identification, the more likely that a person will be oriented toward development of a career and occupational ideology. The other form of identification is a commitment to or an identification with the employing *organization* (local). This is usually associated with the individual's assimilation and acceptance of the values and ideology of the organization and development of an organizational career. Yet a third perspective is that these orientations may be combined to yield an additional type of role orientation, termed *"cosmo-local."* The conflict between occupational and organizational commitments have been recorded in numerous research findings (Glaser 1964; Goldberg 1976; Gouldner 1957; Jauch, Glueck & Osborn. 1978; Kornhauser 1962; Tuma & Grimes 1981); it is not the intention of this chapter to discuss them.

We draw on the typology proposed by C. Hulin and H. Triandis (1981) in classifying valued outcomes and work role identification for this study. The first of their four classification facets is whether the outcomes/roles depend on *task performance* or are *environmentally related*. This facet distinguishes task from environment as separate levels of outcomes. The second facet distinguishes between preferences for outcomes that are *internally mediated* against personal standards and preferences for outcomes that are *externally mediated* against standards of external agents. The third facet distinguishes between outcomes that are *symbolic* and are *concrete*. Examples of symbolic outcomes include information, service to others, and status. Examples of concrete outcomes include money and promotions (although in some respects money and promotions undoubtedly include a symbolic element as well as being concrete). The fourth and final facet is whether the outcome is *particularistic* or *universalistic*. Outcomes that are particularistic depend on the person receiving them. Examples include praise, recognition, status, and service to others. Universalistic outcomes include those that are not dependent on who receives them. Examples include money and information.

Additionally, the levels of analysis distinction (personal agents versus institutional agents) made by R. Dubin, R. A. Headley, and T. C Taveggia (1976) provided additional guidance. Recognition of this level of analysis distinction can aid in interpreting and understanding why particular work outcomes or work roles group together. In addition, the distinction between outcomes of work and functional attachments of work made by V. H. Vroom (1964) has helped in classifying outcomes. Vroom recognized that the functional properties involved in work roles have a different character from other outcomes. These functional characteristics are a type of purpose that provides an attachment between the worker and society. These work role functions provide opportunities for occupants to experience a continually changing environment, to play an active part in inducing environmental change, and, by so doing, to use and develop further personal skills.

Work may also serve a moral purpose for the worker, such as the opportunity to serve others, protect others, or protect fundamental legitimate institutional or societal values. Examples include persons in occupations such as medicine or law enforcement who provide critical services to society. Soldiers who perceive their role as defenders of freedom provide an example of an occupation that protects critical societal values. Because these functional attachments are at different levels of analysis and are each of a different character, it is useful to retain the distinction.

With these variations in mind we can now classify the work attributes of valued work outcomes and work role identifications included in the present study.

VALUED WORK OUTCOMES

Table 9.1 shows the number of points assigned to each valued work outcome by the target groups and the national sample representing the labor force in Israel. Two work outcomes were perceived to be of about equal importance: income, and interesting and satisfying. Both were assigned about 24–30 percent of the points (out of 100) and were ranked either as first or second. Teachers were an exception to this trend. While ranking work as interesting and satisfying first (37.2 points), they regarded societal service as more important than income (ranked second and third respectively). For ease of visualization, results of valued work outcomes for the national sample and the combined sample of all target groups are presented in Figure 9.1.

The *income-producing outcome* of work was ranked first by the national sample and the self-employed, as well as by manual and lower-level occupations (textile workers, tool and die makers, white-collar workers, and the unemployed).

The *intrinsic outcome* of working ("working is interesting and satisfying") was seen as most important (was assigned most points) by chemical engineers, teachers, temporary workers, the retired, and students. It was selected as the second most important work outcome by the national sample (25.9 points).

The *societal service* outcome of work is ranked third in importance by the national sample. It is similarly viewed by chemical engineers, tool and die makers, the retired, and students.

The *interpersonal outcome* of working ("permitting you to have interesting contacts with other people") is viewed as the fourth most important work outcome by the national sample. Temporary workers, the self-employed, and white-collar workers ranked it higher than the other target groups.

The *time-occupying outcome* of work is of relatively minor importance. It is ranked fifth by the national sample. Some target groups find this work outcome relatively more important than other groups. Understandably so do the unemployed. Finally, in order of general importance, the *status and prestige* outcome

Table 9.1
Number of Points Assigned to Work Outcomes and Rankings by National and Target Groups Samples

Sample	Working gives status & prestige	Working provides income	Working keeps one occupied	Working permits interesting contacts	Working is useful to serve society	Working is interesting & satisfying
Chemical	12.9	22.8	5.0	10.4	13.0	35.4
Engineers	(4)	(2)	(6)	(5)	(3)	(1)
Self-	10.2	30.3	11.7	15.4	8.0	24.4
Employed	(4)	(1)	(5)	(3)	(6)	(2)
Teachers	11.5	12.9	6.6	11.2	19.8	37.2
	(4)	(3)	(6)	(5)	(2)	(1)
Temporary	11.2	21.8	11.8	15.7	9.9	26.9
Workers	(5)	(2)	(4)	(3)	(6)	(1)
Textile	9.8	32.5	13.1	12.6	9.5	20.0
Workers	(5)	(1)	(3)	(4)	(6)	(2)
Tool & Die	10.8	29.8	10.7	10.9	11.8	23.9
Makers	(5)	(1)	(6)	(4)	(3)	(2)
White	13.7	27.3	11.5	13.8	10.1	21.3
Collar	(4)	(1)	(5)	(3)	(6)	(2)
Retired	12.9	18.9	10.1	13.0	15.9	29.5
	(5)	(2)	(6)	(4)	(3)	(1)
Unemployed	9.3	23.6	14.1	12.1	11.7	21.8
	(6)	(1)	(3)	(4)	(5)	(2)
Students	13.4	18.9	13.6	16.3	16.6	25.9
	(6)	(2)	(5)	(4)	(3)	(1)
All Target	11.6	23.9	10.8	13.1	12.6	26.3
Groups Combined	(5)	(2)	(6)	(3)	(4)	(1)
National	8.4	30.5	9.3	10.1	13.3	25.9
Sample	(6)	(1)	(5)	(4)	(3)	(2)

Notes:
Owing to rounding, the points assigned to the six outcomes do not always total 100 exactly.
Rankings are given in parenthesis.

of work is last. White-collar workers, chemical engineers, teachers, and the self-employed assign this outcome relatively more importance than the other groups.

Further support for the reality and meaning of the importance of these outcomes of working derives from the responses to question 28B: "I would like you to tell me, in your own words, what is most important to you about working." Content analysis of these open-ended responses from the national sample shows the pattern displayed in Table 9.2.

Although there was a wide range of other responses, none was mentioned by more than 4 percent of the respondents. The ranking of the first two reasons nicely replicates findings from responses to the valued work outcomes question.

Thus, two highly valued work outcomes or functions of work emerge. First, it seems clear that for a majority of individuals a key underlying rationale for

Figure 9.1
Number of Points (out of 100) Assigned to Work Outcomes by National and Target Groups Samples

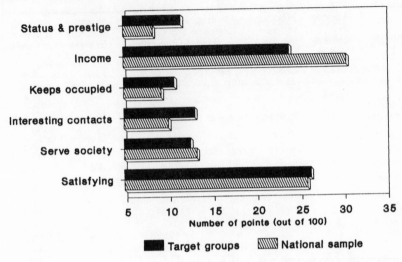

working is that it provides an income needed for a livelihood. Second, performing work perceived to be intrinsically interesting and satisfying is for many individuals an important outcome of work. However, this does not imply that there is a uniform evaluative framework among individuals as to what makes work intrinsically interesting and satisfying; it means only that being able to perceive one's working situation as intrinsically interesting and satisfying is a valued outcome or function of work.

WORK ROLE IDENTIFICATION

Six work roles were ranked according to their significance and importance to the individual. The results of these rankings by the target groups as well as the

Table 9.2
Support for Functions of Work in Order of Importance in the National Sample

Response Category	Response Percentage
Income to support family	27
Like my work or like working	20
Accomplishment or creativeness	14
Contact with people/feeling of belonging	13
Gives meaning or goals to life	9
Service to others or contribution to society	7
Self-realization or growth	5
Moral obligation	4

national sample are presented in Table 9.3. Overall the role of "tasks one does while working" was most significant. It was ranked either first or second by the national sample, and by most of the target groups, with the exception of teachers (third) and the self-employed (fifth). The role of "money" was relatively important for the national sample, the self-employed, and temporary workers (ranked second); it was of greatest significance for textile workers and tool and die makers, who ranked it first. The "product or service" role was ranked third by the national sample. Overall, it was also ranked third by the combined target groups samples, with the self-employed and teachers ranking it first. The "occupational/professional" identification was ranked fourth by the national sample and was relatively unimportant for the target groups, with the exception of chemical engineers and teachers, who ranked it second. The identification with "people" was ranked fifth by the national sample as well as by the combined target groups sample. Finally, the identification with "company or organization" was the least important work role for the national sample and for all target groups (it was unanimously ranked sixth and last by all).

The relationship between work role identification and demographic variables was previously found to be important in an earlier analysis (Chusmir 1982).

Table 9.3
Rankings of Work-Role Identification

Target Groups	Tasks	Company/ Organization	Product/ Service	People	Occupational/ Professional	Money
Chemical Engineers	1	6	4	5	2	3
Self-Employed	5	6	1	3	4	2
Teachers	3	6	1	4	2	5
Temporary Workers	1	6	5	4	3	2
Textile Workers	2	6	3	5	4	1
Tool & Die Makers	2	6	3	5	4	1
White Collar	1	6	2	3	5	4
Retired	1	6	2	3	4	5
Unemployed	1	6	2	5	4	3
Students	2	6	3	5	2	4
All Target Groups Combined	1	6	3	5	2	4
National Sample	1	6	3	5	4	2

Note: 1 = most significant, 6 = least significant.

Because of this, such an analysis was undertaken for the national sample. The picture that emerges reveals that the role of "tasks" was most important for both men and women, for every age category (young, middle, and old) and at every educational level (primary, secondary, some college and university degree). One notable exception is that people with a university degree ranked "occupational/professional" identification as equally important to "tasks."

In relation to the distinction made in the literature between identification with the organization that one is a member of or with one's profession, our data clearly show that profession or occupation is significantly more important than the employing organization. Among the target groups samples, the highest ranking allotted to "occupational/professional" identification by any group was attributed to chemical engineers and teachers (ranked second by both). Both target groups are the most professional groups in the target groups sample population. Identification with company or organization is actually lowest for every sample studied, even the less professional groups.

CONCLUSION

It is clear that most of the individuals participating in this study expressed the view that providing an income for themselves and their families is the dominant underlying reason or rationale for working. In this sense, it could be correctly stated that the major reason why people work is to secure an income that would enable them to acquire whatever is needed or desired. It is also apparent, however, that there are other important and highly valued outcomes or roles provided by work. The "tasks" that are performed at work emerged as another dominant role. It is clear that the content of work or the tasks performed are critical to individuals. This provides a direct signal to organizations regarding the character of jobs and the tasks meted out to their employees. Consequently, organizations have to make special efforts to provide their employees with meaningful and motivating tasks. This also has an implication regarding the design of tasks or their redesign for the future. A deliberate, planned structuring or restructuring of how tasks and work are executed may increase employees' motivation, involvement, and efficiency and, as a result, improve their performance.

Another important outcome of work is its expressive dimension. The capacity of work to make provisions for noninstrumental rewards and outcomes is important for this study population. Hence, people work to obtain outcomes that are expressive or intrinsic, such as interesting and satisfying tasks, or jobs that provide a feeling of achievement or challenge. The management of expressive work aspects is a challenge for managers and organizations. This ties in well with the issue of task/job design. Organizations ought to design tasks for their employees in such a manner that expressive work outcomes, in addition to the instrumental ones, arise as a result of applying effort to assigned tasks.

Service to society or customers is an additional work outcome/role identification item of relative importance. This means the importance attached to providing service to others or to society at large. Such an approach is typical of occupations or professions that provide service to others, or of individuals with idealistic values and norms.

This chapter draws attention to the multidimensional nature of work, its outcomes and roles, and stresses the importance of viewing work in this way.

10

Work Goals

An investigation of the sort of goals individuals seek from work may shed light on the fundamental question of why people work. A useful way of understanding what is important to people in their working life is to focus on a uniform set of work goals, or facets of work, and to ascertain how important each of them is to individual workers.

There is a vast literature that is relevant to the operationalization of work goals, and it covers the subject of job satisfaction, work values, work needs, and incentive preference. F. Herzberg and others (1957) reviewed 16 studies in which employees had been presented with job facets to be rated in terms of their importance. The samples in the 16 studies reported varied markedly, although there was some dissimilarity in terms of the sets of job facets investigated and the particular types of ratings or rankings employed. From the results of these studies Herzberg and his colleagues constructed a detailed composite of the ranking of the importance of 14 job facets; the ranking was provided by 11,000 workers who were heterogeneous in regards to education, sex, occupation, and level of skill, among other things. These facets comprised the following items: security, interest, opportunity for advancement, appreciation, company management, intrinsic aspects of job, wages, supervision, social aspects of job, working conditions, communication, hours, ease (from intrinsic aspects of job), and benefits.

Some years later, D. Weiss and others (1964) constructed the Minnesota Importance Questionnaire (MIQ), which was designed to measure 20 vocationally relevant need dimensions (to accompany the MSQ) referring to specific reinforcing conditions found to be important to job satisfaction. The needs are ability, utilization, achievement, activity, advancement, authority, company policies and practices, compensation, co-workers, creativity, independence, moral values, recognition, responsibility, security, social service, social status, supervision–human relations, supervision-technical, variety, and working conditions.

Data collected by L. W. Porter (1964) show that for over 1,900 managers sampled, the higher-order needs (social, esteem, autonomy, and self-realization) are the most important. Other data from the study show that the managers are most satisfied with the lower-order needs (security, pay). Thus it follows that these lower-order needs should be the least important. Other data suggest that pay and certain lower-level needs are rated as more important by workers than by managers (Porter & Lawler 1965).

E. E. Lawler (1971) reviewed 43 studies in which pay importance was rated, and found that its average ranking was third. R. P. Quinn (1971) found that importance ratings of 23 job facets provided by a national probability sample of 1,533 American workers indicated that no single job facet was preeminently important. According to the mean scores of workers on five summary indices, the most important general aspect of the workers' jobs was having sufficient resources to perform adequately. This was followed, in order of decreasing importance, by receiving adequate financial rewards; doing challenging, self-enriching work; having pleasant co-workers; and having an undemanding job.

Quinn's (1971) study has comparable facets for 12 of the 14 facets ranked by Herzberg and his colleagues (1959). There is a connection between how important employees say job facets are and how much job facets influence overall job satisfaction (Vroom 1964). Satisfaction with pay and with supervision seem to have particularly strong influences on overall satisfaction for most people (Lawler 1973).

Most studies comparing occupational groups have shown systematic differences in the importance rating of various job facets (Friedlander 1965; Hinrichs 1968; Hofstede 1972), although others have shown substantial agreement among diverse employee groups (Ronan 1970; Stracevich 1972). A. I. Kraut and S. Ronen (1975) found occupation to be an important predictor of an employee's intent to stay with an organization.

Since M. Haire, E. E. Ghiselli, and L. W. Porter's (1966) study of national differences in managerial thinking, we have witnessed a flurry of cross-national comparative studies focusing on work goals, values, and attitudes (e.g., England 1978; Hofstede 1976; Kelley & Worthley 1981; Kraut 1975; Ronen & Shenkar 1985).

For example Haire, Ghiselli, and Porter (1966) and D. Sirota and M. J. Greenwood (1971) found similarities in the order of the importance of job facets among different nationalities. Kraut and Ronen (1975) also found relatively little difference in the importance of various job facets from country to country. W. J. Bigoness and G. Hofstede (1987) collected data on work goals from 13 national groupings at two points in time 14 years apart. They found that the rankings of the importance of ten work goals remained highly similar over the period of the study. For both samples job challenge, job freedom, good relations with one's superior, and advancement opportunities were the four most important work goals. On the other hand, there are also studies reporting divergence and national differences. B. Bass and L. Eldridge (1973) found that successful managers in Denmark emphasize societal concerns in decision making, whereas successful U.S., British, and German managers strongly value a profit motive in their decision making.

G. H. Hofstede (1980) surveyed employees working in 40 countries for a multinational company. He reported significant national difference across four dimensions of culture, which were labeled power distance, uncertainty avoidance, individualism, and masculinity. British managers were found by R. N. Kanungo and R. W. Wright (1983) to place far greater importance on individual achievement and autonomy than did French managers, whereas French managers placed greater importance on competent supervision, sound company policies, fringe benefits, security, and comfortable working conditions. P. J. Dowling and T. W. Nagel (1986) found that Australian business majors place great emphasis on extrinsic values whereas their American counterparts stressed self-fulfillment, responsibility, and other intrinsic factors.

Regarding sex differences, results support the frequently quoted generalization that women are more oriented than men to the interpersonal aspects of their jobs (Centers & Bugental 1966; Hardin, Reif & Heneman, 1951; Herzberg et al. 1957; Kilpatrick, Cummings, & Jennings 1964).

THE STRUCTURE OF WORK GOALS

The procedure for measuring the importance of work goals was adopted after pilot experimentation had been carried out with several formats. Respondents were presented with the following question:

32. What about the nature of your working life? How important to you is it that your work life contains the following:

32A   –A lot of opportunity to LEARN new things
32B   –Good INTERPERSONAL relations (super-visors, co-workers)
32C   –Good opportunity for upgrading or PRO-MOTION
32D   –CONVENIENT work hours
32E   –A lot of VARIETY
32F   –INTERESTING work (work that you really like)
32G   –Good job SECURITY
32H   –A good MATCH between your job requirements and your abilities and experience
32I   –Good PAY

32J   –Good physical working CONDITIONS (such
        as light, temperature, cleanliness, low noise
        level)
32K   –A lot of AUTONOMY (you decide how to do
        your work)

Respondents were asked to rank these items by first selecting the most important item, then the least important, and so on until they had finally ranked all 11 work goals.

It was necessary first to enquire about the underlying structure of work goals, as was done for the general meaning of work structure in Chapter 6. The factor analysis procedure used consisted of principal components factor analysis of the 11 work goals importance scores. After iteration, factors with eigenvalues exceeding 1.0 were rotated to simple structure by the varimax procedure. Factor loadings with an absolute value greater than 0.35 were used in defining factors. Three factors explained 49 percent of the common variance in the 11 work goals in the sample. Table 10.1 identifies factors and presents factor loadings for the 11 work goals in the national sample. The dimension identified and the items comprising the dimensions are as follows (see Table 10.1):

I. *Expressive Dimension*
   E. A lot of variety
   F. Interesting work
   H. A good match between your job and your abilities
   K. A lot of autonomy

II. *Economic and Comfort Dimension*
   D. Convenient work hours
   I. Good pay
   J. Good physical working conditions
   A. Opportunity to learn new things
   K. A lot of autonomy

III. *Learning, Interpersonal, and Improvement Dimension*
   C. Good opportunity for upgrading and promotion
   B. Good interpersonal relations

With some minor differences similar dimensions (factors) were also found in the international study on the meaning of working (MOW-International Research Team 1987).

THE RELATIVE IMPORTANCE OF
INDIVIDUAL WORK GOALS

It is useful to consider every work goal separately and enquire into the relative importance of each. The basic data for this analysis are the mean rank of each

Table 10.1
A Varimax Solution of Factor Loadings on Work Goals for the National Sample

Work Goal	Factor I Expressive	Factor II Economic & Comfort	Factor III Learning, Interpersonal & Improvement
a. Opportunity to learn			.51
b. Interpersonal relations			.48
c. Opportunity for upgrading/promotion			.56
d. Convenient work hours		.38	
e. Variety	.62		
f. Interesting work	.58		
g. Job security			
h. Match person & job	.49		
i. Good pay		.60	
j. Working conditions		.55	
k. Autonomy	.42		
Eigenvalue	2.45	1.68	1.22
% of Explained Variance	22.3	15.3	11.1

of the 11 work goals utilizing the national sample data. Table 10.2 presents these data in terms of mean ranks and in terms of ranking of the 11 mean ranks. The table also presents rankings by age categories as well as sex and educational levels.

"Interesting work," "interpersonal relations," and "good pay" are the most dominant in order of importance. "Working conditions," "job security," and "variety" were the least important work goals in the national sample. A generally similar finding was also reported in D. Elizur's (1984) study of Israeli samples.

As shown in Table 10.2 there is similarity among work goals rankings by the three age groups and systematic age effects. "Interesting work" and "good pay" are again on top of the list. However, the importance of pay increases with age. "Opportunity to learn" is consistently less important as age increases. "A good match between your job requirements and your abilities and experience" was rated eighth in importance for the younger age groups and sixth for the oldest age groups. A likely reason for this finding is that young workers may be more eager to experiment with different work settings and roles and have not crystallized their work personalities to the same extent as longer-term workers. The more important rankings given to "variety" and "learning opportunity" by the youngest workers would lend some support to this explanation. In many industrialized countries, the higher rankings of "job security" by the older age group may signify the greater impact of actual and potential unemployment for this age group in recent years.

Table 10.2
Work Goals Ranking by National Sample, Age Categories, Sex, and Educational Levels

Work Goal	National Sample	Age Category			Sex		Educational Level			
		<30	30-50	50>	Male	Female	Primary	Secondary	College	University
a. Opportunity to learn	5	4	4	5	5	3	10	4	4	2
b. Interpersonal relations	2	2	3	3	3	2	2	2	3	4
c. Opportunity for Upgrading/ promotion	8	5	7	10	6	8	7	6	10	7
d. Convenient work hours	7	6	6	9	9	4	8	9	8	11
e. Variety	11	9	11	11	11	10	11	11	9	5
f. Interesting work	1	1	1	2	2	1	4	3	1	1
g. Job security	10	11	9	8	7	11	8	9	8	11
h. Match between Person & Job	6	8	8	6	8	7	9	10	5	3
i. Good pay	3	3	2	1	1	5	1	1	6	8
j. Working conditions	9	10	10	7	10	9	3	8	11	10
k. Autonomy	4	7	5	4	4	6	6	5	2	6

Note: Rank 1 is the *most* important work goal while rank 11 is the *least* important work goal.

The importance of a lot of autonomy at work increases with age. The work goals rankings for males and females also show similarities and differences (Table 10.2). "Interesting work" and "interpersonal relations" are high for both groups. Work goals noticeably higher for males than females are "pay," "opportunity for upgrading and promotion," and "job security." These items are economic and comfort work goals that are traditionally found to be more important for males than females (Beutell & Brenner 1986; Brenner & Tomkiewicz 1979; Schuler 1975). In contrast, items for which females' rankings deviate remarkably in importance from that of males were " opportunity to learn" and "convenient work hours." Both of these work goals were also found to be significantly different (and in the same direction) for the combined national samples of the countries participating in the MOW study (Harpaz 1990). "Opportunity to learn" may be in accord with the increase of females in the labor force of industrialized societies and their need to learn in order to receive equal treatment to males. However, "convenient work hours" may be a reflection of the female's traditional role conflict between work and family responsibilities (Wiersma 1987).

Some of the explanations for the principal difference found between men and women in regard to work goals can be related to a distinction in the orientations of the sexes to work as a life role. It has been suggested that the socialization of women to sex roles causes them to regard work as being less central to their lives (Ritzer 1972; Saal 1978). S. D. Saleh and M. Lalljee (1969) found that men perceived their occupation to be more central to their lives than did women. And H. B. Presser and W. Baldwin (1980) have claimed that working women experienced a role conflict between their expected role as homemaker and their role as a full-time career-oriented worker.

Some trends could also be observed with regard to educational levels (Table 10.2). The higher the level of education, the greater the importance assigned to " interesting work," "match between a person and job," "opportunity to learn," and "variety." On the other hand, the lower the educational level, the more importance is given to "good pay" and "working conditions." There are less noticeable variations on the rest of the work goals. Hence there is a clear preference for expressive work goals among the highly educated respondents, whereas those with lower educational levels more vividly value the economic and comfort dimensions of work.

RANKING OF WORK GOALS BY TARGET GROUPS

The importance rankings of work goals by each target group are shown in Table 10.3. As was reported in the occupational literature some substantial differences exist in the rated importance of work goals by the target groups in our sample. "Interesting work" is overall the most important work goal in this population. Tool and die makers and textile workers assign less importance to this goal, whereas "good pay" is highly important for them. "Good pay" was

Table 10.3
Work Goals Ranking by Target Groups Samples

Work Goal	Students	Chemical Engineers	Self-Employed	Teachers	Temporary Workers	Textile Workers	Tool & Die	White Collar	Retired	Unemployed	Total Target Groups
Opportunity to learn	4	2	10	3	2	11	1	1	6	5	4
Good interpersonal relations	5	5	2	2	3	6	4	3	2	4	2
Good opportunity for promotion	3	7	11	11	7	3	3	4	9	8	7
Convenient work hours	10	11	9	6	5	7	7	8	8	3	8
Lot of variety	11	3	8	7	8	10	10	5	11	10	9
Interesting work	1	1	1	1	1	4	5	2	1	2	1
Good job security	7	9	7	8	11	4	9	10	4	5	10
Match requirements & abilities	6	8	5	4	9	8	8	7	3	11	5
Good pay	2	6	4	10	4	1	2	6	5	1	3
Good physical working conditions	9	10	6	9	10	2	11	11	7	9	11
A lot of autonomy	7	4	3	5	6	9	6	9	10	7	6

Note: Rank 1 is the *most* important work goal while rank 11 is the *least* important work goal.

ranked relatively high by the other groups (third overall), although it varied and assumed the least importance for the teachers. Good "interpersonal relations" was the second overall salient work goal and "opportunity to learn" ranked fourth overall (ranked first by tool and die makers and white-collar employees, tenth by the self- employed). Some work goals that were ranked overall as very low by the combined samples were relatively more important to some groups than for the rest. Examples were "variety" for chemical engineers (third) and "job security" for retired (fourth) and unemployed (fifth).

Our target groups samples reveal a general similarity in the importance rankings of work goals as well as some target-group-specific differences. The findings from the Israeli target groups data are generally similar to those found in the other countries participating in the MOW project (See MOW-International Research Team 1987). The extent to which these effects are functions of occupational role expectations, actual work experience, and similarities among target groups because of the selection criteria or because similar kinds of individuals (that is, target groups) attract each other is difficult to specify and the reader is referred to Chapter 13 for further exploration.

WORK GOALS ACCORDING TO DIFFERENT ORGANIZATIONAL LEVELS

Another approach to a consideration of work goals is to examine them from the perspective of organizational level. For this purpose respondents were divided into three organizational levels: employees, supervisors, and managers. Results of the analysis by organizational level are presented in Table 10.4. "Interesting

Table 10.4
Work Goals Rankings by Organizational Levels

Work Goal	Organizational Level		
	Employee	Supervisor	Manager
a. Opportunity to learn	7	4	6
b. Interpersonal relations	2	2	2
c. Opportunity for Upgrading/promotion	10	7	8
d. Convenient work hours	4	9	11
e. Variety	11	10	10
f. Interesting work	3	1	1
g. Job security	9	8	7
h. Match between Person & Job	8	6	5
i. Good pay	1	3	4
j. Working conditions	6	11	9
k. Autonomy	5	5	3

work" is most important for supervisors and managers and only third for employees. For the latter, "good pay" was the most dominant work goal. A consistent trend regarding pay was observed in this sample. This goal assumes increasing importance as one moves down the organizational levels, and thus, for employees it is of much greater importance than it is for managers.

Although "good pay" is apparently very important at all organizational levels, it featured less prominently in the thinking of workers situated higher up in the organization. Managers, who enjoy higher pay, probably perceive it to be less important than their subordinates and consequently rank it lower. In his study of managers, Lawler (1971) found a similar trend; he also cites other studies that report comparable results. These findings led him to suggest that the distinctions in the eminence of pay at different organizational levels may stem from job factors such as pay level and other rewards related to higher-level positions.

The second most important work goal for all organizational levels was unanimously "good interpersonal relations." Items that assumed greater importance the higher one's position in the organizational echelons were "match between job requirements and abilities," "opportunity for upgrading and promotion," and "job security." On the other hand, work goals assuming more importance at lower organizational levels were "convenient work hours" and "working conditions."

These findings are generally in line with what traditional management literature asserts are important work factors among managers (Huse 1979; Mintzberg 1973).

CONCLUSION

It is apparent through various analyses that most persons regard interesting work to be the main rationale for working. The nonfinancial rewards of work seem to be powerful incentives that are currently highly valued by workers in Israel as well as in various other countries (Harpaz 1990). Moreover, the expressive dimension of work goals was evaluated as more important than the economic dimension in six out of the seven countries that took part in the MOW project (MOW-International Research Team 1987). Nevertheless, the role that income plays in people's lives cannot be overlooked. Pay is evidently another cardinal work goal for individuals. In this regard it can be acknowledged that people work mainly to secure an income that allows them to purchase the things they desire in either the present or the future.

The reasons and rationales for working are distinctly multidimensional and interactive and must be viewed accordingly. Moreover, learning about what workers want from their jobs, or what is more important for them, may turn up essential information for effective human resources management. It may shed some light on such questions as why some people invest greater effort in their work and others less. Additionally, it may account for why individuals are satisfied with some jobs and occupations but not with others, or why they should find some work situations attractive and others less so. Finally, such information provides a basis for practical suggestions concerning the ways in which work organization may be optimally designed, or redesigned, for the individual as well as for organizational and societal purposes both currently and in the future.

11

Defining the Concept
of Work

Defining the concept of work has been a concern of social scientists of various
disciplines for a long time. It is little wonder that the term *work* has taken on a
multiplicity of meanings ranging from totally instrumental to purely expressive
(Kaplan & Tausky 1974). Although, superficially, work appears to be a distinct
realm of life and activity, it is not easy to find criteria by which to distinguish
it effectively from other activities. There are as yet no useful typologies of those
characteristics that identify or signify when an activity one is engaged in is or
is not considered to be working.

Evidence of the difficulty in defining the concept of work is in the *American
College Dictionary*, which gives 46 noun and verb definitions of *work*. Other
prominent dictionaries, such as the *Oxford Universal Dictionary* and *Webster's
Third International Dictionary,* as well as the Even-Shoshan Hebrew dictionary,
each devote over a page of explanation to this topic.

Part of the complexity in defining work results from the very fact that work
does not have the same meaning and function for all people. For some it is an
instrument through which they derive their basic survival and sustenance, while
for others it serves as a mechanism through which self-expression and other
social needs are fulfilled. Another complexity in the definition of work is that
it takes on different meanings at different times, and in different places, societies,
and cultures (Tilgher 1962). Finally, the meaning of work is shaped by the
workplace or by the various activities and relationships found within specific
work settings. The social context of the workplace is particularistic and one
within which workers construct meanings and relationships that are often unique
(Miller 1980).

A work definition measurement procedure was developed by reviewing the
general conceptual and empirical literature on work definitions and the meanings
of work. Three classes of concepts emerged from this review: (1) broad rationales

or reasons for being engaged in working, (2) personal outcomes or states that result from performing or engaging in working activities, and (3) constraints or controls related to the context or performance of working activities (England & Harpaz forthcoming).

Within the category of *broad rationales or reasons* for working, many authors focus on working in terms of its economic rationale. R. Firth (1948) suggested that "income producing activity" covers a general definitional use of the term *work*. E. Friedman and R. Havighurst (1954) saw one function of work as maintaining a minimal level of sustenance. R. Dubin (1958) noted that by work we mean continuous employment in the production of goods and services for remuneration. N. Anderson (1961) defined work as an "activity of some purpose" or, in more direct terms, as time given to a job for which one is paid. L. Braude (1975) stated that work may be viewed as that which a person does in order to survive; work is simply the way in which a person earns a living. G. Miller (1980) defined work as the various ways in which human beings attain their livelihoods. Other major rationales for working have also been suggested. Friedman and Havighurst (1954) and M. Donald and R. Havighurst (1959) noted that one function of work is to serve or benefit society. The authors of *Work in America* (Special Task Force 1973) as well as M. Fox and S. Hesse-Biber (1984) and R. H. Hall (1986) have defined work as an activity that produces something of value for other people. B. R. Salz (1955) defined work as an activity one does in the execution of a task or project.

Personal outcomes or states that result from engaging in work comprise a variety of notions. R. S. Weiss and R. L. Kahn's (1960) definition, one of the few attempts to define work empirically, noted that one fifth of the men interviewed in their sample defined work as an activity that requires physical or mental exertion. P. Warr (1981) and Fox and Hesse-Biber (1984) also regard employment as providing outlets for physical or mental energy. N. C. Morse and R. C. Weiss (1955) identified a sense of belonging as a personal outcome of working; interviewees noted that working gives them a feeling of being tied into wider society. Work is also seen as a source of identity and peer-group relations (Friedman & Havighurst 1954; Steers & Porter 1975). S. Shimmin (1966) noted that one distinguishing feature of work is that it is not enjoyable. Support for this idea was also advanced by Weiss and Kahn (1960), who defined work as activity performed but not enjoyed. This notion may also be reflected by language usage. The Hebrew word for work, *avodah*, is derived from the same root as *eved*, meaning a slave. However, Firth (1948) warned against representing work as simply something people do not like doing.

Finally, other authors have identified a range of notions that are *constraints or controls* relating to the context or performance of work activities. Miller (1980) noted that the context of meaning about work that has most occupied sociologists of work in this century is that of the workplace. Anderson (1961) identifies "time given to a job" as important. Thus, both where and when work takes place are potential defining elements. L. S. Hearnshaw (1954), Weiss and Kahn (1960), and Friedman (1961) identify elements of obligation, control, and restraint when defining work. Accountability, compulsion, and being directed by others are also suggested as potential defining elements of working.

It is easy to see why Firth (1948) concludes that any definition of work must to some extent be arbitrary. In practice, an activity which one person defines as work may be considered leisure by another. What seems to be significant about the MOW project formulation of the measurement of work definition is that it attempts to include major conceptual elements identified in the literature, and it relies on the views of those actually working. Moreover, it was standardized based on pilot studies for all countries participating in the international MOW project. The work definition item finally utilized in the MOW project—which provides the basic data for this chapter—is as follows:

49. Not everyone means the same thing when they talk about working. When do you consider an activity as working? Choose four statements from the list below which best define when an activity is "working".

   A. if you do it in a working place.
   B. if someone tells you what to do.
   C. if it is physically strenuous.
   D. if it belongs to your task.
   E. if you do it to contribute to society.
   F. if, by doing it, you get the feeling of belonging.
   G. if it is mentally strenuous.
   H. if you do it at a certain time (for instance from 8 until 5).
   I. if it adds value to something.
   J. if it is not pleasant.
   K. if you get money for doing it.
   L. if you have to account for it.
   M. if you have to do it.
   N. if others profit by it.

The preceding question resulted from pilot studies conducted on different versions of the item involving some 26 defining elements. The reason respondents were asked to "choose four statements" also comes from the results of the pilot study. When respondents were asked to choose the statements that defined a given activity as work, 61 percent chose either three or four statements. The choice of four statements occurred nearly three times as frequently as the choice of three statements. In other cases, the number of statements chosen ranged from two to ten; none was used by more than 6 percent of the pilot group (England & Harpaz forthcoming). The benefits gained by using a standardized four-statements defining task for respondents seemed greater than the relatively small amount of information lost by the standardization. It also should be noted that the "definition of working" item occurred rather late in the questionnaire (about two thirds of the way through) and that the preceding context implied but never directly stated that employment served as the general referent for working.

Table 11.1
Distribution of Work Definitions Ranking and Frequency Percentage Chosen by Target Groups and National Sample

Variable	Students	Chemical Engineers	Self-Employed	Teachers	Temporary Workers	Textile Workers	Tool & Die	White Collar	Retired	Unemployed	Total Target Groups	National Sample
a. Do in working place	23.30 (9)	18.90 (8)	47.80 (2)	17.80 (8)	23.30 (8)	50.00 (2)	31.90 (4)	36.70 (4)	27.80 (5)	17.80 (10)	29.50 (5)	29.56 (5)
b. Someone tells to do	5.60 (12)	5.60 (13)	6.70 (13)	3.30 (13)	10.00 (12)	14.40 (11)	13.20 (8)	10.00 (12)	5.60 (13)	20.00 (7)	9.40 (13)	13.88 (12)
c. Physically strenuous	10.00 (11)	8.90 (12)	20.00 (9)	11.10 (9)	11.10 (11)	24.40 (8)	26.40 (7)	5.60 (13)	17.80 (9)	34.40 (3)	17.00 (10)	19.92 (9)
d. Belongs to task	55.60 (2)	55.60 (2)	43.30 (3)	63.30 (1)	47.80 (2)	31.10 (6)	4.40 (13)	48.90 (1)	62.20 (1)	46.70 (2)	49.80 (2)	50.37 (2)
e. Contribute to society	44.40 (4)	37.80 (5)	26.70 (7)	51.10 (3)	36.70 (4)	41.10 (3)	48.40 (2)	31.10 (6)	57.80 (3)	32.20 (4)	40.70 (3)	40.11 (3)
f. Feeling of belonging	36.70 (5)	26.70 (7)	18.90 (10)	36.70 (6)	30.00 (6)	18.90 (10)	28.60 (5)	21.10 (8)	23.30 (8)	26.70 (5)	26.70 (7)	23.81 (7)
g. Mentally strenuous	31.10 (6)	36.70 (6)	28.90 (5)	36.71 (5)	25.60 (7)	6.70 (12)	28.60 (5)	34.40 (5)	25.60 (6)	20.00 (7)	27.40 (6)	24.97 (6)
h. Do at certain times	26.70 (8)	12.20 (11)	27.80 (6)	14.40 (10)	31.30 (5)	33.30 (4)	12.10 (10)	22.20 (7)	15.60 (11)	17.80 (10)	21.30 (9)	15.98 (11)
i. Adds value	27.80 (7)	43.40 (3)	16.70 (11)	34.40 (7)	23.29 (9)	23.30 (9)	12.10 (10)	21.10 (8)	17.80 (9)	20.00 (7)	24.00 (8)	22.33 (8)
j. Not pleasant	1.25 (14)	1.40 (14)	2.20 (14)	--	--	1.15 (14)	1.05 (14)	3.30 (14)	3.30 (14)	2.10 (14)	1.40 (14)	1.48 (14)
k. Get money for it	74.40 (1)	71.10 (1)	78.90 (1)	54.40 (2)	80.00 (1)	87.80 (1)	80.20 (1)	74.40 (1)	60.00 (2)	64.40 (1)	72.60 (1)	68.04 (1)
l. Account for it	12.20 (10)	13.30 (9)	14.40 (12)	6.70 (12)	8.90 (13)	3.30 (13)	12.10 (1)	16.70 (11)	8.90 (12)	7.80 (13)	10.40 (12)	12.28 (13)
m. Have to do it	4.40 (13)	13.28 (10)	22.20 (8)	10.00 (11)	12.20 (10)	25.60 (7)	13.20 (8)	17.80 (10)	25.60 (6)	16.70 (12)	16.10 (11)	16.30 (10)
n. Others profit by it	47.80 (3)	38.90 (4)	33.30 (4)	45.60 (4)	37.80 (3)	33.30 (4)	40.70 (3)	38.90 (3)	42.20 (4)	23.30 (6)	38.20 (4)	33.97 (4)

Note: Number in parentheses denotes ranking position within a category.

IMPORTANCE OF WORK DEFINITIONS

The ranking of work definitions by the target groups and national samples are presented in Table 11.1. The role of money in defining work is prominent in both samples employed in this study. A similar pattern of ranking is also observed in each population. The highest ranked definitions were (1) belongs to task, (2) contribute to society, (3) others profit by it, and (4) do in working place. Since the responses are quite similar for both populations, the rest of the analyses presented in this chapter will focus on the national sample only.

The national sample was broken down according to three organizational levels: employees ($n = 455$), supervisors ($n = 311$), and managers ($n = 179$).

Table 11.2 presents a breakdown of the three organizational levels according to the four major occupational categories prevalent in the sample population. Employees represent about half the sample. However, the occupational groups are fairly evenly represented among the organizational levels. An analysis was carried out to examine how individuals ranked the 14 work definition statements and to see how these varied according to organizational levels. The results are presented in Table 11.3.

For simplification purposes only, the five most frequently chosen responses will be discussed here. Table 11.4 shows the responses to be highly uniform across the three organizational levels and in relation to the total sample responses. The definition most Israelis, by far, considered as work was "if you get money for doing it" (K). While this was the dominant response at all organizational levels, there was a significant difference ($p < .001$) among organizational levels in the actual number of points assigned to this category. The higher the organizational level, the less the emphasis given by respondents to the economic function of work as expressed through the "money" definition. The second most

Table 11.2
Breakdown of Organizational Levels According to Four Major Occupational Categories (in percentages)

Occupational Category	Organizational level [a]			
	Employee n = 455	Supervisor n = 311	Manager n = 179	Total n = 973
Professionals	16.6	26.6	11.4	18.6
Clerical and Administration	21.2	26.5	46.3	27.8
Services	23.0	19.6	20.5	21.9
Manual Workers	23.4	16.6	12.6	19.0
Others	15.7	10.6	9.1	12.7

Note: [a]The n size at organizational levels is slightly reduced owing to some missing responses.

Table 11.3
Distribution of Work Definitions Ranking and Frequency Percentage Chosen for National Sample and According to Organizational Levels

Definition of work	National Sample	Organizational Levels[a]			χ^2
		employee	supervisor	manager	
	n = 973	n = 455	n = 311	n = 179	
a. Do in working place	(5)[b] 29.56	(4) 33.19	(7) 25.72	(7) 26.97	5.65*
b. Someone tells to do	(12) 13.88	(12) 16.08	(13) 11.90	(11) 11.73	
c. Physically strenuous	(9) 19.92	(6) 23.79	(9) 18.33	(10) 12.65	10.37**
d. Belongs to task	(2) 50.37	(2) 46.81	(2) 55.95	(2) 49.72	6.20*
e. Contribute to society	(3) 40.11	(3) 36.92	(3) 40.84	(3) 46.93	
f. Feeling of belonging	(7) 23.81	(8) 20.44	(6) 26.05	(6) 28.49	5.87*
g. Mentally strenuous	(6) 24.97	(7) 20.66	(5) 27.97	(5) 30.73	9.18**
h. Do at certain times	(11) 15.98	(11) 17.14	(10) 15.11	(9) 14.53	
i. Adds value	(8) 22.33	(9) 19.78	(8) 24.12	(8) 25.70	
j. Not pleasant	(14) 01.48	(14) 01.54	(14) 00.64	(14) 02.79	
k. Get money for it	(1) 68.04	(1) 75.38	(1) 64.31	(1) 55.87	25.48***
l. Account for it	(13) 12.28	(13) 12.53	(12) 12.86	(13) 10.61	
m. Have to do it	(10) 16.30	(10) 18.90	(10) 15.11	(11) 11.73	
n. Others profit by it	(4) 33.97	(5) 29.89	(4) 36.66	(4) 39.66	6.97*

Notes:
[a] n size at organizational levels is slightly reduced owing to some missing responses.
[b] number in parentheses denotes ranking position within a category.
* $p < .05$;   ** $p < .01$;   *** $p < .001$.

expressed definition of work in the total Israeli sample, as well as by respondents at all organizational levels, was "if it belongs to your task" (D). The third definition selected by all was "if you do it to contribute to society" (E). Again, a trend can be noted where the higher the occupational level, the greater the number of persons who selected this category. The next most preferred definition in the national sample as well as by supervisors and managers was "if others profit by it" (N). While employees selected "do it in a working place" (A), as with the previous definition the higher the organizational position, the greater the importance assigned to the "others profit" definition ($p < .05$). Finally, in the fifth most popular definition, a departure can be noted from the general

Table 11.4
Top Five Ranked Definitions of Work in Israel

Rank of Definition	National Sample	Organization Level		
		Employee	Supervisor	Manager
	n = 973	n = 455	n = 311	n = 179
1	K	K	K	K
2	D	D	D	D
3	E	E	E	E
4	N	N	N	N
5	A	A	F	G

Definitions of work:
K - if you get money for doing it
D - if it belongs to your task
E - if you do it to contribute to society
N - if you have to do it
A - if you do it in a working place
F - if by doing it you get the feeling of belonging
G - if it is mentally strenuous

Note: The n size at organizational levels is slightly reduced owing to some missing responses.

homogeneity observed so far at the various organizational levels. The total sample population, as well as employees, adopted "if you do it in a working place" (A) (ranked fifth and fourth respectively). Supervisors and managers picked as their fifth definition "if it is mentally strenuous" (G).

On the whole, the order of ranking of the top five definitions was very homogeneous among organizational levels. It is worth noting that Israelis associate work with money before considering it as a societal variable.

THE RELATIONSHIP BETWEEN WORK DEFINITIONS AND DEMOGRAPHIC VARIABLES

Three major demographic variables—sex, age, and educational level—were examined to assess their relationship with work definition preferences. Although, in general, the ranking order of responses remained similar regardless of the specific demographic variable, the actual frequencies varied among different groups. Significantly more males ($n = 538$) chose "if it is physically strenuous" ($p < .01$), whereas females ($n = 399$) chose "if it belongs to your task" (p

< .05). These differences were probably because more males are involved in physical work than females and because women's jobs are usually more narrowly defined than men's. Males also allotted more points to "if you get money for doing it" (K) and "if you have to do it." This may be a reflection of the current situation in which Israeli men still perform the traditional role as the breadwinner of the family to a much greater extent than women.

Age was divided into three categories: (1) up to 30 years old ($n = 248$), (2) between 31 and 50 ($n = 477$), and (3) 51 years and up ($n = 209$). No statistically significant differences were found among the rankings or frequencies of work definitions of the various age groups. However, some trends are worth noting regarding the following definitions: "if it is physically strenuous" (C) was considered more important with increased age. These differences may be associated with the type of work that individuals do at different ages or with their current job. People performing physical work will tend to relate and define work as being physically strenuous. This apparently was the situation for older employees, who allotted more points to this category than did the younger cohorts (for example, in response to the question "Does your job require too much of you physically?" older employees received a score of 2.30 [on a scale of 1 to 4] while young respondents received a score of 2.20). A similar trend was also noticed regarding the definition "if you do it to contribute to society" (E). Older people tended to associate more with this category. This may imply that young Israelis are less inclined to think of their work in terms of a contribution or service to society than the older generation, which has a more favorable attitude to societal values. Finally, the "money" (K) definition also varied by age group: the younger the group, the more importance attached to money.

Respondents were divided according to four educational levels: primary school ($n = 179$), secondary school ($n = 436$), some college ($n = 172$), and university degree ($n = 151$). "If it is physically strenuous" (C) and "if you do it at a certain time" (H) received fewer points the higher the level of education ($p < .01$). On the other hand, more points were awarded to the definitions "if it is mentally strenuous" (G) and "if you have to account for it" (L) ($p < .001$) with higher educational level. It is apparent that the first two definitions (C and H) are associated with jobs that are usually carried out by employees who in most cases have attained lower educational achievements. Hence, they are more likely to define work in this manner. At the same time, individuals with higher educational achievements would be more inclined to hold positions at higher organizational echelons and would therefore identify more readily with definitions such as "mentally strenuous" (G) and "account for" (L). Likewise, similar patterns were found with the definitions "if it belongs to your task" (D), "if it adds value to something" (I), and "if others profit by it" (N).

In sum, these demographic variables did not affect the rankings of work definitions per se. There was, however, a consistent variation in emphasis among the different groups. These variations appeared to be related to the type of work typically performed by the different groups.

CLUSTERING WORK DEFINITION CONCEPTS

A large number of work definition concepts are advanced in the literature. All have been considered and treated in the present chapter. However, to contribute to the future discussion of this issue, it seems appropriate to try to cluster work definitions into a smaller number of dimensions with much internal similarity. Smallest Space Analysis (SSA), a nonmetric, multidimensional scaling technique, was utilized for this purpose. It provides a geometric presentation of the variables (work definitions) as points in Euclidean space, so that distances in this space are inversely related to correlations (Guttman 1968). It also identifies clusters by finding interrelated groups of correlation coefficients. A set of coordinates is calculated for locating the cases as points in space, yielding a basic configuration (Lingoes 1972). The Guttman-Lingoes Smallest Space Analysis computer program (SSA-I) was employed in the present analysis.

Table 11.5 is a matrix representing correlation coefficients among the 14 work definition concepts. It indicates the relative similarity between the definitions. The correlations are rather low and some even have a negative sign. An important feature of SSA is the space diagram, which enables the interrelations among all variables to be viewed simultaneously and the same information is more easily digested. For every pair of work definitions a value is calculated that is the distance between the points that represent them in the space. The larger the similarity coefficient between two definitions, the smaller the distance between their points in the space. The space representing the points may have a number of dimensions.

The program determined that it was not possible to place the points in a two-dimensional space in a manner that would represent the matrix perfectly. Table 11.6 presents the coordinates calculated and used for a three-dimensional space diagram. The Coefficient of Alienation, indicating the average goodness-of-fit for all points simultaneously, is .26. Adding a dimension (that is, utilizing three instead of two dimensions) reduced the coefficient dramatically from .38 to .26. (Coefficient of Alienation varies between 0 and 1. A perfect fit is represented by the value 0 [Porat 1974]). A graphic representation of the three-dimensional space of Table 11.6 is portrayed in Figure 11.1.

A close observation of the SSA analysis identifies three major groupings or clusters of work definition concepts. The first includes the following definitions:

E. if you do it to contribute to society

K. if you get money for doing it

It is interesting to note that these were among the two most frequently selected work definitions in the sample population. Although they differ in content, they represent the most basic properties and functions of work. The economic and instrumental aspects of work are beyond doubt. This definition is selected most frequently by most people, and in most of the countries studied (MOW-Inter-

Table 11.5
Coefficients of Similarity among 14 Work Definition Concepts

Work Definition	a	b	c	d	e	f	g	h	i	j	k	l	m	n
a. Do in working place	0.0													
b. Someone tells to do	0.09	0.0												
c. Physically strenuous	0.03	0.33	0.0											
d. Belongs to task	0.02	-0.14	-0.13	0.0										
e. Contribute to society	-0.21	-0.15	-0.14	-0.03	0.0									
f. Feeling of belonging	-0.14	-0.15	-0.14	-0.01	0.15	0.0								
g. Mentally strenuous	-0.19	-0.05	0.11	-0.06	0.04	-0.07	0.0							
h. Do at certain times	0.09	-0.02	0.00	-0.09	-0.14	-0.13	-0.13	0.0						
i. Adds value	-0.17	-0.13	-0.12	-0.07	0.06	0.01	0.10	-0.14	0.0					
j. Not pleasant	-0.02	0.02	0.04	-0.09	-0.08	-0.05	0.09	0.02	0.02	0.0				
k. Get money for it	0.05	0.03	-0.08	-0.05	-0.19	-0.11	-0.15	0.07	-0.15	-0.07	0.0			
l. Account for it	-0.02	0.02	-0.05	-0.08	-0.15	-0.14	-0.08	0.10	-0.13	0.03	0.05	0.0		
m. Have to do it	0.02	0.00	0.01	-0.06	-0.12	-0.08	-0.12	-0.07	-0.11	0.02	0.04	-0.13	0.0	
n. Others profit by it	-0.20	-0.13	-0.21	-0.13	0.12	0.05	-0.09	-0.16	0.08	0.02	0.02	-0.06	-0.17	0.0

Table 11.6
Guttman-Lingoes Smallest Space Coordinates for a Three-Dimensional Space Diagram of Work Definition Concepts

Work	Dimension		
Definitions	Length (X)	Width (Y)	Height (Z)
a. Do in working place	10.6	4.1	-91.3
b. Someone tells to do	-20.7	95.5	-21.5
c. Physically strenuous	-2.2	-56.2	87.7
d. Belongs to task	-25.7	-67.8	32.7
e. Contribute to society	-66.6	15.1	-41.3
f. Feeling of belonging	51.4	70.1	-24.9
g. Mentally strenuous	59.7	46.8	-100.0
h. Do at certain times	29.7	-100.0	-35.8
i. Adds value	-18.1	34.4	75.2
j. Not pleasant	-100.0	-68.5	-42.8
k. Get money for it	-90.9	33.5	7.9
l. Account for it	70.8	52.6	48.8
m. Have to do it	100.0	-16.9	13.2
n. Others profit by it	66.6	72.9	-4.4

Note: Guttman-Lingoes Coefficient of Alienation = 0.26 in 13 iterations.

national Research Team 1987). It is the single definition most closely associated with work. Yet the social aspect is prominent too. Contribution to society may signify norms and values toward expressive aspects of work and society at large. In this respect, work may be perceived as providing social identity attaching one to the mainstream of social life.

The second cluster contains the following definitions:

A. if you do it in a working place
B. if someone tells you what to do
C. if it is physically strenuous
D. If it belongs to your task
H. if you do it at certain times
I. if it adds value to something

These definitions have several similar dimensions that cluster them together. The cluster demarcates work in a certain specified area (definition A), where a task has to be executed (D) and performed at designated times (H). In addition, it points to the hierarchical authority that is part of most jobs (B) and to the physical strains of work (C). Finally, a phenomenon characteristic of many low-level jobs is noted. This is that assignments are carried out in order to complete a larger task. Thus, each step superimposes some additional component or adds value (I) until the final product/task is completed. It seems that the definitional characteristics in the second cluster would be descriptive of low-level manual work.

The third cluster incorporates the following definitions:

Figure 11.1

Graphic Representation of the Three-Dimensional Space of 14 Work Definition Concepts (coordinates presented in Table 11.6)

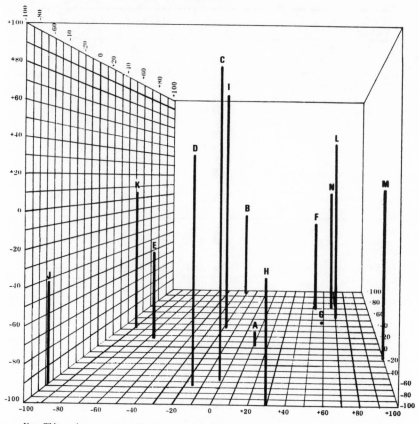

Note: This graph paper was provided by the Israel Institute of Applied Social Research

F. if by doing it you get a feeling of belonging

G. if it is mentally strenuous

L. if you have to account for it

N. if others profit by it

Having to account for a task (L) or a job may provide a sense of responsibility and importance to a person. It may show that an organization furnishes employees with meaningful jobs. In turn, such a job may create a feeling of belonging (F) and commitment to the organization. Such conditions often place mentally strenuous (G) demands on a person. An additional attribute of such (and other) jobs is the likelihood that one is working for others, and as a result others profit (N) most from one's work.

If the second cluster was peculiar to manual, low-level jobs, the third cluster is typical of jobs with more responsibility, probably of a managerial nature at a higher level in the organization.

Two work definition concepts did not seem to belong to any of the main clusters. These were (J), if it is not pleasant, and (M) if you have to do it. Both were generally ranked very low (J was ranked fourteenth and last, and M was tenth) and selected by only a few respondents. Although both may be characteristic of many jobs, they do not seem as important as most other definitions of work.

By using the SSA technique it was possible to reduce the relatively large number of available work definitions to a more refined and practical number. In sum, the 14 definitions dominating the literature may be reduced to three major clusters or definitions.

CONCLUSION

From the various analyses defining work, as employed in this chapter, some general conclusions may be reached. Some definitions obviously dominate the scene while others are less important.

A phenomenon observed is the strong emphasis given by the respondents to the definition linking money with work. Does this mean that Israelis today have highly instrumental attitudes toward work? To test this possibility the relationship between the "money" definition was examined in relation to indices considered to be central in the model attempting to study the meaning of working. The "money" definition showed a correlation of .28 ($p < .0001$) with the extrinsic orientation (economic) index and $- .09$ ($p < .05$) with the intrinsic index, but also ($- .11$, $p < .0001$) with the obligation index. Although these correlations are relatively low, their directions may point to some trends. Obligation, as described in Chapter 5, is an index stressing the contribution to organizations and society through work and other activities, as against receiving from them. The findings in this sample may indicate a trend away from the norm of contribution that prevailed in Israeli society only a few decades ago (Eisenstadt 1969). To some extent it may also confirm the assumption that Israelis today may be economically oriented and thus relate firmly to work in an instrumental sense.

The evident association between money and work implies the instrumental role played by money in people's lives. Nevertheless, although money is apparently very important at all organizational levels, less points were assigned to it by those situated in higher echelons of the organization. Managers who enjoy higher pay probably perceive it as less important than their subordinates and consequently attributed less weight to it. In his studies of managers, E. E. Lawler (1971) found a similar trend; he also cited other studies reporting such results. These led him to suggest that the distinctions in the importance of pay at different organizational ranks may stem from job factors such as pay grades and other rewards related to higher-level positions. Nevertheless, the association of money with work was the most important component in every respondent's perception of work. This trend was particularly noticeable among young individuals and those in the employed category.

Managers and lower-level employees also differed consistently in other ways, in what traditionally would be considered managerial as opposed to lower-level organizational norms. Such trends consistently occurred for most (10 out of a total of 14) definitional characteristics, with five of them statistically significant ($p < .05$ to $p < .001$). As hypothesized, persons situated higher in organizational echelons tended to give greater consideration to what is typically considered to be managerial perceptions and attitudes toward work and its relationships. These were contributions to society (E), feelings of belonging (F), mentally strenuous (G), adds value (I), and others profit by it (N). On the other hand, they attached less importance to the following definitional traits: someone tells you what to do (B), physically strenuous (C), do at specific times (H), get money for it (K), and have to do it (M). Consequently, Israeli managers fit closely with what is considered the traditional role of the manager in the managerial literature (e.g., Huse 1979; Mintzberg 1973).

By using the SSA technique it was possible to reduce the abundance of available definitions to a more practical and consistent set of definitions. The 14 broad work definition concepts suggested by the literature were clustered into three major categories.

The following are the general definitional characteristics that emerged:

1. Work is associated with economic/instrumental aspects of life as well as being perceived as a contribution to society.

This category could be labeled as the most prevalent definition of work.

2. Work is a directed activity executed in the frameworks of a specific locality and time, it is physically strenuous, and it adds value to something (for example, a task or job).

The dimensions composing this classification seem to represent mainly occupations associated with low-level jobs or manual work.

3. Work is a function to be accounted for, creates a feeling of belonging, is mentally strenuous, and profits others.

This conception consists of items most closely related to higher-level jobs providing some degree of responsibility. These are most likely associated with managerial positions.

Narrowing down a wide range of work definition attributes into fewer categories will enable future research to focus on the association between these central definitions of work and some other important behavioral aspects of work such as productivity or motivation.

In sum, the activity commonly referred to as "work" still continues to take on different and multiple meanings, and it still affects the lives of contemporary individuals directly or indirectly.

12

Meaning of Work Patterns

The issue addressed in this chapter is the ways in which dimensions of work meanings can be combined so that certain patterns associated with work meanings emerge.

The construction of MOW patterns may enable one to identify different MOW patterns or profiles that may characterize the population under study. It may be used for classification of occupational groups as an indication of the prevailing patterns in Israeli society as well as for comparisons of profiles of the labor force in different countries.

As was observed in the MOW heuristic model (Chapter 4, Figure 4.1), the meaning of work has been conceptually defined in terms of five major domains: (a) work centrality, (b) societal norms, (c) valued work outcomes, (d) work goals, and (e) work role identification. The five domains were measured by means of 39 variables. The same 39 variables were also instrumental in the development of six central MOW indices employed in constructing the MOW patterns. These were the following:

- *Work centrality*. The evaluative belief that work is important and significant in one's life.

- *Entitlement norm*. The normative belief that all individuals should be provided with certain outcomes from their organizations or society.

- *Obligation norm*. The normative belief that all individuals have a duty to contribute to society through work and working.

- *Economic* (function of work). Valued work outcome preference for income.

Portions of this chapter are derived from Itzhak Harpaz, "Meaning of Working Profiles of Various Occupational Groups," *Journal of Vocational Behavior* 26 (1985): 25–40.

- *Intrinsic* (or expressive working outcomes). Valuing working that allows for self-expression.
- *Contacts*. Valuing good interpersonal contacts through working and social relations in a work setting.

FORMATION AND VALIDATION OF
MEANING OF WORK PATTERNS

Chapter 6 depicts the structure of the meaning of working in Israel. The method used there to obtain the MOW structure also served as an empirical validation procedure for the indices developed from the five MOW domains. The 39 variables constituting these domains were submitted to a factor analysis (varimax) procedure. The latter yielded 14 factors with eigenvalues greater than 1.0, which accounted for 62.2 percent of the total variance. More than 50 percent (50.3 percent) of the total variance was accounted for by six of the indices employed in the present study. Consequently, these results support the validity of the indices extracted.

MOW patterns were obtained through a cluster method (the terms *cluster* and *pattern* are used interchangeably in this chapter). Cluster analysis categorizes variables or objects (persons) into subsets or clusters. The multidimensional hierarchical clustering method proposed by J. A. Hartigan (1975) was utilized in the present study. It is based on the assumption that given variables, objects, and people will form into groups or categories that are more similar or closer to each other than they are to variables outside or in another cluster.

The data utilized for the cluster analysis were from the target groups samples, thus enabling us to distinguish work patterns according to occupational distributions. The general structure of clusters in the target groups will also be contrasted with the national sample to examine its representation.

MEANING OF WORK PATTERNS

Results of cluster solutions, *F* ratios, and means are presented in Table 12.1. To eliminate scaling differences, indices were constructed in a standardized form. The *F* ratio compares the variance within a cluster with the overall variance. The smaller the *F* ratio, the more likely will a "true" or stable cluster be obtained (that is, the distances among points within a cluster are smaller than the distances among points between clusters).

Clusters 6 and 3 were those which dominated in the overall population. They included, respectively, 40.5 percent and 22.7 percent of our respondents. Cluster 6 ($n = 363$, 40.5 percent) represented the MOW pattern of persons who viewed work centrality as being of high importance to them. They showed relatively high intrinsic orientation while putting low emphasis on economic or extrinsic propensity. Entitlement was another item of relatively high importance, while

Table 12.1
Meaning of Work Patterns/Clusters of Ten Target Groups and the National Sample

Meaning of Work Index		Patterns/Clusters							Target Groups Grand Mean	National Sample Grand Mean
		1	2	3	4	5	6	7		
Work Centrality	F	1.01	1.31	0.66	1.43	1.18	0.79	0.98		
	$\overline{X}$	45.18	45.72	51.40	49.77	44.22	51.65	49.55	49.94	51.43
Obligation	F	1.17	1.03	0.99	1.57	0.88	0.65	0.65		
	$\overline{X}$	49.77	52.01	51.00	51.46	52.49	50.71	31.87	49.84	49.99
Entitlement	F	1.41	1.07	0.93	1.22	0.70	0.90	0.92		
	$\overline{X}$	50.18	50.96	40.16	49.77	52.88	52.47	43.59	50.67	50.11
Intrinsic Rating	F	1.55	0.57	1.01	1.57	1.22	0.78	0.78		
	$\overline{X}$	45.70	46.55	47.43	53.29	51.88	51.37	53.40	50.15	51.73
Economic	F	1.05	.93	0.74	1.23	0.73	0.89	1.15		
	$\overline{X}$	46.76	48.25	51.77	47.51	41.05	47.39	47.80	48.32	51.16
Contacts	F	1.16	1.22	0.91	0.91	1.15	0.92	1.09		
	$\overline{X}$	50.59	50.04	48.48	48.34	50.91	50.37	50.53	49.87	51.61
Target groups Total n		79	101	204	39	46	363	64		896
%		8.8	11.3	22.8	4.4	5.1	40.5	7.1		100
National Sample Total n		94	103	183	48	87	387	66		968
%		9.7	10.6	18.9	4.9	8.9	39.8	6.8		100

Notes:
[a] the smaller the *F* ratio, the more stable an index is for a specific cluster.
[b] $\overline{X}$ = index mean.

obligation was low. Cluster 3 ranked second in its size (*n* = 204, 22.7 percent) and was composed of individuals who were ranked highest on the economic index (extrinsic orientation). They still saw work centrality as prominent, but slightly less so than individuals in cluster 6. However, intrinsic predispositions were quite low in this group. Cluster 2 was the third dominant pattern of MOW (*n* = 101, 11.3 percent). It was composed of persons with low work centrality and low intrinsic orientation.

The remaining patterns or clusters were less important in this population and were composed of about 25 percent of the remaining sample. Cluster 1 (*n* = 79, 8.8 percent) was composed of persons with low emphasis on work centrality, intrinsic orientation, and economic tendencies. However, contacts with other people was an important characteristic of this cluster. Cluster 7 ($n = 64$, 7.1 percent) included persons with very low obligation to society; at the same time they also did not want much from it (low on entitlement). Work centrality in this group was found to be moderate. Clusters 5 and 4 each consisted of about only 5 percent of the sample ($n = 46$ and $n = 39$ respectively). Both showed a moderate to low propensity toward work centrality and were high on both obligations and entitlements.

As may be observed from Table 12.1, the distribution of the seven clusters in the national sample is very similar to the results obtained in the target groups samples. Hence the discussion of clusters/patterns in this chapter may be applicable to the total Israeli society as well.

Table 12.2 presents the distribution of the ten target groups along the resulting seven MOW clusters or patterns. The most notable observation from this table was the inclusion of 58 percent of the chemical engineers, 48 percent of tool and die makers, 48 percent of self-employed, and 36 percent of the teachers in the most dominant cluster (cluster 6), while textile workers dominated (45 percent) the second cluster (cluster 3).

Three significant MOW patterns that represent approximately 75 percent of the sampled population have emerged: (1) individuals who have high levels of work centrality, an intrinsic work orientation, and obligations to organizations and society; (2) individuals with high work centrality and a strong extrinsic inclination; (3) people with low work centrality and low intrinsic tendencies.

The leading and most dominant pattern, comprising more than 40 percent ($n = 363$) of the sample population, was that of individuals with high levels of work centrality and high intrinsic work orientation. These individuals emphasize entitlements relatively strongly while deemphasizing obligations. In other words, they showed a greater tendency to receive from society and the workplace than to contribute to it. Our findings are an indication of a movement away from the norm of obligations, voluntary activities, and contributions of the individual to society, which was highly valued in Israeli society only a few decades ago (Eisenstadt 1969). The finding seems to be in accordance with Israeli social observers and sociological reports (Eisenstadt 1969; Shapira 1977). This trend has been noted by other writers and seems to occur also in other Western societies (Levitan & Johnson 1982; Rotenstreich 1980). Such a state of affairs may prevail as a result of their growing affluence, which has had a pervasive influence on attitudes toward work (Levitan & Johnson 1982), and their desire to attain personal rewards (entitlements) for the efforts and contributions (obligations) they make to their organizations and society (Rotenstreich 1980). Furthermore, some authors have noted that an individual's inability to determine or control socio-political and economic events may contribute to a feeling of powerlessness (Levin 1960; Middleton 1963; Neal & Rettig 1963; Seeman 1975). This, in turn, may be an additional factor affecting the erosion in individual obligations to society. According to N. Rotenstreich (1980), this global trend is strongly no-

Table 12.2
Distribution of Target Groups within the Meaning of Working Patterns/Clusters

Target Group	Patterns/Clusters							
	1	2	3	4	5	6	7	Total
Students	4	9	29	1	2	37	8	90
Temporary Workers	8	10	19	6	5	34	8	90
Self-Employed	10	8	10	5	8	43	6	90
Chemical Engineers	1	7	17	5	2	49	7	88
Teachers	9	7	6	6	9	41	11	89
Tool & Die Makers	3	9	24	4	3	44	4	91
White Collar	4	14	26	2	2	35	7	90
Textile Workers	3	10	45	2	0	27	1	88
Unemployed	22	17	16	3	4	22	6	90
Retired	15	10	12	5	11	31	6	90
Total	79	101	204	39	46	363	64	896
(%)	8.8	11.3	22.8	4.4	5.1	40.5	7.1	100

Note: $\chi^2 = 173.03$, $p < 0.001$.

ticeable in present-day Israel owing to the wish of the Israelis to attain some personal rewards (entitlements) for the continuous efforts and contributions (obligations) they make to the total society, that is, for long military duty, lifelong service in military reserves, and high levels of taxation in almost every aspect of life, for example.

Most of the target groups were concentrated in cluster 6—the dominant pattern. Most notable were the chemical engineers, tool and die makers, self-employed, and teachers; all belong to occupations with relatively higher prestige, status, pay, and professionalism within our total sample.

The second leading MOW pattern (cluster 3) resembles the dominant one (cluster 6) in the emphasis that individuals put on work centrality. Here, however, work centrality appears to be associated with an extrinsic orientation. These workers value economic factors but attach low importance to intrinsic factors. This contrasts with the orientation of the dominant pattern (cluster 6), where centrality is a link to intrinsic factors rather than to an economic index. Hence, although work centrality is quite important in both clusters, it can probably be attributed to different sources. Considerable attention has been given in the literature to the relationship between work centrality involvement and intrinsic orientation, whereas little is reported about research on the relationship between the former and extrinsic orientation (Kanungo 1982a; Rabinowitz & Hall 1977). R. N. Kanungo (1982a) suggests that this situation exists because researchers have ignored extrinsic needs because they believe that an intrinsic, and not extrinsic, orientation is a necessary condition for work centrality/involvement. The present study shows, however, that in fact there are situations or circumstances in which work centrality might be associated with extrinsic factors. It is quite conceivable that workers with extrinsic need orientation may perceive a work setting as having the potential for providing them with the fulfillment of such a need; therefore, work would assume a central role in the lives of such persons.

Dominating this pattern are textile workers (51 percent) who are semiskilled laborers and are employed at entry-level positions in their organizations. Other groups associated with this pattern (although more of their co-workers are classified in the dominant work pattern) are white-collar employees (29 percent) who are low-and semiskilled and also hold positions that are low service functions. A third group represented in this category are tool and die makers (26 percent) who are highly skilled blue-collar employees. The common denominator for these target groups is their being either manual workers and/or situated in low-level positions in their organizations. Also part of this MOW pattern are students not yet active in the labor force but who are preparing to enter the world of work.

The two patterns may have different implications for organizations. If organizations wish to create or maintain environments favorable to their employees, they should try to find out what factors may be related to high work centrality and thus try to provide them for their employees. To maintain or create high work centrality for each type, organizations should make specific and appropriate provisions for their members who value extrinsic rewards while making different provisions for those favoring intrinsic ones. Determining what type of work setting is most highly appreciated by employees could occur through an evaluation of the present workforce or during the selection process for new employees (Lawler 1973).

The third noticeable pattern (cluster 2) is composed of people with low work centrality levels. These individuals attach low importance to the intrinsic aspects that work provides, having a moderate to high inclination toward an extrinsic orientation. This relatively small group of workers (11.3 percent) is formed mainly by individuals belonging to low- and semiskilled groups such as the unemployed, white-collar employees, textile workers, temporary workers, and retirees. In terms of its size, it is clearly not a significant group in this sample and probably will not be of great concern for policy makers.

The data suggest that work has a central role in the lives of more than 63 percent of the sampled population. Work centrality thus seems to assume a central role for the major part of this population. This was viewed favorably and is encouraging in relation to the reports of the decline in the work ethic. In light of previous findings on work centrality, it appears that maintaining or establishing high levels of work centrality would be beneficial to organizations and workers alike.

13

Consequences of the
Meaning of Work

This chapter considers the consequences of certain patterns of the meaning of work; we ask about the attitudes, values,and fancies people have on the subject. Workers make various judgments and decisions at the workplace or away from it on the basis of their value system and preferences. How these decisions differ depends on people's work values and the strength of their values. Given variations in job requirements, composition of jobs, and rewards from work, what job decision preferences do people with different work values make? Finally, the complexities of both individuals and work need to be recognized. Not only do people affix several meanings to work,but working itself also has multiple facets and consequences. Acknowledging this, additional questions are introduced about the consequences of work meanings. In particular, how do individuals with different patterns or profiles on several work meanings contrast in regard to the multiple consequences of work?

Some answers to these questions are provided here through the investigation of the relationship between the meaning of work and work consequences. The evidence presented is relational; therefore, consequences do not necessarily imply causality. However, a postulate bearing on this research,and indeed a basic assumption in most behavioral science research, is that many people have some freedom of choice in relation to certain aspects of work. Disclosures made by individuals provide an indication of the range of consequences associated with the meanings they assign to work.

Three types of consequences will be examined in this chapter: (1) work involvement, (2) job preferences, and (3) MOW patterns or profiles. The analysis

The structure of various issues in this chapter are based on Chapter 12 in MOW-International Research Team, *The Meaning of Working* (1987).

of the first two were conducted on the national labor force sample, while the last involved the target groups data only.

WORK INVOLVEMENT

In this section two aspects of decisions relating to work are examined. One is nonfinancial employment commitment to work, meaning that if the economic necessity for working is eliminated, people would opt to continue working anyway. The second decision concerns the extent of involvement with or amount of time devoted to work. The first issue uses the lottery question. Justification for its use stems from the theory of labor supply that argues that the supply of labor is increasingly affected by noneconomic factors (for example, psychological and sociological) as the influences of economic factors for working approximate to zero. The lottery question and various analyses concerning it were carried out and elaborated in Chapter 7, thus requiring no further theoretical discussion here.

Four MOW variables expected to correlate with an individual's preferences about continuing to work are work centrality, an obligation norm, pay or economic (instrumental) orientation, and expressive orientation. The properties of work centrality discussed in Chapters 4 and 7 include identification with work, involvement with work, and commitment to work. It is to be expected that individuals with increasingly higher levels of work centrality would state that they would continue to work even when it is not an economic necessity. Those who feel it is an obligation or a duty of individuals in society to work are also more likely to indicate that they would continue to work than are people not assenting strongly to this norm. It may also be anticipated that people appreciating outcomes from work, such as autonomy, a match between their skills and their work, interesting work, and variety in their work are more likely to indicate that they would continue working. At the same time, these expressive values suggest that work provides a challenge or an avenue for self-expression through continued work involvement. Conversely, people who value pay or who have a firm economic orientation are unlikely to indicate that they would continue working once the economic necessity to work had been removed. Hence it may be hypothesized that work centrality, obligation norms, and expressive orientation all correlate positively, and that economic orientation correlates negatively with the responses of people to the lottery question, thus indicating a wish to continue working.

The amount of time a person dedicates to work is of concern for several reasons. An important factor pertains to the implications of the number of working hours on nonworking time, such as time available for spending with family, leisure undertakings, and other desired activities.

The amount of time devoted to work is presumed to be an indication of the centrality of work and involvement with work in the life of the person. According to this hypothesis the longer the time spent at work, the more central work is to the person. On the other hand, there could be a distinct possibility that a person spends long hours at work because work provides much needed income.

Support for the former proposition is found in the present study from the relationship between the average number of working hours per week and the number of points assigned to work. The self-employed, textile workers, and chemical engineers worked about an average of 50 hours per week or more. They were also the groups that allotted more points to "work" than any other target group. Most marked here were the self-employed, who work an average of 52.5 hours per week and assigned 37 points (out of 100) to "work" (even more than to "family"), thus indicating its centrality to them.

A. Gechman and Y. Wiener (1975) also found a significant relationship between personal time devoted to work and job involvement. W. E. Oates (1978) in his book *Confession of a Workaholic* defines a workaholic as a person working 50 to 60 hours per week. He claims that such people find a great deal of satisfaction from their work and life.

Conceptually a reciprocal causal relationship may be acknowledged between the meaning of work and measures of time involvement in work. The time involved in work is both influenced by and influences the meaning of work. There are five postulated MOW variables that relate to working hours. First, work centrality should correlate positively with hours of work. Individuals who identify with work, are involved in work, and are committed to work for whatever reason are likely to devote more hours to work. Second, individuals who value pay highly or who are economically oriented are likely to spend more time at work. Since the amount of regular and overtime pay is frequently determined by the number of hours that one actually works, people who value pay are likely to participate more in work to secure greater remuneration. Third, individuals who seek expressive outcomes from work (variety, autonomy, interesting work, and a match between their skills and their work) have a propensity to work longer hours. The prominence of interpersonal contacts and social interaction can also form a notable element associated with the extent of involvement in work. Nevertheless,the direction of the relationship between interpersonal value and work involvement may be contingent on situational variables that affect the magnitude and quality of social interaction allowed or compelled by work roles (Vroom 1964). Lastly, obligation norms may enforce a situation of increased work involvement. Individuals inclining toward this norm would probably tend to work long hours as part of their sense of social duty and responsibility. In sum, the time committed to the workplace, as measured by the length of the average work week, depends on work centrality, obligation norm, economic orientation, expressive orientation, and interpersonal contacts.

Table 13.1 displays the results of a multiple regression analysis with the specified MOW variables as independent variables and measures of work involvement as dependent variables. The size of the standardized beta (β) weights indicates the MOW variable's relative contribution to the prediction or explanation of the involvement score of respondents in the national labor force.

Although relatively small, some of the results confirm the hypotheses advanced here. Variables contributing most to the explained variance in work involvement

Table 13.1
Relationship between Meaning of Work Central Variables and Measures of Work Involvement in the National Sample

Central M O W Variables	Work Involvement Measure	
	Lottery Question	Hours Work Per Week
	β	β
Work Centrality	.168*	.217*
Obligation Norm	.076*	.044
Economic Orientation	-.181*	.307*
Expressive Orientation	.041	.125*
Interpersonal Contacts	-.009	.051
R^2	.091*	.097*

Note: * $p < .05$

or noninvolvement are work centrality and economically oriented work values. The findings show that the higher the work centrality among individuals, the more inclined they would be to continue working even if it was no longer required. Conversely, the more attached one is to economic goals, the less likely one is to continue working. In addition, people with strong obligation norms to organization and society have a greater propensity to continue working. The most universal prototype of a person in the Israeli labor force who would stay employed rather than give up working is a person with high work centrality, low economic values, and high obligation norms.

The general model of labor market involvement, expressed by working hours, is somewhat different. People with strong economic orientation, high work centrality, and expressive orientation tend to work longer hours. Only work centrality emerged as a consistent predictor of work involvement, measured here by two independent methods. As shown previously in other chapters (for example, Chapter 7) work centrality is an important and highly valued work-related concept for this population.

JOB PREFERENCES

This section concentrates on work values in relation to distinct job types differing in content and reward features. Two sets of jobs or job images are contrasted, and in both respondents have to make a choice by selecting one of them. In the first set (questions 33 to 36), job A offers the same pay the person is now receiving, but the person has freedom in deciding how the work should be performed. On the other hand, job B does not allow any autonomy but offers gradual pay increases, starting at 10 percent and rising to 50 percent, compared with current pay levels. Faced with these two positions, respondents have to select either job A or job B or choose a third option stating indifference in regard to both jobs. The second set (questions 37 to 40) is similar to the first in that it presents two jobs. However, job A offers similar pay to what is currently being received but emphasizes and offers autonomy, ability, skill utilization, and interesting work. Conversely, none of the peculiarities particular to job A are present in job B; it nevertheless proposes pay increases ranging from 10 percent to 50 percent in relation to what is currently received.

In forming these judgments it is important to consider some features of the choice procedure several writers (e.g., Locke 1969; 1976; Mahoney 1979a; 1979b) have advanced concerning jobs and the content of their values:

• values affect what people want to attain from their job or work.

This characteristic of values serves as a criterion in the decision-making process concerning preferences for various job features. In forming these judgments two components of the choice process are important:

• perceptions of some peculiarity or amalgamation of job characteristics and
• reciprocity between one's perceptions of job features and one's value system.

In addition, part of the decision-making process also depends on the

• prominence and value of the outcome for a person.

Hence, in evaluating job choices, one can be considered to be evaluating the gap between the distinguishing characteristics of jobs and one's value standards and the importance of these standards in relation to other criteria. Another important attribute of values applicable in the present study is that

• values may have a balanced or optimal level.

Values may change in importance in relation to the amount of a job feature an individual already possesses. For example, pay may be important up to a certain level of increase, but additional pay accretions may be valued less than other appraised job features, such as expressive items. As a consequence, a person might be willing to give up noneconomic job features such as autonomy or interesting work for additional pay provided that the pay is at such a level that it is more attractive than these or other expressive job features. The proportion of monetary increase required to bring about a change in preferences (pay versus expressive features) is an important consideration. It is estimated that an increase of 30 percent over current pay is needed before a person would tend to change job preferences from an expressive to an instrumental orientation (Jacques 1965; Kuethe & Levenson 1964; Mahoney 1979b).

An individual's evaluation of contrasting features of work and jobs was measured by asking respondents to rank, or to rate and rank, these features on an importance scale. For each person a difference between preference for either instrumental or expressive job features was then calculated, for example, in the differences between the individual's evaluation of pay relative to autonomy. People were then classified into seven categories depending on the difference scores. These categories ranged from those for which *pay* has a very important value and *autonomy* is nonessential, to those at the opposite end of the scale where autonomy is all-important and pay is not. It should be noted that the equilibrium point is conceptually important. This category includes people who are balanced in their values; they emphasize pay and autonomy about equally. This middle category is the zone where increasing values of one job characteristic (such as pay or autonomy) relative to other job features are being initiated.

These options for work or job features and outcomes were not selected randomly. Findings presented in Chapter 6 disclose that regard for aspects of expressive orientation in jobs (that is, autonomy, abilities-job match, and interesting work) are found among significant numbers of people in Israel as well as in various other countries (MOW-International Research Team 1987). The same can be said in relation to an evaluation of pay.

Tables 13.2 and 13.3 present the results for the national labor force for the two sets of job images (pay versus autonomy). The results of these analyses are summarized and presented in Figures 13.1 and 13.2. These figures show the general pattern in the national labor force sample. The results in Figure 13.1 are for the first set of job images where jobs and the work values contrast pay and autonomy (questions 33 to 36).

First, it can be observed that individual differences in the relative importance of pay and autonomy are associated with large differences in preferences for jobs that differ on these characteristics. With a 30 percent pay increment the differences between the two extreme groups (7 to 10 and -7 to -10) in their preference for job B (job containing instrumental features) is approximately 70 percent. At the 50 percent pay increment the difference between these two groups in preferences for job B increases to approximately 85 percent. This was also the change in preferences for job B, from pay equal to the present pay to pay 50 percent more than present pay, for the group with the highest pay-autonomy score (7 to 10). A change of approximately 30 percent in preferences for job B across the four job images was discerned for the group with the highest pay-autonomy score (-7 to -10).

A second general finding shown in Figures 13.1 and 13.2 is that the slope of the job preference line for groups that value pay more than autonomy increases dramatically at a 30 percent pay increment. This supports the expectation that relative value importance can be observed in terms of the slope of the preference line. In contrast, and as expected, the slope of the job preference lines is not as steep for all three groups that value autonomy more than pay.

There is also evidence from Figures 13.1 and 13.2 and Tables 13.2 and 13.3 supporting an equilibrium view of values and motivation, namely, that the currently perceived importance of a work value depends partially on the number of

Table 13.2

Percentage of National Sample Response at Each Level of Valued Working Outcomes and Their Job Preference with Each Increase in Pay

Work Values Difference Score[b]	Pay Equal			Job choice[a] Job B 10% More Pay			Job B 30% More Pay			Job B 50% More Pay		
	A	I	B	A	I	B	A	I	B	A	I	B
High Autonomy *Low Pay*												
-7 to -10 (n = 16)	100.0	0.0	0.0	100.0	0.0	0.0	100.0	0.0	0.0	100.0	0.0	0.0
-4 to -6 (n = 96)	96.6	0.0	3.1	94.8	0.0	5.2	83.3	0.0	16.7	68.7	0.0	31.3
-2 to -3 (n = 142)	96.5	0.0	3.5	94.4	0.0	5.6	84.5	0.0	15.5	68.3	0.0	31.7
Balanced -1 to 1 (n = 279)	97.8	0.0	2.2	90.6	0.0	9.4	74.8	0.0	25.2	58.7	0.0	41.3
2 to 3 (n = 132)	90.1	0.0	9.9	80.2	0.0	19.8	61.3	0.0	38.7	46.9	0.0	43.1
4 to 6 (n = 148)	94.6	0.0	5.4	76.3	0.0	23.7	54.0	0.0	46.0	40.5	0.0	59.5
7 to 10 (n = 42)	85.7	0.0	14.3	64.3	0.0	35.7	22.2	0.0	73.8	14.3	0.0	85.7
High Pay *Low Autonomy*	95.2	0.0	4.8	86.5	0.0	13.5	69.8	0.0	30.2	64.6	0.0	45.4

Notes:

$\chi^2_1 = 121.35; p = .0001$

$r_{vp}^1 = .32$

[a] Features of job A: Same pay as present job and respondent decides how to do work.
Features of job B: Pay increase increment and hardly any room for decisions about work and procedures.

[b] Difference Score = Pay Rank − Autonomy Rank.

lr_{vp} = Spearman correlation between value difference score and preference for job B.

outcomes presently possessed. In both figures the slope of the job preference line becomes steeper at a higher rate between a 10 percent and 30 percent pay increase for the groups valuing pay more than autonomy or the average of the three features. But between a 30 percent and 50 percent increase in pay, the slopes of the preference lines for these groups are not as steep. By contrast, the slope of the job preference line becomes steeper between the 10 percent and 30 percent increments for the groups valuing autonomy alone or autonomy, match, and interesting work more than pay. But the slope of the preference lines for these expressive groups becomes steeper still between 30 percent and 50 percent pay increments. This may be interpreted as an indication of substitution effects. For groups with relatively high pay, the attractiveness of further increases in

Table 13.3

Percentage of National Sample Response at Each Level of Valued Working Outcomes and their Job Preference in Each Increase in Pay

Work Values Difference Score[b]	Pay Equal			Job B 10% More Pay			Job B 30% More Pay			Job B 50% More Pay		
	A	I	B	A	I	B	A	I	B	A	I	B
High Autonomy Low Pay -9, -6 (n = 47)	95.7	4.3	0.0	95.7	4.3	0.0	89.6	4.2	6.3	78.7	4.3	17.0
-3, -5.7 (n = 149)	95.4	3.3	1.3	94.7	1.3	4.0	89.5	2.6	7.9	80.0	2.7	17.3
1 - 2.67 (n = 151)	94.8	1.3	3.9	89.6	1.9	8.4	82.4	2.0	15.7	68.9	2.6	28.5
Balanced -.67, .67 (n = 120)	96.0	3.2	0.8	92.1	2.4	5.6	81.6	3.2	15.2	67.2	4.1	28.7
1 to 2.67 (n = 144)	94.5	1.4	4.1	85.7	2.7	11.6	74.0	3.4	22.6	56.2	3.4	40.4
3 to 5.7 (n = 224)	91.5	3.6	4.9	80.4	3.1	16.4	60.2	4.0	35.8	44.4	2.7	52.9
6 to 9 (n = 50)	82.7	3.8	13.5	60.0	4.0	36.0	34.0	2.0	64.0	25.5	2.0	72.5
Pay High, Low Intrinsic	93.6	2.8	3.7	86.6	2.6	10.9	74.2	3.1	22.7	60.4	3.0	36.6

Notes:

$\chi^2 = 126.24$; $p = .0001$

$r_{vp}^{1} = .33$

[a]Features of job A: Same pay as present job, autonomy to decide, good skill match, like work activities.

[b]Difference Score = Pay Score $- \overline{X}$ (Autonomy + skill match + interesting work value scores).

$1r_{vp}$ = Spearman correlation between value difference score and preference for job B.

pay may be limited by the increased preference for autonomy alone or the three expressive job features. For groups scoring relatively high on autonomy or on the three expressive characteristics, a 50 percent pay increase is important enough to increase the rate of substitution of pay for a loss of autonomy alone, or for the three expressive job characteristics. Finally, the data have shown that a majority of the people in each group valuing autonomy alone or autonomy, job requirements-competence match, and interesting work more than pay do not switch their job preferences from job A to job B even with a 50 percent pay increase. These values appear to be a powerful set of working outcomes for a significant percentage of workers in the national labor force.

With regard to practical applications, in the job preferences for many workers pay increases do not seem to substitute for a loss of autonomy or autonomy,

Figure 13.1
Percentage of National Sample at Each Level of Valued Working Outcomes Who Choose Job B with Each Increase in Pay (Job A: high autonomy; Job B: low autonomy)

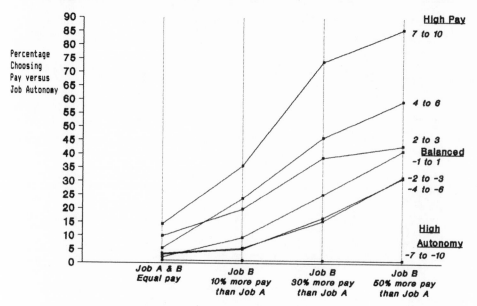

Note: Difference Score = Pay Rank - Autonomy Rank.

job-competence match, and interesting work. Most powerful of all in terms of preferences and choice are jobs with high degrees of autonomy or the three expressive characteristics and high pay increments. This is a situation often found in compensation practices for managerial and professional jobs where pay and pay increases are based on features of decision autonomy (decision frequency, size of decision in terms of resources or time commitment, and decision responsibility). To summarize, the relative preferences of individuals for pay and autonomy alone or autonomy, skill match, and interesting work do relate to the choices of jobs stated. The slope of the preference line for jobs with increasing increments of pay used to offset the loss of autonomy, or jobs with the three expressive features, depends, to a significant extent, on the relative importance of work values for a person as well as the magnitude of the pay increase.

MEANING OF WORK PATTERNS

In this section, the earlier discussion of the patterns or profiles of work meanings is extended to the multiple consequences associated with these patterns. The basis for the present analysis is the MOW patterns that were identified and described in Chapter 12.

There are five major classes of consequences included in this analysis:

Figure 13.2

Percentage of National Sample at Each Level of Valued Working Outcomes Who Choose Job B with Each Increase in Pay (Job A: high expressive; Job B: low expressive)

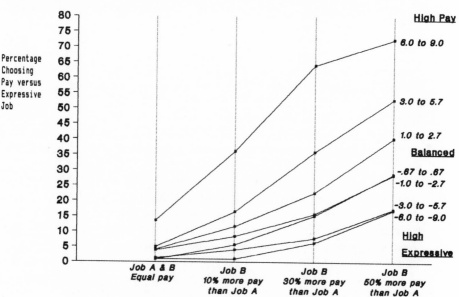

Note:

(1) Expressive job characteristics scores include the mean of autonomy, ability/job match and interesting work rating.

(2) Difference Score = Pay Rank - average (Autonomy + skill match + interesting work values scores).

1. The first class includes two measures of *work involvement:* the lottery question (question 48A) and average length of a person's work week (question 4). Characteristics of both have been described earlier in this chapter and also in Chapter 7.

2. The second category of consequences consists of people's *preferences* for the set of job images, also described earlier in this chapter. Here we restrict the consequences to the individual's preferences when pay was 30 percent greater than present pay in each set of decisions (questions 35 and 39). The decision to include only responses at the 30 percent increase was based on theoretical reasoning (Mahoney 1979b), as described earlier in this chapter, and because the job preferences begin to differ significantly at this pay increase level for people with contrasting work values.

3. The third type of consequence includes three *affective- emotional* measures. The first is an index of occupational satisfaction. It is based on the respondents' answers to two questions: whether they would choose the same or a different occupation if they were to start over (question 50A), and if they would recommend their occupation to their children (question 50B). The second of the measures asked individuals to indicate how frequently they worry about work in their free time (question 55). The third of the affective-emotional measures asks individuals about their reaction to a situation in which they would work fewer hours and draw commensurately less pay (question 68).

4. The fourth class is concerned with *social participation* and asks people whether or not they would participate in company-organized group activities outside of working hours (question 54).

5. The final class of consequences is *future* rather than present oriented and asks respondents how important work will be to them in the next five to ten years as compared with the importance of work at the present time (question 66A).

Therefore, the consequences associated here with patterns of work meanings include those concerned with attachment to work, preferences for jobs, affective-emotional responses to work and work policies, social participation, and future importance of work. The task of this section is initially to identify and describe MOW patterns and then to examine differences in the multiple consequences associated with each pattern.

Cluster analysis for the purpose of extracting meaning of work patterns or profiles was employed on the combined samples of our ten target groups. A detailed description of this procedure may be found in Chapter 12. The analysis resulted in describing seven major clusters or profiles prevailing in Israeli society. However, most of the population was distributed among three main clusters comprising about 75 percent ($n = 668$) of the target groups sample population, so our discussion will focus on these three profiles only. As described in Chapter 12 and Table 13.4, the dominant pattern (cluster 6) consisted of 40.5 percent of the respondents ($n = 363$). It includes people with high work centrality, high entitlement norm, moderate obligation norm, low economic orientation, high expressive orientation, and moderate interpersonal contacts value. Included in this pattern were 58 percent of the chemical engineers, 48 percent of the tool and die makers, 48 percent of the self-employed, and 36 percent of the teachers. Second in size was a different pattern (cluster 3), including 22.7 percent of our

Table 13.4
Meaning of Work Patterns of Most Dominant Clusters in Target Groups Samples

Meaning of Work Variable	Cluster 2	Cluster 3	Cluster 6	Grand Mean[a]
Work Centrality	45.72[b]	51.40	51.65	49.94
Obligation Norm	52.01	51.00	50.71	49.84
Entitlement Norm	50.96	40.16	52.47	50.67
Expressive Values	46.55	47.43	51.37	50.15
Economic Orientation	48.52	51.77	47.39	49.32
Contact Values	50.04	48.48	50.37	49.87
n	101	204	363	896
%	11.3	22.8	40.5	100

Notes:
[a] Grand mean of all target groups samples combined.
[b] Numbers are the T-scores in relation to the grand mean and grand standard deviation.

sample ($n = 204$). It is composed of individuals with high work centrality, low entitlement norm, moderate obligation norm, high economic orientation, low expressive orientation, and low interpersonal contacts value. Most notable in this cluster were textile workers, of whom 45 percent were included. The third pattern (cluster 2) comprised 11.3 percent of the respondents ($n = 101$). It comprised people with low work centrality, moderate entitlement orientation, high obligation norm and economic orientation, low expressive values, and moderate interpersonal contacts.

The classes of consequences associated with each of the three sets of MOW patterns are shown in Table 13.5. Adjectives rather than t-scores have been used to represent each pattern or profile.

Although patterns 6 and 3 contain people with high work centrality, these were attributed to different sources (see discussion in Chapter 12). Most notable are high entitlement norm, low economic orientation, and a high expressive orientation in pattern 6 (the most dominant) versus low entitlement norm, high economic orientation, and a low expressive orientation in pattern 3. These different inclinations are further supported by our measures of work involvement, job preferences, and some of the affective-emotional results. Roughly 3.3 times as many respondents in pattern 3 as in pattern 6 would quit working if they suddenly became wealthy. People in pattern 3 also work rather more hours per week (2.5 hours per week), presumably for the extra pay associated with extra working hours. Respondents in pattern 6 show a significant preference for the jobs offering higher autonomy, ability and skill utilization, and interesting work (job A) as compared with jobs offering 30 percent pay increase (job B). Finally, a significantly greater proportion of respondents in pattern 6 report that they worry about work in their free time more frequently than individuals in pattern 3.

People in pattern 2 are noted particularly for expressing low work centrality and low expressive values. This is supported by consequences such as showing the highest tendencies (though not different from group 3) to stop working. In preferences between jobs offering pay and autonomy, they are distributed more equally than respondents in other patterns between the two types of jobs. They also tend to be least involved in company-sponsored activities outside of work hours, albeit not significantly. Similarly, they think that work will be less important in the future, at a higher percentage level, than people in other patterns. Although no significant differences were found among the groups concerning occupational satisfaction, more respondents in pattern 2 than any other pattern indicated a preference for changing jobs (48.5 percent) rather than staying at the same one, as indicated by the lottery question. This may also be related to the low work centrality observed among people in pattern 2.

In summary, differences in emphasis on various MOW patterns probably contribute to the observed differences in consequences such as the decision to work or not to work, job preferences, and some affective emotional responses. From the results it may be concluded that different MOW profiles tend to be

Table 13.5

Classes of Consequences Associated with Meaning of Work for Target Groups Samples

Meaning of Work Variables		Pattern 2	Pattern 3	Pattern 6	Significance Test
Work centrality		low	high	high	
Obligation norm		high	moderate	moderate	
Entitlement norm		moderate	low	high	
Expressive orientation		low	low	high	
Economic orientation		moderate	high	low	
Interpersonal contacts		moderate	low	moderate	
Consequences:					
A. *Work Involvement* (%)					
1. Lottery question					
Stop working		12.1	11.8	3.6	$F = 8.41$
Continue working		87.9	88.2	96.4	$p < .0001$
Continue - same job		39.4	47.8	52.6	
Continue - different job		48.5	45.7	43.7	
2. Average work week (hrs.)		43.1	45.7	43.3	$F = 2.07$
B. *Job preferences* (%)					
1. 30% higher pay or autonomy					
Prefer job A (autonomy)		50.8	21.9	95.4	$\chi^2 = 262.4$
Prefer job B (pay)		49.2	78.1	4.6	$p < .0001$
2. 30% higher pay or autonomy match and interesting work					
Prefer job A (autonomy)		63.4	37.4	96.9	$\chi^2 = 209.6$
Prefer job B (pay)		36.6	62.6	3.1	$p < .0001$
C. *Affective-Emotional*					
1. Occupation satisfaction					
percent choosing, or	mean	1.92	1.88	1.94	$F = 3.61$
recommending same	S.D.	.78	.79	.76	$p = .69$
occupation					
2. Worry about work in	mean	2.84	2.59	2.93	$F = 4.69$
free time?	SD	1.24	1.21	1.21	$p < .01$
Never-occasionally	% distri-	33.3	49.6	29.5	
Often-very often	bution	66.7	50.4	70.5	
3. Attitudes-emotional					
reaction to working	mean	1.57	1.63	1.54	$F = .608$
less hours for less pay	SD	.91	.93	.89	$p = .54$
Against-indifferent	% distri-	71.6	68.4	73.0	
Moderately for-in favor	bution	28.4	31.6	27.0	
D. *Social participation in*					
company-sponsored activities	mean	2.26	2.39	2.45	$F = 1.84$
outside work hours	SD	.78	.73	.71	$p = .16$
No	%	20.0	14.5	12.5	
Maybe	distri-	33.8	31.5	30.0	
Yes	bution	46.2	53.9	57.5	
E. *Future Importance of work*	mean	2.15	2.29	2.24	$F = 1.94$
	SD	.58	.58	.54	$p = .14$
Less important	%	10.2	7.4	5.3	
Same as MOW	distri-	64.8	56.1	65.2	
More important	bution	25.0	36.5	29.5	

associated with differences on multiple work outcomes. The meaning of work is perceived to be multifaceted, with these multiple meanings shaping complex profiles.

CONCLUSIONS

Major conclusions that can be drawn from this chapter regarding the consequences of the meaning of work are the following:

• The best predictors of continued work involvement or noninvolvement are work centrality and economic-oriented work values.

• The best predictors of the extent of labor market involvement in terms of hours of work are economic orientation, work centrality, and expressive orientation work values.

• The more important pay and instrumental work aspects are to individuals relative to expressive perspectives, the more the individuals prefer jobs in which they forego expressive characteristics for pay increases.

• The power of money is denoted by the high expressive value groups' increasing rate of preference for the jobs with a 30 to 50 percent pay increase.

• Sources of work centrality may be related to expressive as well as to economic orientations. In both instances different patterns emerge with different implications for such consequences as work involvement, job preferences, and affective-emotional outcomes.

One clear conclusion to be drawn from the present research is that not only do people attribute many meanings to work, but the patterning of those meanings also varies. Preceding chapters have shown that the pattern of work meanings varies in a manner that can be related to characteristics of the individual, dispositions and quality of their career experience, and their occupation, in addition to other causes. What emerges is a portrait of a complex person with an intricate pattern of work meanings. An outlook such as this has been advanced previously by E. Schein (1980), who viewed a complex person with patterns of work meanings and values changing with age, stage of vocational development, and changes in jobs and work environments, as well as other influences.

Another important conclusion is that both *economic* (pay) and *expressive* characteristics of jobs are important and powerful work values. Both contribute to and influence in major ways the job preferences of people. A case can be made for using both as principal potential motivational agents in influencing people's job preferences taking account, also, of the role of individual differences.

Finally, MOW patterns help in organizing the many consequences of work and working. The multiple patterns of work meanings and the consequences associated with each pattern also provide a general set of models of a complex person, models which apply to the labor force and target groups samples in an advanced industrial society such as Israel.

14

The Meaning of Work: Summary and Relevance for Israeli Society

The focus of the research presented in this volume has been the meaning of work for a national sample of the labor force and for ten selected target groups. Several important findings have resulted from the various analyses carried out on the data.

GENERAL FRAMEWORK OF THE MEANING OF WORK

The general framework delineating the dominant meaning of work in Israel emerging from the conceptualization and analyses presented and discussed in this book is displayed in Figure 14.1. This chapter first provides a general overview of this model with a brief presentation of the major findings. A discussion relating the findings to earlier research follows, with some implications resulting from the research completing the chapter.

Work Centrality

Work centrality emerges as the most important concept in this model. It is related in some way or another to every other variable presented and discussed throughout this project. It is the most salient and fundamental variable in understanding the meaning of work.

That work is central to the lives of the participating samples was determined through the following results:

- Work is second only to family in life role importance. While family received 43 percent of responses in the national sample, 28 percent placed *work* as most important among five life roles (family, working, community, religion, and leisure). A similar general trend was also present among the ten target groups samples.

Figure 14.1
General Framework of the Meaning of Work in Israel

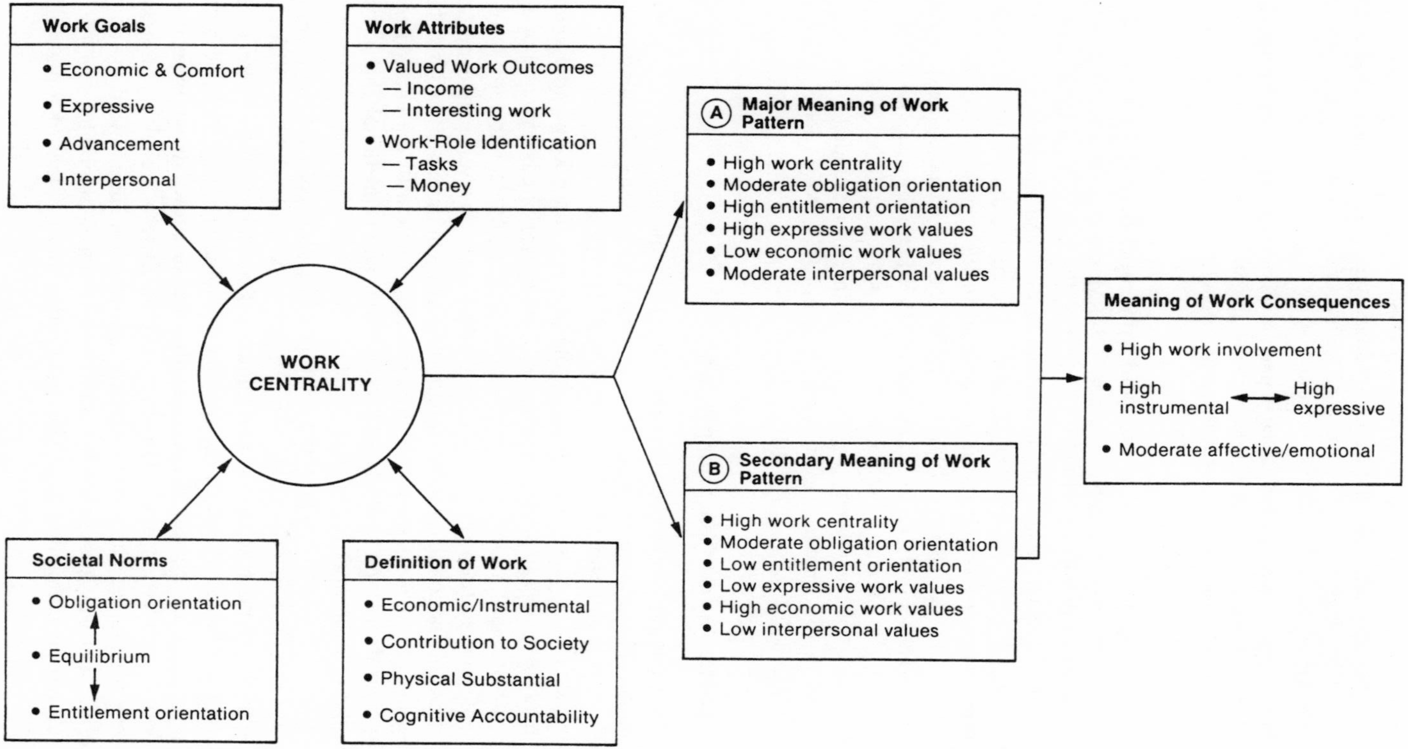

Work Goals
- Economic & Comfort
- Expressive
- Advancement
- Interpersonal

Work Attributes
- Valued Work Outcomes
  — Income
  — Interesting work
- Work-Role Identification
  — Tasks
  — Money

WORK CENTRALITY

Societal Norms
- Obligation orientation
- Equilibrium
- Entitlement orientation

Definition of Work
- Economic/Instrumental
- Contribution to Society
- Physical Substantial
- Cognitive Accountability

Ⓐ **Major Meaning of Work Pattern**
- High work centrality
- Moderate obligation orientation
- High entitlement orientation
- High expressive work values
- Low economic work values
- Moderate interpersonal values

Ⓑ **Secondary Meaning of Work Pattern**
- High work centrality
- Moderate obligation orientation
- Low entitlement orientation
- Low expressive work values
- High economic work values
- Low interpersonal values

Meaning of Work Consequences
- High work involvement
- High instrumental ↔ High expressive
- Moderate affective/emotional

- In the national sample an overwhelming portion of respondents (87.5 percent) indicated that they would choose to continue working even if they no longer had any financial reason for doing so. In the combined samples of target groups, this proportion was even higher, at 92.5 percent.

- In response to the question "How important will work be to you in the next five to ten years?" 91 percent in the national sample and about 93 percent in the combined ten target groups samples indicated that work would have equal or greater importance in comparison with the present time.

These findings, which are in accord with earlier findings by Israeli researchers (e.g., Krau 1984; Kremer & Weiner 1974; Mannheim & Rein 1981; Mannheim & Schiffrin 1984; Shamir 1986b; Shefi 1986; Yuchtman-Yaar 1984) clearly imply that individuals have a strong attachment to work and that working is a prominent life role. Within the context of labor discontent and changes in values and attitudes toward work that have occurred in the industrialized world over the past few decades (Kerr 1979; Levitan, Mangum & Marshall 1981; Ritzer 1977; Special Task Force 1973; Yankelovich 1979), policy makers and employing organizations should view these findings on the Israeli labor force positively. The results of the present project seem plainly to contradict some reports of a decline in the importance of work (Bacon 1975; Near, Rice & Hunt 1980; Robinson 1977; Vecchio 1980).

Societal Norms Concerning Work

Two central work-related norms have been discussed and analyzed in this volume. These were considered as general expressions of equitable exchange rates concerning what should be received through working—*entitlements*—and what should be contributed through the process of working—*obligations*. The general overview of societal norms concerning working is a picture of a relative degree of equilibrium or balanced norms with a tendency toward an obligation orientation. Retired people, textile workers, and the self-employed show the highest inclination toward the obligation norm. On the other hand, teachers, and tool and die makers show the strongest agreement with the entitlement norm. No clear distinction could be observed based on occupational characteristics or on the type of work carried out.

A solid balanced category between the obligation and entitlement norms generally emerged in this population. Different degrees of this equilibrium were displayed by the teachers, white-collar workers, tool and die makers, and temporary workers, as well as the national sample. This may indicate a prevalent equity value in this population, namely, that just rewards are expected for the efforts expended on work. However, overall there is, relatively, a greater tendency toward the obligation norm and a lower tendency toward the entitlement norm. This was also generally confirmed in our demographic analysis of sex, age, and educational levels. The emerging pattern is that of a high obligation orientation among men, among older members of the work force, and among the less-educated members of the labor force.

The relatively high value placed on the obligation norm is an indication of the continued existence of the traditional work ethnic. Hence, it may be concluded that the latter is a widespread norm in Israeli society.

Work Attributes

Valued work outcomes and work role identification were both identified as important *work attributes* for individuals. Utilizing different measurement approaches revealed major work attributes that were valued by workers and of significance to them. The prominence of *income* again emerges as the first and most important work attribute in this study. It appears as the most desirable valued work outcome, as expressed in the statement "working provides an income that is needed." It received more than 30 percent of responses in the national labor force. It also emerged as a very close second to work role identification ("tasks I do while working") in the national sample.

The valued work outcome of "working itself is basically interesting and satisfying to you" emerges as yet another important feature of work. One in every four people sees this outcome as most important in working life.

There is a clear distinction between the type of employees who selected *income* (or economic, extrinsic rewards) and those who chose *interesting and satisfying* (expressive, intrinsic rewards) as their first or second preference. Typically, groups such as manual laborers and those engaged in lower-level occupations such as textile workers, tool and die makers, white-collar workers, and the unemployed picked income as their most important work outcome. The self-employed also followed a similar pattern. This finding is quite logical. For all of these occupational categories the economic aspects of work are essential either for survival (self-employed) or for obtaining their most basic needs. It seems that only after securing income does interesting and satisfying work become important for these occupations, ranking it second. A different perception is expressed by higher-level occupations (such as chemical engineers or teachers) or groups with specific attitudes toward work such as retired or temporary workers. The latter are loosely attached to the labor force on ideological grounds; apparently money is second only to interesting and satisfying work for them, otherwise they would probably seek full employment. Interesting and satisfying aspects of work are more important for groups that are able to satisfy their lower-level needs. Sufficient income usually enables fulfillment of these needs, hence their main interest is in attainment of higher-order needs expressed by interesting and satisfying work (for example, autonomy, variety, responsibility, recognition, achievement).

The *tasks* one does while working form yet another important work attribute with which people identify. It is the most important work role in the national sample. Eight of the target groups ranked it either first or second in importance. Obviously, the nature of the tasks one performs are of special concern for the individual.

Work Goals

An evaluation of the relative importance of the various goals people seek from work may provide valuable information concerning the nature of the jobs people prefer or the organizations in which they may seek to participate. *Interesting work* is, by far, the most dominant work goal in this study. With slight variations it appears as the most salient among the participating samples. *Good pay* was ranked second overall and very close to interesting work, indicating its instrumentality for working people. Both of these work dimensions concede that the typical orientation of people toward their work may be quite intricate universally. What emerges here is a picture of workers who are viewed neither as exclusively expressive nor completely economic. Such a complex and compound portrait has been demonstrated by the Israeli worker's characteristic high concern with both expressive and economic aspects of work.

Comparing these findings with those of previous studies reveals some resemblance to the study by F. Herzberg and others (1957), which found importance rankings generally similar to those of our findings. There is also a very close similarity between the findings of the present study and those of R. P. Quinn (1971), where interesting work was ranked first and good pay came very close behind (although not second as in the present study).

Both of these work goals were included in two distinct factors that clustered together several related items. Interesting work was part of the *expressive* factor including such work goals as a lot of variety, opportunities to learn new things, considerable autonomy, and a good match between one's job requirements and one's abilities and experience. The second major factor, termed *economic and comfort*, included the work goals of good pay, good job security, convenient work hours, and good physical working conditions.

Two additional work goals emerged as independent factors. One was an *interpersonal* dimension and included the work goal of good interpersonal relations. People valuing such a goal are particularly concerned with social relationships such as love, friendship, and approval of others. A final factor was *advancement*, containing the work goal of good opportunity for upgrading and promotion. Such a factor is usually described in the literature as part of an economic or an external organizational variable. It seems that for the Israeli sample its importance was enough to warrant a specific factor. Advancement probably has a special meaning for Israeli workers. While it obviously provides the usual economic rewards, however large or small, it also provides a sense of accomplishment indicating one's value to the organization, self-esteem, as well as one's significance for others outside of work organizations.

Definitions of Work

The definition of work or how workers perceive the activity they engage in for about a third of their life may be seen as closely related to work centrality. Work may be central because it provides an income that is needed to obtain various goods and services, and so work will be defined as an activity that provides money. Similarly, work may be central or marginal for a variety of reasons that may be associated with how one sees the sphere of work and that consequently shape one's definition of it.

Fourteen statements previously discussed in the literature and describing work-related attributes were presented to our respondents (Chapter 11). As expected, through the economic reasoning revealed by the various analyses employed in this book, the statement "if you get money for doing it" is highly prominent. More than 68 percent in the national sample and close to 73 percent in the combined samples of the target groups selected this definitional statement. A similar general trend was also found for other countries participating in the MOW study (MOW-International Research Team 1987). These results are explained by the fact that money is a powerful reward that can satisfy many human needs. It is valued by individuals in society because it not only makes provisions for satisfying basic demands for subsistence but also symbolizes several things people cherish, such as material possessions, status, power, and self-reliance. Money is a versatile neutral stimulus that achieves its importance from its relationship with other valued outcomes in life. As a result, the selection of this definitional statement should be viewed quite naturally for most workers.

Another important definitional characteristic of work in Israeli society is "you do it to contribute to society." Such a definition and its position in relation to the other statements indicates the relevance and importance accorded to society. This is particularly noticeable among retired workers, who selected this definition significantly more frequently than the other target groups or the national sample. This is probably related to their value system, with the strong work ethic and collectivist ideology, emphasizing self-sacrifice, giving to rather than receiving from society. The teachers in our study also closely resemble this pattern. A third general definitional characteristic emerged, generally depicting work as a directed activity carried out within the framework of a specific locality and time, physically strenuous, and adding value to something. Although the economic/ instrumental and social aspects of work are universal attributes of work, fundamental to a significant number of people, it seems that the directed work characteristics are restricted to individuals employed mainly in traditional organizations, with low skills and involved in low-level jobs. Hence, their perception of work is obviously inclined toward such a definition. This definition may be labeled *physical substantial*.

Contrary to the latter definition, it seems that the final major pattern of work definitions is a function of a different perception about work. Here work is discerned as an activity to be accounted for, creating a feeling of belonging, an activity which is mentally strenuous and from which others profit. It is most likely that the preceding portrayal of work is part of the world of work as seen through the eyes of people in managerial positions, occupying highly skilled jobs along with greater responsibility and situated at higher organizational status. *Cognitive accountability* is the best indicator and label of this definitional perspective.

A major conclusion that can be drawn from the analysis of work definitions is that most individuals in our sample make a distinction among different features of work when they define it. A substantial number of respondents relate to it either in economic/instrumental terms or as a contribution to society. Others also identify work as an activity associated with substantial physical labor or with cognitive accountability. Moreover, only a very minor proportion of respondents see work as an unenjoyable or unpleasant activity when they attempt to elaborate the aspects that differentiate work from other activities. This finding contradicts the assertion made by S. Shimmin (1966) and R. S. Weiss and R. L. Kahn (1960) that one of the distinguishing features of working activities is that people perform them but do not enjoy them.

Meaning of Work Patterns and Consequences

Two central MOW patterns emerge from this study. The principal feature that characterizes both is the high work centrality expressed by individuals. Equally, a moderate obligation norm was also observed in each of the patterns. Nevertheless, the composition of these patterns differed regarding the other MOW variables. In the first and largest pattern (cluster 6) individuals expressed a high entitlement norm, low economic orientation, high expressive values, and a moderate level of interpersonal contact. In contrast, in the second pattern (cluster 3) a low entitlement norm, high economic orientation, low expressive value, and low interpersonal contact were found to go together.

From organizational and societal perspectives, it is encouraging to know that a major proportion of the labor force sees work as a central element in their total life. However, implications should be drawn from the results of other related MOW variables that probably shape and influence the high work centrality. What is depicted here is that *individual differences* play a major role, accounting for different needs, values, and norms. This appears to be the central explanatory variable for the phenomenon that although work is central for most Israelis, different factors may lie at its foundation. Here, work centrality is part of a pattern containing high expressive value along with a low economic orientation for more than 40 percent of the total target groups sample population. Hence, work or jobs that allow one to fulfill expressive needs are of chief concern to these employees. Obviously, the management of organizations needs to provide such opportunities to this type of employee. In our study, this pattern was typical of professional or relatively highly skilled occupations; it thus seems to be a property of such groups. Conversely, work centrality is associated with high economic orientation and low expressive values for about a quarter of the total target groups sample population.

These suggestions are further supported by the data provided through an analysis of the MOW consequences. For example, a very significant proportion of respondents in the high economic–low expressive pattern proportion (cluster 3) expressed a wish to stop working if this was no longer economically necessary. In addition, the same people were found to spend more time at work, apparently for the supplementary income furnished by additional working hours. By contrast, workers belonging to the high expressive–low economic pattern (cluster 6) showed a significant preference toward jobs allowing high autonomy, ability and skill utilization, and interesting work in opposition to jobs proposing greater economic gains (a 30 percent pay increase).

Another related MOW consequence is work involvement. It was found that work centrality and economically oriented work values were the best predictors of work involvement. In addition, people with a strong obligation norm showed the greatest propensity to remain employed even if working was not required any longer. However, of all the MOW variables utilized in this project, only work centrality emerged as a consistent predictor of work involvement.

A final important consequence regarding the meaning of work has to do with instrumental as well as expressive features of jobs. It was clearly observed that people who prefer the instrumental or economic aspects of work tend to choose jobs that offer more pay rather than jobs mainly offering expressive attributes. On the other hand, most people who value such expressive facets as autonomy, a match between job requirements and competence, and interesting work higher than instrumental aspects do not switch their expressive predisposition even if presented with a 50 percent increase in pay. As a consequence a conclusion to be drawn from this study is that both economic and expressive characteristics of work are important and powerful work values.

IMPLICATIONS

This study on the meaning of work in Israel has produced a wealth of data that have been presented throughout this volume. In this section some of the more general implications to be elicited from the most consistent findings will be discussed.

Work centrality consistently emerges as the most salient aspect in this study. This is a fundamental concept in the meaning of work in the life of Israeli workers.

The prevalence of high work centrality throughout this project should be viewed as encouraging to employing organizations and policy makers because of its relationship with other desired organizational outcomes. Work centrality, often used interchangeably with other terms (for example, central life interest, job involvement, ego involvement, job satisfaction, intrinsic motivation, work role involvement; see Rabinowitz & Hall 1977) was found to be associated with some important organizational variables. For example, researchers such as R. J. Aldag and A. F. Brief (1975), D. T. Hall, B. Schneider, and H. T. Nygren (1970), R. N. Kanungo (1982a), T. Lodahl and M. Kejner (1965), B. Mannheim (1980), F. E. Saal (1978), and R. S. Schuler (1975) have found a positive correlation between work centrality and job satisfaction. Other findings showed that more involved workers tend to spend more time and effort on the job than workers who are less involved (Hall & Foster 1977; Hall et al. 1978). T. A. Beehr and N. Gupta (1978), G. F. Farris (1971), J. L. Koch and R. M. Steers (1978), and A. L. Siegel and R. A. Ruh (1973) have all asserted that participation in decision making was found to be positively related to work centrality. Finally, there are also some indications pointing to the relationship between work involvement and performance (Hall et al. 1978; Vroom 1962). If possible, then, employers and organizations should provide employees with work settings that will lead to high work centrality levels. These settings might take into consideration the amount of autonomy, control, and influence a person has on the job (Bass 1965; Tannenbaum 1966; Vroom 1962), the feeling that one is making important contributions to organizational success (Bass 1965), a chance to utilize one's abilities (Lawler & Hall 1970), work challenge (Hall 1971), and opportunities for the satisfaction of the individual's need for achievements, belonging, and self-esteem (Patchen 1970).

Through the various measures employed in this study, two opposing variables consistently emerge as important in the structure of the meaning of work. These are *economic* or *instrumental* versus *expressive* inclinations toward work. Both indicate a different and opposing orientation toward work, implying that several needs are provided by work or may be fulfilled through working.

The expressive dimension of work is represented in this study by facets like interesting work, variety, autonomy, and opportunity to learn new things. All of these items deal with the human need to be productive, competent, self-actualizing, and achievement oriented. A characteristic of work goals or outcomes of an expressive nature is that successful task performance becomes a source of satisfying these work goals. Unlike lower-level needs (such as those described by Maslow 1954), the strength of expressive dimensions can increase as a result of a satisfying or gratifying experience. Expressive work goals can become a continuous source of motivation, since their contentment is directly related to job performance (Herzberg et al. 1959; Saleh & Grygier 1969). Expressive goals are also claimed to satisfy higher-order needs (Slocum 1967).

The attributes of the economic and comfort work goals dimensions are the opposite of those of the expressive factor. The goals or rewards are *acquired* from the organization and are externally mediated by someone other than the worker (for example, the employee's supervisor) and are usually associated with the satisfaction of lower-level needs (in the Maslowen conception; Dyer & Parker 1975). The economic or instrumental aspects utilized in this study were various forms of compensation for work. These included the *valued work outcome* of "working provides you with an income that is needed," the *work role identification* of "the money I receive from my work," and the *work goal* of "good pay." An additional instrumental aspect was job security.

Organizations may affect the behavior of their members by using appropriate management to satisfy their needs. The first task facing organizations is to identify these basic needs. Once organizations achieve this goal, they should match important work goals or work attributes with these needs. Assuming that the needs of individuals at the workplace are matched with desirable outcomes, the motivation to work will be enhanced. This task may be accomplished by the proper design of tasks, jobs, and organizational environment so that desirable work outcomes may induce and reinforce motivational behavior.

The role of pay or income is clearly apparent as one of the major work outcomes desired by workers. This finding has immediate implications for organizational decision makers.

Pay is a powerful motivator that can satisfy several subsistence and higher-order needs. Dissatisfaction with pay may lead to a number of dysfunctional behaviors. Employees tend to reduce their commitments to organizational endeavors when they are not satisfied with what they receive from the organization. Pay dissatisfaction may be manifested in forms of low motivations, absenteeism, turnover, or sabotage. These undesirable behaviors contribute to low productivity and other high costs. Nevertheless, the importance of pay varies. If organizations want to utilize pay as a motivator, the following should be carefully considered. First, the importance of pay varies. Pay or income may be important to a person who strives to achieve satisfaction of lower-level needs such as physiological or security needs. But as a person becomes reasonably satisfied with these needs, pay may lose its importance unless it can be instrumental in satisfying others. Economic rewards are usually considered to have stronger impact on satisfying lower-level needs, since they are more essential for survival. As a result, they are more applicable for low-skilled workers at lower organizational levels or entry positions. The reason may be that higher-level and more highly skilled jobs usually provide more and better opportunities to satisfy higher-order needs. In addition, higher-level and more highly skilled jobs usually pay more than lower-level and unskilled jobs.

Related to this is a second variation of pay importance. The importance of income depends on how much a person receives. The more money one gets, the less important pay is (Lawler 1971; Lawler & Porter 1963). As satisfaction with pay rises less importance is attached to it. As the marginal utility of additional income decreases, it will take more money to make a raise meaningful to highly paid employees. This is closely related to a third variation in pay importance, which has a clear organizational implication. Income varies as a function of job levels. Managers tend to value pay less highly than workers (Centers & Bugental 1966; Ronan 1970). This was distinctly noted in our analysis of the importance of work goals according to organizational levels. Thus, an important requirement for management is the development of motivational methods and strategies other than monetary rewards to motivate relatively highly paid employees continuously. These are obviously expressive rewards, and their importance has been well established in this study.

Another important result with a different organizational implication is the emphasis placed upon *expressive or intrinsic orientation*. Thus, employment in a work context that allows the facilitation of such aspects may be fruitful for those who value or who have a great need to achieve expressive or intrinsic goals. Moreover, when work is interesting and challenging, people are motivated to perform more than is required to justify their instrumental gains. They exert extra effort to achieve a sense of accomplishing something worthwhile and of fulfilling their potential. Various studies have shown the motivational consequences of jobs with expressive content (Hackman & Oldham 1975; Herzberg et al. 1959). The existence of such job factors influences the psychological status of workers and may influence their affective reactions toward the job. This in turn eventually affects work motivation and job performance. Intrinsically motivated employees are interested in the expressive aspects of work (interesting work, autonomy, advancement), not necessarily for the sake of obtaining greater financial rewards or more power, but because these expressive rewards are associated with intrinsically motivating jobs. Employees whose expressive-oriented work behaviors are persistently reinforced will most likely remain in the organization as productive workers to a greater degree than will those who have high expressive needs but who are not continuously challenged in their work situations. When expressive needs are not reasonably satisfied over a period of time, employees may develop negative attitudes that may result in undesirable behavior. I. Harpaz (1983) reviewed the literature on the consequences of dissatisfaction and classified their effects on three different levels: individual, organizational, and societal. At the individual level such factors as frustration, aggression, counterproductive behavior (for example, sabotage), drug use, withdrawal from the labor force, physical health, and life satisfaction are listed. At the organizational level factors such as turnover, absenteeism, grievances, and poor performance were found to be associated with dissatisfaction. Finally, on the societal level, it was found that dissatisfaction may impose a burden upon society and its resources, cause underutilization of human resources, be related to low national productivity and the high cost of goods and services, and restrict political activity.

These outcomes may bring about higher costs, low productivity, and poor product quality in organizations and society, and in many instances they probably cause business failure. Therefore, making jobs more interesting and challenging to those seeking such positions is crucial not only for satisfying the needs of workers but also for maintaining productive organizations.

In order for organizations to benefit more from expressive-oriented employees, as well as to maintain high motivation among them, various practical measures should be considered. These would mostly focus around diversified methods to structure, design, or redesign tasks, jobs, and work settings in such a way that it will allow meeting expressive needs.

Several approaches are available to create innovative and expressive work systems. It is not within the scope of this chapter to elaborate on these or to evaluate their relative strengths, weaknesses, or cost. Nevertheless, we may find among these such systems as various approaches to job design, job enrichment, job enlargement, a condensed work week, flexitime, participative work methods (such as industrial democracy), goal setting, and responsibilities. These are just some of the approaches available for enhancing expressive orientation.

The importance of *interpersonal contacts* is a work goal of considerable significance in Israel. Social relations and social interaction take place wherever people are grouped together. Social needs are basic to human beings. Aspects such as social interaction or the social support of fellow workers or of an employer may be critical to well-being at the workplace. Interpersonal factors may affect motivation in many complex and diverse ways. They seem to influence both expressive and instrumental orientations (Lawler 1971). A superior is usually situated in a role that influences both expressive and instrumental rewards. A superior may determine how much or how often financial rewards are received and the rate of promotion. Simultaneously, the quality of the social or human interaction between leaders and subordinates may also be affected by the ability or willingness of the superior to interact with employees. Since superiors occupy such an important position in organizations, it should be the concern of organizations to train and develop their managerial staff with respect to their interpersonal and human skills. Interpersonal contacts are capable of satisfying such relation-oriented needs as affiliation, companionship, and emotional support. The motivation of employees may be influenced by their ability to satisfy such needs. Moreover, organizations should also make provision for social interpersonal contacts among their employees rather than restrict them. This may enable workers to interact, receive mutual support from their fellow workers, or fulfill interpersonal needs not provided by their superiors.

A consistent finding in this study has been the importance that people place on the *tasks* they do. This was considered the most important work role identification in the national sample and was viewed similarly among almost all the target groups. Since tasks are considered to be of such importance to individuals, and tasks are at the heart of a job, they should be carefully designed by organizations. In this respect L. W. Porter, E. E. Lawler, and J. R. Hackman (1975) contended that jobs should be adequately "whole" so that workers could perceive that they achieve or create things of value to themselves and to others. Such a job, according to Porter and his colleagues (1975), would be high on task identity. Hence, organizations should make an effort to structure jobs or tasks to be meaningful and worthwhile for their occupants. According to A. Turner and P. Lawrence (1965), jobs that contain task identity are distinguished by (1) a very clear cycle of perceived closure—the job provides a distinct sense of beginning and ending a transformation ("doing something") process; (2) the high visibility of the transformation to the worker; (3) the high visibility of the transformation in the finished product; and (4) a transformation of considerable magnitude (Turner & Lawrence 1965: 157).

Societal norms concerning work and working clearly reflect the general norms and values prevalent in society. In this study we have shown that a relative degree of *equilibrium* or balanced norms with a tendency toward an *obligation* norm exists. People with a high obligation toward organizations or society tend to contribute more to both, since giving rather than receiving is a core value for them. A balance or equilibrium between obligations and entitlements may echo a state wherein involvement or contribution is based on a *calculative* disposition. Namely, people feel obligated to the point where they perceive that their contributions and efforts (obligations) are being recognized and fairly rewarded (entitlements). In a sense, this is in accord with various notions of social or organizational justice and equity theory (Adams 1963; Homans 1961).

In a society still in its formative stages and with a constant need to increase productivity, it would be beneficial to employ a workforce with a high obligation norm. However, norms are beyond the control of organizations. Norms develop over time and are part of the social, political, and cultural structure of a society. People join organizations with a set of established and given norms. If obligation norms need to be emphasized or developed, this may be achieved through the educational system. Another avenue is through personal examples provided by political, labor, or management leaders and by those who mold public opinion. In the current state of affairs, it would be advantageous to organizations to try to determine the norms held by prospective employees. If possible, and other things being equal, those with high obligation norms should be preferred to those low on obligation or high on entitlement or those in a state of equilibrium regarding their work-related norms.

The definition of *working* is not presented in this study as one of the major meanings of work variables. It is viewed as parallel to the MOW model presented in Chapter 4 rather than being an integrated part of it. Nevertheless, how an individual defines work may also indicate what the meaning of work is to that person or what is considered important, or what the individual seeks from work. Through an examination of what is considered as working, it is apparent that the economic/instrumental aspect of work is the most dominant definitional concept of work. Similarly, societal contribution is another important attribute of working.

These findings are congruent with the variables that emerged as important in the MOW model. It adds support to the significance of these variables in the life of the Israeli worker.

Considerations Regarding Demographic Variables

Throughout this study, analyses have been conducted in relation to three major demographic variables: sex, age, and educational level. Some major implications regarding these are discussed in this section.

Differences between the sexes in relation to the meaning of work have been noted in this research. Significant differences were observed between the work centrality of men and the work centrality of women. Various measures employed consistently showed that work is more important to men than to women. In addition, if the time devoted to work as an indicator of work involvement/ centrality (as presented in Chapter 13) is considered, there is a significant difference in the national labor force between men (48.02 hours per week) and women (34.10 hours per week). In the rankings of *work goals* the emphasis given to different aspects between the sexes is most noticeable. Work goals such as "pay," "opportunity for upgrading and promotion," and "job security" are strikingly ranked as more important by men than women. Conversely, work facets such as "convenient work hours" and "opportunity to learn" are distinctly more important for women. Convenient work hours may represent the traditional role conflict between the time women have to allocate for work and their family responsibilities, whereas the opportunity to learn may be a reflection of the rise in the number of women in the labor force and their desire for learning and development in order to achieve parity with men.

Differences were observed between the sexes with respect to *societal norms.* Men are significantly more *obligation* oriented than women. The effect of sex is distinctly larger on the obligation norm in comparison with the *entitlement* norm.

Finally, with respect to *work attributes,* men allot more points (33.2 out of 100) to the *valued work outcome* of "working provides you with an income that is needed" compared with women (26.7). Women place greater importance on outcomes such as "interesting contacts with other people" or "interesting work." Similarly, while men rank "money they receive from work," as their most important *work role identification,* women rank it only fifth. Here women as compared with men again show their stronger preference for "people they work with."

The various analyses conducted in this volume point to some shared values of men and woman regarding work. However, some major differences were also noted, as summarized. These lead us to conclude that

1. work is more central to men than to women;

2. men value instrumental aspects of work more than women;

3. men have a greater obligation to work than women;

4. convenient work hours are an important work goal for women; and

5. women have a stronger preference for social contact at work.

Several explanations have been advanced to explain some of the variations disclosed here. U. Leviatan (1985) summarized some of the most salient accounts put forward in the literature. These are the following: (1) Differences in work centrality between the sexes may be related to differences in their educational levels. People with lower education also have lower centrality. Since women generally have less schooling than men, their work centrality also tends to be lower. (2) Most studies include women employed in part-time or in temporary employment. For such women work is less central. (3) The dual role of women (work and home) creates a problem in which women exert a great deal of effort with their home chores, a fact that detracts from the efforts needed at the workplace, thus making the workplace less central. (4) Women work mostly in lower-status jobs or jobs that do not allow them to fulfill several needs. To overcome frustration women lower their expectations of work. (5) Women have different attitudes about and expectations of work because of the "social direction" they receive through sex role socialization from childhood to adulthood. These social influences affect what women expect from work in terms of development and achievements. Alternatively they express themselves in the family domain and in social interaction.

It has been claimed that, biologically, women are expected to find satisfaction in their families as opposed to work. According to this assertion, sex differences will persist regardless of the efforts taken to solve women's social and environmental problems. Besides these issues, women face discrimination in the workforce that may be related to and affect their attitudes toward work. Two general types of discrimination are frequently encountered by women: One is job entry: restricted entry to entry-level jobs, failure to recruit women for certain positions, and lower starting salaries for women (Arvey 1979; Stumpf et al. 1980; Terburg & Ilgen 1975). The other is differential treatment: once women enter the workforce, they may be subjected to discrimination in how they are treated in such areas as job placement, promotional opportunities, salary increases, and other human resources decisions.

All the preceding explanations for sex differences regarding work call for some policy implications. If, as has been found in this study, women's work centrality, work involvement, and other attitudes toward work are lower or different from those of men because of differential conduct or external, environmental treatment by society, then a specific policy implication exists. In other words, society and organizations ought to act in order to change these conditions. Change can be achieved through legislation, education, favorable treatment, various affirmative action programs, or training and development programs. Society and organizations will need to reach out to women, since they have begun to take on an increasingly important role in the labor force. If society and organizations wish to utilize women more efficiently in the labor force as well as to make work more meaningful for them, certain steps will need to be taken. Otherwise, the different meaning that women attach to work will continue to affect them seriously.

Various analyses were conducted with different *age* categories. The sample population was divided into three levels: under 30, 30 to 50, and over 50 years of age. Significant differences were noted in relation to age. Work centrality was relatively low in the younger category, rising with age. Moreover, through the work involvement measure, it was revealed that a higher proportion of young workers (age 20–29) would stop working if work were no longer a requirement. The magnitude of these figures regarding young people's attitude toward work is enhanced when our data, collected in the early 1980s, are compared with the response of young people to a similar question a decade earlier. We noted a substantial increase (from 6.3 percent to 15.4 percent) in the desire of young people to stop working. These findings indicate that work is less central in the life of young people and has probably become less important since the 1970s. On balance, work is significantly more central in the life of the older workforce and apparently gaining in its importance for that group in comparison with previous years.

Several issues are of utmost concern. What will be the nature of the workforce in the future if its current young people perceive work as less important? If centrality of work is linearly correlated with age, as found in this study, then policy makers should not be alarmed. As young people mature, it is most likely that work will be perceived to be more important, with all the outcomes and implications associated with this. However, if the work ethic is deteriorating among the young, various steps will need to be considered by those making policy for society and its institutions. At the macro level, society will have to evaluate if it is disseminating the correct values to its younger generations. A well-controlled research project will be needed in order to examine the causes of such relatively new attitudes in Israeli society.

If at the societal level solutions to the problems of work centrality are very complex, at the micro level they may be more realistic. Scrutinization of the relative importance of *work goals* might provide some solutions to the problem of work centrality among young people. For instance, we can observe that "opportunity to learn new things," "opportunity for upgrading and promotion," and "variety" are consistently more important for younger workers than for their older counterparts. If organizations can create work settings containing these and other work facets that are relatively more important for the young, this may also affect their work centrality positively.

Most encouraging to policy makers is the finding that work is very central in the life of older people. With life expectancy increasing, older workers should be considered as very valuable and important human resources. Their skills and experience should be utilized better by organizations for mutual advantage. In order to maintain this present favorable attitude among older workers, organizations should see that they are provided with work goals that seem to be important to them. These are mainly "good pay," "work autonomy," a "good match between a person and a job," and "good working conditions."

The claim that older workers are valuable to organizations and society receives additional support when we examine *societal norms*. While entitlement norms do not seem to be related to age, obligation norms clearly increase with each age category, with the lowest scores in the youngest age group and highest among the oldest. Hence, a higher work commitment might be expected and a greater contribution made by older employees, regardless of whether this is a cohort or a maturation effect.

A final demographic variable considered is *educational level*. Usually closely associated with sex and age, this variable did not reveal significant differences in relation with some of our MOW variables. For example, no relationship was observed between educational level and work centrality. Some significant trends were found in the relationship between education and work goals. Highly educated employees express a clear preference for expressive work goals. Such were "interesting work," "match between a person and a job," "opportunity to learn" and "variety." On the other hand, the lower the educational level, the more importance attached to economic and comfort dimensions of work (for example, "good pay" and "working conditions"). As noted earlier, in order to maintain a motivated and satisfied workforce, organizations should try to make an effort to provide these valued work goals.

A final consideration regarding education may be inferred from our data. Although no relationship was observed between educational level and entitlement norm, it was disclosed that the lower the educational level, the higher the obligation norm. People with higher education usually occupy the better-paid, higher-skilled, and more responsible jobs in the organization. They tend to be more professional, thus their orientation may be directed to their profession or occupation and less to their organization. In contrast, people with lower educational levels tend to be the opposite of those with better education. For both of these, policy makers need to apply different methods to create (among the highly educated) or maintain (among the lower educated) their obligation orientations. Again, by attending to the special needs to their diversified workforce, organizations might be able to achieve their own goals.

CONCLUSION

The pattern that emerges from this extensive research project is that of a complex and multidimensional meaning of work in Israel. Different motives and preferences were noted for work centrality, work goals, work attributes, and societal norms. All of these characteristics affect the ways in which individuals define work or shape their meaning of working. To create or improve organizational functioning, suggestions for changes or plans for organizational design should treat the characteristics of workers as contingencies. All suggestions or implications advanced in this chapter are derived from the diversity and complexity observed in individuals. These are a reflection of the current Israeli labor force. However, it should be noted that jobs that are challenging and interesting at one time may not be the same in the future. Similarly, the interest in instrumental aspects of work may shift to other work values. Hence, workers cannot be taken for granted. Organizations have the task of constantly enquiring about their employees' work values in order to try to match these with desired organizational outcomes and rewards. Knowledge of values, attitudes, goals, and preferences of employees and of potential workers is necessary to design organizations that are good at surviving in times of rapid technological change, scarce resources, and other environmental uncertainties.

Epilogue

It is only in the last few decades that objective data on the meaning of work have been collected and recorded. Before that the notion of work and its meanings were available only through philosophical and religious writings.

This volume has shown that work means different things to different people. A review of the meaning of work in Israel through the ages revealed that work also has different meanings at different times. Hence, its meaning is in a process of constant change varying from peripheral to extremely important. Among Israelis of the 1980s it is clear that work is a central element in their lives. It is perceived as such because work is an essential and fundamental human activity, an instrumental, as well as expressive activity, and it provides directly or indirectly for central human needs. There is probably no other single activity that consistently demands and provides as much emotionally, physically, and cognitively as work.

Although the commitment to work and the centrality of work constitute an important element of the work ethic, its presence does not necessarily ensure another component of the work ethic, namely, motivation on the job, or the readiness to exert an effort at work. From our discussion of why people work, and from the data presented in this volume, it is apparent that people work for a variety of reasons. These may be instrumental, socio-psychological, or perhaps derive from some kind of a human urge or instinct, but they need not necessarily lead to highly motivated job performance. It is a primary task of society and organizations to channel human work centrality in the most appropriate way to enable them to achieve their requirements and goals.

Appendix I

Meaning of Work Questionnaire

Three questionnaires were utilized in the study: (1) for the nonworking samples of unemployed and retired, (2) for the students sample, and (3) for all the working samples. Because the first two are virtually similar to the third, with the appropriate modifications for nonworking people, only the third questionnaire is presented here.

✱✱✱

PLEASE CIRCLE THE NUMBER BESIDE THE RESPONSE OF YOUR CHOICE AND FILL IN THE BLANKS, WHERE APPROPRIATE.

✱✱✱

First, some questions about your present work situation.

1. What type of work (job) do you presently do? _____
_____

2. Is your position primarily:
   1 Non-Supervisory
   2 Supervisory
   3 Managerial

3. Are you a member of the following types of organizations?
   NO   YES
   3A   1   2   Trade Union
   3B   1   2   Professional Association
   3C   1   2   Employers Association

4. On the average, how many hours a week do you work (including overtime)?
   __ __ hours

5. On the average, how much time do you spend travelling to and from work (both ways) each day?
   __ __ __ minutes

6. Now about your working schedule:
6A Is your work schedule primarily:
   1 day
   2 night
   3 swing shift (partly day, partly night)
   4 shift changes regularly
6B Are your work hours primarily
   1 regular
   2 varied
6C During the last 12 months, have you worked weekends at least half of the time?
   1 no
   2 yes

7A Have you been unemployed in the last 5 years?
    1 no
    2 yes
7B If yes, for how many months in the past 5 years?
    __ __ months
7C If yes, for how many months in the past 12 months?
    __ __ months

> Now, some questions about your present job.

8. Which statement best describes your present job? (Please circle <u>one</u> number)
   1 I often do the same things over and over or use the same piece of equipment or procedure almost all the time.
   2 There is some variety in my job. I use different pieces of equipment or procedures.
   3 I do many different things, use a wide variety of equipment or procedures.

9. Which statement best describes your present job? (Please circle <u>one</u> number)
   1 There is hardly any room for me to make decisions about my work and its procedures.
   2 I make some of the decisions about my work and some are made for me.
   3 I decide myself how to do my work.

10. Which statement best describes your present job? (Please circle <u>one</u> number)
    1 Mistakes in my work do not have serious consequences for the organization or for other people.
    2 Mistakes in my work may have somewhat serious consequences for the organization or for other people.
    3 Mistakes in my work may have serious consequences for the organization or for other people.

11. Which statement best describes your present job? (Please circle <u>one</u> number)
    1 Doing my job I really can't learn something new.
    2 Sometimes I can learn something new doing my job.
    3 My work gives me the opportunity to learn many new things.

12. Which statement best describes your present job? (Please circle <u>one</u> number)

    1 In fact, I do my work alone.

    2 I work with some other people, but this is not a big part of my job.

    3 Working with other people is a very big part of my job.

13. Which statement best describes your present job? (Please circle <u>one</u> number)

    1 There is almost no chance during the work day to talk to other people about non-business topics.

    2 Sometimes I do have the opportunity during the work day to talk to other people about non-business topics.

    3 There is almost always an opportunity during the work day to talk to other people about non-business topics.

14.[2] Do you sometimes have to do your work in dangerous circumstances?

    1 no

    2 yes

15.[2] Do you sometimes have to do your work in unhealthy circumstances?

    1 no

    2 yes

16.[2] Does your job require <u>too</u> much of you physically?

    1 It never does.

    2 It seldom does.

    3 It sometimes does.

    4 It often does.

17.[2] Does your job require <u>too</u> much of you mentally?

    1 It never does.

    2 It seldom does.

    3 It sometimes does.

    4 It often does.

18.[2] How much of your past experience, skills and abilities can you make use of in your present job?

    1 Very little.

    2 A little.

    3 Quite a lot.

    4 Almost all.

19.[2] Which of the following statements best describes your relationship with your supervisor?

1   He does not inform me at all about his decisions.
2   He informs me after he has made his decisions.
3   He usually asks for my advice before making decisions.
4   We usually make decisions jointly.
5   He allows me to make most decisions on my own.

Now we would like to ask you some questions about jobs you have held in the past and about your work history.

20.[2] Is your present job your first job?
1   no
2   yes (If <u>yes</u>. go to question 23.)

21.* Let's start with your first <u>full time</u> job that lasted 12 months or longer.

21A __ __ What type of occupation was it? _____

_____

21B __ __ What made you choose this job? _____

_____

21C __ __ What was the name of the organization or company where you worked? _____

_____

21D   How long did you work in this job?
__ __ years.

22.* Now, for each <u>full time</u> job after your first job and up to but <u>not including</u> your present job, could you provide the following information:

22A Second Job
22A1 __ __ • Type of job (occupation) _____

_____

22A2 __ __ • Length of time on the job __ __ years

---

*NOTE: For temporary workers, Questions 21 and 22 refer only to full time <u>steady</u> jobs that lasted 12 months or longer. If no steady job has been held, go to Question 23.

22A3 __ __ • Major reasons for leaving the job _____

_____

22B Third Job
22B1 __ __ • Type of job (occupation) _____

_____

_____

22B2 __ __ • Length of time on the job __ __ years
22B3 __ __ • Major reasons for leaving the job _____

_____

22C Fourth Job
22C1 __ __ • Type of job (occupation) _____

_____

_____

22C2 __ __ • Length of time on the job __ __ years
22C3 __ __ • Major reasons for leaving the job _____

_____

22D Fifth Job
22D1 __ __ • Type of job (occupation) _____

_____

_____

22D2 __ __ • Length of time on the job __ __ years
22D3 __ __ • Major reasons for leaving the job _____

_____

22E Sixth Job
22E1 __ __ • Type of job (occupation) _____

_____

_____

22E2 __ __ • Length of time on the job __ __ years
22E3 __ __ • Major reasons for leaving the job _____

_____

22F Seventh Job
22F1 __ __ • Type of job (occupation) _____

_____

_____

22F2 __ __ • Length of time on the job __ __ years
22F3 __ __ • Major reasons for leaving the job _____

_____

23. Now considering your present job (occupation):
23A __ __ • What made you choose this job? _____

__ __ _____

__ __ _____

23B   • How long have you worked in your present job?

         __ __ years

23C   • What is your monthly <u>net</u> income from your present job?

         __ __ __ __ (dollars) per month

Now, looking at your total working history as a whole, please describe it in the following aspects.

---

24. Compared to your present occupational group (colleagues), where did you start your work career?

    1   Lower than my occupational group.

    2   About the same as my occupational group.

    3   Higher than my occupational group.

25. Would you describe your work career as having ups and downs (either large or small)?

25A   1   no

       2   yes

25B If yes, were the ups and downs:

       1   small

       2   large

26. Considering my whole work history until today in relation to where I started:

    1   It is marked by some decline

    2   It has remained approximately on the level where I started

    3   It has improved somewhat

    4   It has improved a great deal

27. On the whole, how satisfied are you with your work history until now?

    1   Very dissatisfied

    2   Somewhat dissatisfied

    3   Neutral

    4   Somewhat satisfied

    5   Very satisfied

> For the next set of questions, we would like you to think about what
> working means to you at the present time. Please remember we are
> not referring only to your present situation. We are interested in
> knowing what beliefs and values you personally have regarding work-
> ing as a result of your total working life.

28B • First of all, I would like you to tell me, in your own words, what is
most important to you about working.

___ ___ _____

___ ___ _____

_____

_____

28C • Is there anything about working that really bothers you?

___ ___ _____

___ ___ _____

_____

_____

28.   To help explain what working means to you, please assign a total of
100 points, in any combination you desire, to the following six
statements. The more a statement expresses your thinking, the more
points you should assign to it. Please read all the statements before
assigning points.

28A1 ___ ___ Working gives you status and prestige.

28A2 ___ ___ Working provides you with an income that is needed.

28A3 ___ ___ Working keeps you occupied.

28A4 ___ ___ Working permits you to have interesting contacts with other
people.

28A5 ___ ___ Working is a useful way for you to serve society.

28A6 ___ ___ Working itself is basically interesting and satisfying to you.
(100 Total)

29.   How important and significant is working in your total life?

| One of the least important things in my life | 1 2 3 | 4 of medium importance in my life | 5 6 7 | One of the most important things in my life |

30.   Assign a total of 100 points to indicate how important the following
areas are in your life at the present time.

30A   __ __ My leisure (like hobbies, sports, recreation and contacts with friends)

30B   __ __ My community (like voluntary organizations, union and political organizations)

30C   __ __ My work

30D   __ __ My religion (like religious activities and beliefs)

30E   __ __ My family

(100 Total)

31.   When you think of your working life, which of the following aspects of working seem <u>most</u> significant and important to you? Please rank these items from 6 = most significant to 1 = least significant.

31A   __ The tasks I do while working

31B   __ My company or organization

31C   __ The product or service I provide

31D   __ The type of people with whom I work

31E   __ The type of occupation or profession I am in

31F   __ The money I receive from my work

32.   What about the nature of your working life? How important to <u>you</u> is it that your work life contains the following:

		Do not write in this space
32A	–A lot of opportunity to LEARN new things	32A __ __
32B	–Good INTERPERSONAL relations (supervisors, co-workers)	32B __ __
32C	–Good opportunity for upgrading or PROMOTION	32C __ __
32D	–CONVENIENT work hours	32D __ __
32E	–A lot of VARIETY	32E __ __
32F	–INTERESTING work (work that you really like)	32F __ __
32G	–Good job SECURITY	32G __ __
32H	–A good MATCH between your job requirements and your abilities and experience	32H __ __
32I	–Good PAY	32I __ __
32J	–Good physical working CONDITIONS (such as light, temperature, cleanliness, low noise level)	32J __ __
32K	–A lot of AUTONOMY (you decide how to do your work)	32K __ __

<u>First,</u>   Look over the items above to get an idea of what they are.

Second,   Determine which of the items is <u>most</u> important in your work life. Then write the capitalized portion of that item on the line of the rating scale which represents its importance in your work life.

Third,   Cross the first item you selected off the list.

Fourth,   Select the item which is <u>least</u> important in your work life. Decide how important it is in your work life and write the capitalized portion of that item on the line of the rating scale which represents its importance in your work life. Cross out that item.

Fifth,   Now from the remaining list, select the item which is most important to your work life and repeat the process. Then select the item that is least important to your work life and repeat the process for that item. Do this until <u>all</u> of the items are written on the scale and all are checked off the list.

Note: You may choose to write <u>more than one item</u> on a line if you decide that they are of equal importance to your work life.

Extremely Important	15	_____
	14	_____
	13	_____
Very Important	12	_____
	11	_____
	10	_____
Important	9	_____
	8	_____
	7	_____
Of Some Importance	6	_____
	5	_____
	4	_____
Of Little Importance	3	_____
	2	_____
	1	_____

Now, we would like you to tell us which choice you would make in the following situations.

33. Imagine that two jobs are available to you. Let's call them job A and job B. You have to take one of them.

JOB A	JOB B
If you take this job, you will have the same pay as you have now.	If you take this job, you will have the same pay as you have now.
You will decide yourself how to do your work.	There will be hardly any room for you to make decisions about your work and its procedures.

  1 It would be more or less the same to me to have either job.
  2 I would prefer job A.
  3 I would prefer job B.
*IF JOB B IS PREFERRED, GO TO QUESTION 37.

34. Now let's say you have to take one of these two jobs.

JOB A	JOB B
If you take this job, you will have the same pay as you have now.	If you take this job, you will have 10% higher pay than you have now.
You will decide yourself how to do your work.	There will be hardly any room for you to make decisions about your work and its procedures.

  1 It would be more or less the same to me to have either job.
  2 I would prefer job A.
  3 I would prefer job B.
*IF JOB B IS PREFERRED, GO TO QUESTION 37.

35. Now imagine that you have to take one of these two jobs:

JOB A	JOB B
If you take this job, you will have the same pay as you have now.	If you take this job, you will have 30% higher pay than you have now.
You will decide yourself how to do your work.	There will be hardly any room for you to make decisions about your work and its procedures.

    1 It would be more or less the same to me to have either job.
    2 I would prefer job A.
    3 I would prefer job B.
*IF JOB B IS PREFERRED, GO TO QUESTION 37.

36. Now let's say you have to take one of these two jobs:

JOB A	JOB B
If you take this job, you will have the same pay as you have now.	If you take this job, you will have 50% higher pay than you have now.
You will decide yourself how to do your work.	There will be hardly any room for you to make decisions about your work and its procedures.

    1 It would be more or less the same to me to have either job.
    2 I would prefer job A.
    3 I would prefer job B.

37. Now let's say you have to take one of these two jobs:

JOB A	JOB B
If you take this job, you will have the same pay as you have now.	If you take this job, you will have the same pay as you have now.
In this job you will decide yourself how to do your work.	There will be hardly any room for you to make decisions about your work and its procedures.
You will fully use your skills and abilities.	There will be little opportunity for you to use your skills and abilities.
You will do something you really like.	You will not do something you really like.

1   It would be more or less the same to me to have either job.
2   I would prefer job A.
3   I would prefer job B.
*IF JOB B IS PREFERRED, GO TO QUESTION 41.

38. Now let's say you have to take one of these two jobs:

JOB A	JOB B
If you take this job, you will have the same pay as you have now.	If you take this job, you will have 10% higher pay than you have now.
In this job you will decide yourself how to do your work.	There will be hardly any room for you to make decisions about your work and its procedures.
You will fully use your skills and abilities.	There will be little opportunity for you to use your skills and abilities.
You will do something you really like.	You will not do something you really like.

1   It would be more or less the same to me to have either job.
2   I would prefer job A.
3   I would prefer job B.
*IF JOB B IS PREFERRED, GO TO QUESTION 41.

39. Now let's say you have to take one of these two jobs:

JOB A	JOB B
If you take this job, you will have the same pay as you have now.	If you take this job, you will have 30% higher pay than you have now.
In this job you will decide yourself how to do your work.	There will be hardly any room for you to make decisions about your work and its procedures.
You will fully use your skills and abilities.	There will be little opportunity for you to use your skills and abilities.
You will do something you really like.	You will not do something you really like.

    1   It would be more or less the same to me to have either job.
    2   I would prefer job A
    3   I would prefer job B.
*IF JOB B IS PREFERRED, GO TO QUESTION 41.

40. Now imagine that you have to take one of these two jobs:

JOB A	JOB B
If you take this job, you will have the same pay as you have now.	If you take this job, you will have 50% higher pay than you have now.
In this job you will decide yourself how to do your work.	There will be hardly any room for you to make decisions about your work and its procedures.
You will fully use your skills and abilities.	There will be little opportunity for you to use your skills and abilities.
You will do something you really like.	You will not do something you really like.

1   It would be more or less the same to me to have either job.
2   I would prefer job A.
3   I would prefer job B.

41. Now let's say you have to take one of these two jobs:

JOB A	JOB B
This job will permit you to have as much leisure time as you have now.	This job will permit you to have less leisure time than you have now.
It will bring you the same pay as you have now.	It will bring you 10% higher pay than you have now.
There will be little opportunity for you to use your skills and abilities.	There will be little opportunity for you to use your skills and abilities.
You will not do something you really like.	You will not do something you really like.

1   It would be more or less the same to me to have either job.
2   I would prefer job A.
3   I would prefer job B.
*IF JOB B IS PREFERRED, GO TO QUESTION 43.

42. Now let's say you have to take one of these two jobs:

JOB A	JOB B
This job will permit you to have as much leisure time as you have now.	This job will permit you to have less leisure time than you have now.
It will bring you the same pay as you have now.	It will bring you 30% higher pay than you have now.
There will be little opportunity for you to use your skills and abilities.	There will be little opportunity for you to use your skills and abilities.
You will not do something you really like.	You will not do something you really like.

1 It would be more or less the same to me to have either job.
2 I would prefer job A.
3 I would prefer job B.

43. Now let's say you have to take one of these two jobs:

JOB A	JOB B
This job will permit you to have as much leisure time as you have now.	This job will permit you to have less leisure time than you have now.
It will bring you the same pay as you have now.	It will bring you the same pay as you have now.
There will be little opportunity for you to use your skills and abilities.	In this job you will fully use your skills and abilities.
You will not do something you really like.	You will do something you really like.

1   It would be more or less the same to me to have either job.
2   I would prefer job A.
3   I would prefer job B.
*IF JOB B IS PREFERRED, GO TO QUESTION 46.

44.   Now imagine that you have to take one of these two jobs:

JOB A	JOB B
This job will permit you to have as much leisure time as you have now.	This job will permit you to have less leisure time than you have now.
It will bring you the same pay as you have now.	It will bring you 10% higher pay than you have now.
There will be little opportunity for you to use your skills and abilities.	In this job you will fully use all your skills and abilities.
You will not do something you really like.	You will do something you really like.

1   It would be more or less the same to me to have either job.
2   I would prefer job A.
3   I would prefer job B.
*IF JOB B IS PREFERRED, GO TO QUESTION 46.

45. Now imagine that you have to take one of these two jobs:

JOB A	JOB B
This job will permit you to have as much leisure time as you have now.	This job will permit you to have less leisure time than you have now.
It will bring you the same pay as you have now.	It will bring you 30% higher pay than you have now.
There will be little opportunity for you to use your skills and abilities.	In this job you will fully use your skills and abilities.
You will not do something you really like.	You will do something you really like.

1 It would be more or less the same to me to have either job.
2 I would prefer job A.
3 I would prefer job B.

46.   And now the last choice about jobs A and B, you have to take one of
these two jobs:

JOB A	JOB B
This job will permit you to have as much leisure time as you have now.	This job will permit you to have less leisure time than you have now.
It will bring you 30% higher pay than you have now.	It will bring you 30% higher pay than you have now.
There will be little opportunity for you to use your skills and abilities.	In this job you will fully use your skills and abilities.
You will not do something you really like.	You will do something you really like.

1   It would be more or less the same to me to have either job.
2   I would prefer job A.
3   I would prefer job B.

47.   On this page are some work-related statements that people might
make. We would like you to decide whether you agree or disagree
with each of these statements depending on your personal opinions.
If you strongly agree with a statement, please circle the number 4; if
you agree somewhat with the statement, circle the number 3; and so
on.

	Strongly Disagree	Disagree	Agree	Strongly Agree
47A If a worker's skills become outdated, his employer should be responsible for retraining and reemployment.	1	2	3	4
47B It is the duty of every able-bodied citizen to contribute to society by working.	1	2	3	4

		Strongly Disagree	Disagree	Agree	Strongly Agree
47C	The educational system in our society should prepare every person for a good job if they exert a reasonable amount of effort.	1	2	3	4
47D	Persons in our society should allocate a large portion of their regular income toward savings for their future.	1	2	3	4
47E	When a change in work methods must be made, a supervisor should be required to ask workers for their suggestions before deciding what to do.	1	2	3	4
47F	A worker should be expected to think up better ways to do his or her job.	1	2	3	4
47G	Every person in our society should be entitled to interesting and meaningful work.	1	2	3	4
47H	Monotonous, simplistic work is acceptable as long as the pay compensates fairly for it.	1	2	3	4
47I	A job should be provided to every individual who desires to work.	1	2	3	4
47J	A worker should value the work he or she does even if it is boring, dirty or unskilled.	1	2	3	4

48A Imagine that you won a lottery or inherited a large sum of money and could live comfortably for the rest of your life without working. What would you do concerning working?
   1 I would stop working.
   2 I would continue to work in the same job.
   3 I would continue to work but with changed conditions.

48B __   If 1, why would you stop working and what would you miss
     __   about working?
     _____

     _____

48C __   If 2, why would you continue working in the same job?
     _____

     _____

48D __ __   If 3, what are the changed conditions and why would you
     __ __   continue working?
     _____

     _____

49. Not everyone means the same thing when they talk about working. When do you consider an activity as working? Choose four statements from the list below which best define when an activity is "working".
   A. if you do it in a working place.
   B. if someone tells you what to do.
   C. if it is physically strenuous.
   D. if it belongs to your task.
   E. if you do it to contribute to society.
   F. if, by doing it, you get the feeling of belonging.
   G. if it is mentally strenuous.
   H. if you do it at a certain time (for instance from 8 until 5).
   I. if it adds value to something.
   J. if it is not pleasant.
   K. if you get money for doing it.
   L. if you have to account for it.
   M. if you have to do it.
   N. if others profit by it.

50A If you were to start all over again, would you again choose your occupation or would you choose a different one?
   1 different occupation
   2 same occupation

50B[3] Would you recommend your occupation to your children for their work?

    1 no

    2 yes

50C[3] __ __ Why would you make this recommendation? _____

_____

51A Do you think that people's general attitude toward working will change in the next 10 years?

    1 no

    2 yes

51B __ __ If yes, what will be the nature and direction of change? __

_____

_____

52[3,4] If you had to choose, which would you prefer? (NOTE: NOT APPLICABLE FOR SELF-EMPLOYED OR TEACHERS.)

    1 Stay in your present organization but with a different type of job.

    2 Do the same type of work but with a different organization.

53[4] In your leisure time, how often do you do things that have nothing to do with work?

    1 never

    2 only occasionally

    3 sometimes

    4 often

    5 very often

54.[4] If your company organized group activities outside of working hours, would you participate?

    1 no

    2 maybe

    3 yes

55.[5] How often do you worry about work in your free time?

    1 never

    2 only occasionally

    3 sometimes

    4 often

    5 very often

> Now some items concerning your plans about working in the future,
> about what you expect will happen in the future and what you would
> like to see happen in the future.

56A   Do you intend to change jobs   (FOR <u>TEMPORARY</u>
      within the next 12 months?   <u>WORKERS</u>, THIS MEANS
      1   no   TAKE A <u>STEADY/FIXED JOB</u>)
      2   yes

56B   ___   If yes, what are you looking for in another job? _____
      _____

57.   Do you think it would be easy for you to find a similar job with
      another employer within the next 12 months? (NOTE: NOT
      APPLICABLE FOR SELF-EMPLOYED.)
      1   difficult
      2   not so easy
      3   somewhat easy
      4   easy
      5   very easy

58A   Would you be willing to be retrained for a different job or occu-
      pation than you now have?
      1   under no conditions
      2   only if the economic situation forced me to
      3   under certain conditions

58B   ___   If under certain conditions, please specify _____
      _____

59.   Do you intend to be retrained for a different job or occupation
      during the next 12 months?
      1   no
      2   yes

60.   Do you intend to take part in further training related to your present
      job during the next 12 months?
      1   no
      2   yes
      3   I am already taking part

61.[6] Are you actively trying to be promoted within the next 12 months?
      (NOTE: NOT APPLICABLE FOR SELF-EMPLOYED).
      1   no
      2   yes

62A[6] Do you have any other significant plans regarding working during
        the next five years?

        1   no
        2   yes

62B[6] __ __   If yes, what plans? _____

        _____

63.   In the next 5 to 10 years, do you expect any societal developments
        which could endanger your employment?

        1   no
        2   yes

64.   Are there any societal developments in the next 5 to 10 years which
        are likley to improve your employment situation or make it more
        secure?

        1   no
        2   yes

65.   In the next few years, do you expect the level of pay for your job
        compared to pay for other jobs to:

        1   go down
        2   stay about the same
        3   go up

66A   Compared to the present time, how important will work be to you in
        the next 5 to 10 years?

        1   less important
        2   equal in importance
        3   more important

66B   __ __   What are the reasons for this? _____

        _____

67.   Suppose people were able to work less hours for the same pay in the
        future; which alternative would be most preferable to you? (Pick
        one).

        1   more holidays
        2   less working hours per day
        3   a free afternoon every week
        4   longer periods of education before beginning to work
        5   a year off for further study about every 10 years
        6   less working hours for older workers
        7   earlier retirement

68.   If the general economic situation led to proposals to work less hours
       and earn proportionately less money, how would you feel about
       such proposals?
       1   I would be against them
       2   I don't really care
       3   I would be moderately in favor of them
       4   I would be in favor of them

Now some final questions about you, about your background and
about your family.

---

69.   What is your age?
       __ __ years

70.   What was the highest formal education which you completed? (Circle
       ONE.)
       1   primary school
       2   secondary school or further vocational training
       3   some college or similar vocational training below university
           level
       4   university degree

71.   Did you have a religious education?
       1   no
       2   yes

72.   To what extent are you presently associated with a religion?
       1   no contact
       2   loose contact
       3   close contact

73.   What was the highest formal education received by your parents?
73A   Father
                 1   primary school
                 2   secondary school
                 3   some college
                 4   university degree
73B   Mother
                 1   primary school
                 2   secondary sohool
                 3   some college
                 4   university degree

74. Concerning the community where you spent most of your childhood (to about age 14); was it primarily:
    1 city or big town
    2 village or small town
    3 rural

75. Concerning the community where you presently live; is it primarily:
    1 city or big town
    2 village or small town
    3 rural

76A Are you married and/or living with a partner in a joint household?
    1 no
    2 yes

76B   If yes, is your partner:
       1 not employed and primarily a homemaker
       2 part-time employment and homemaker
       3 employed full time
       4 other

76C __   If other please specify _____
          _____
          _____

77. How many persons do you support financially (including yourself)?
    __ __ __ number

78. In general, how satisfied have you been with your life?

    Very   Very
    Dissatisfied 1 2 3 4 5 6 7 8 9 Satisfied

- THE END -

THANK YOU VERY MUCH.

INTERVIEWER CHECKLIST
To be completed for each respondent.

Interviewer name _____ Date of interview _____

79. Is respondent a citizen of this country?
    1 yes
    2 no

80. __ __ City in which interview was done _____

81A Was interview conducted at
    1 home
    2 workplace
    3 other
81B __ If other, please specify _____

82. Sex of respondent
    1 male
    2 female
    Target group to which respondent belongs _____

83B If self-employed, circle appropriate job type:
    1 craftsman
    2 service (non-craftsman)
    3 commercial (selling product)

84A Indicate nature and size of organization which employs the person:
    1 public
    2 private
84B Organization size at the location where the person works:
    1 under 100 employees
    2 100–299 employees
    3 300–999 employees
    4 1000 or over employees

85. Length of interview
    __ __ __ minutes

86. To what extent did the respondent understand the questions?
    1 clearly understood
    2 reasonably understood most questions
    3 had difficulty with many questions
    4 understood only a few questions

87. Would you describe the respondent's cooperation in the interview as:
    1 high
    2 moderate
    3 low

    Interviewer comments about specific items in the interview (wording problems, understanding problems, resistance to answering) _____

    _____
    _____
    _____
    _____
    _____
    _____
    _____

    Interviewer comments about the respondent and/or the interview in general _____

    _____
    _____
    _____
    _____
    _____
    _____
    _____

Notes

[1] Questions 1 through 27 are deleted in Form C.
[2] Slightly altered in Form B.
[3] Deleted in Form C.
[4] Deleted or worded differently in Form B.
[5] Questions 54–69 not applicable for retired.
[6] Deleted in Form B.

Appendix II

Response Distribution Data for National Sample and Target Groups

The reader should refer to the Meaning of Work Questionnaire (Appendix I) for exact item wording. Items are shortened and/or abbreviated for response distribution presentation.

Variable		Students N = 90	Chemical Engineers N = 90	Self-Employed N = 90	Teachers N = 90	Temporary N = 90	Textile Workers N = 90	Tool and Die N = 91	White Collar N = 90	Retired N = 90	Unemployed N = 90	National Sample N = 973
Q1 Type of Work												
Chemists	%	‡‡	‡‡	‡‡	‡‡	‡‡	‡‡	‡‡	‡‡	‡‡	‡‡	0.4
Teachers	%	‡‡	‡‡	‡‡	‡‡	‡‡	‡‡	‡‡	‡‡	‡‡	‡‡	10.7
Other Prof.	%	‡‡	‡‡	‡‡	‡‡	‡‡	‡‡	‡‡	‡‡	‡‡	‡‡	7.0
Admin and Mgr	%	‡‡	‡‡	‡‡	‡‡	‡‡	‡‡	‡‡	‡‡	‡‡	‡‡	6.2
Clerical	%	‡‡	‡‡	‡‡	‡‡	‡‡	‡‡	‡‡	‡‡	‡‡	‡‡	21.0
Prop-Whlsale and Retail	%	‡‡	‡‡	‡‡	‡‡	‡‡	‡‡	‡‡	‡‡	‡‡	‡‡	2.2
Sales	%	‡‡	‡‡	‡‡	‡‡	‡‡	‡‡	‡‡	‡‡	‡‡	‡‡	1.6
Prop-Cater and Lodging	%	‡‡	‡‡	‡‡	‡‡	‡‡	‡‡	‡‡	‡‡	‡‡	‡‡	1.5
Service	%	‡‡	‡‡	‡‡	‡‡	‡‡	‡‡	‡‡	‡‡	‡‡	‡‡	12.7
Agriculture	%	‡‡	‡‡	‡‡	‡‡	‡‡	‡‡	‡‡	‡‡	‡‡	‡‡	2.6
Spinners and Weavers	%	‡‡	‡‡	‡‡	‡‡	‡‡	‡‡	‡‡	‡‡	‡‡	‡‡	0.9
Blacksmiths-Toolers	%	‡‡	‡‡	‡‡	‡‡	‡‡	‡‡	‡‡	‡‡	‡‡	‡‡	0.9
Construction-Equipment	%	‡‡	‡‡	‡‡	‡‡	‡‡	‡‡	‡‡	‡‡	‡‡	‡‡	14.2
Armed Forces	%	‡‡	‡‡	‡‡	‡‡	‡‡	‡‡	‡‡	‡‡	‡‡	‡‡	3.2
Other	%	‡‡	‡‡	‡‡	‡‡	‡‡	‡‡	‡‡	‡‡	‡‡	‡‡	12.3
**Missing Data	%	100.0	100.0	100.0	100.0	100.0	100.0	100.0	100.0	100.0	100.0	2.6
Q2 Present Position												
Non-supervisory	%	‡‡	23.3	33.4	70.0	72.2	70.0	63.7	81.1	44.5	55.6	46.8
Supervisory	%	‡‡	45.6	24.4	15.6	10.0	24.4	27.5	10.0	31.1	33.3	32.0
Managerial	%	‡‡	27.8	27.8	‡‡	16.7	5.6	8.8	3.3	20.0	5.6	18.4
**Missing Data	%	100.0	3.3	14.4	14.4	1.1	‡‡	‡‡	5.6	4.4	5.5	2.8
Q3 Union Member?	%	‡‡	73.3	38.9	88.9	51.1	88.9	89.0	67.8	61.1	36.7	61.0
Q4 Hours worked per week	Mean	‡‡	49.6	52.5	25.9	30.0	50.2	49.5	44.9	41.9	44.0	42.0
	SD	*	7.7	16.2	5.0	11.8	5.6	5.8	9.5	13.8	15.4	14.7

Q5 Daily travel time — Mean	**	59.4	46.4	39.8	71.8	45.6	60.2	74.8	84.9	62.8	49.6
SD		33.0	32.2	36.7	47.5	93.3	36.9	33.7	118.2	42.2	44.0
Q6A Work Schedule											
day %		94.5	93.4	97.8	86.7	60.0	100.0	100.0	81.1	76.7	87.6
night %		**	1.1	**	1.1	1.1	**	**	2.2	2.2	1.1
swing shift %		2.2	3.3	2.2	7.8	10.0	**	**	11.1	13.3	6.6
shift changes regulary %		2.2	1.1	**	2.2	28.9	**	**	5.6	6.7	4.2
**Missing data %		1.1	1.1	**	2.2	**	**	**	**	1.1	0.5
Q6B Work Hours											
Regular %		91.1	92.2	98.9	71.1	84.4	95.6	98.9	77.8	76.7	82.1
Varied %		**	**	**	**	14.5	**	**	22.2	21.1	17.8
**Missing data %		8.9	7.8	1.1	28.9	1.1	4.4	1.1	**	2.2	0.1
Q6C Work weekends %		16.7	36.7	32.2	23.3	25.6	27.5	3.3	20.0	35.6	62.9
Q7A Unemployed past 5 years %		4.4	11.1	6.7	42.2	11.1	26.4	17.8	25.6	54.4	12.9
Q7B No. of months unemployed in past 5 years — Mean		0.1	1.3	0.5	3.1	0.1	1.4	1.9	12.2	9.8	1.7
S.D.		0.6	6.8	2.2	5.4	5.3	3.8	7.7	23.3	14.8	7.1
Q7C No. of months unemployed in past 12 months — Mean		**	0.1	**	1.5	0.2	0.7	0.3	2.0	5.4	0.5
S.D.		**	0.9	**	3.1	1.3	1.5	1.0	4.4	5.1	3.3
Q8 Variety											
Much repetition %		7.8	48.9	5.6	47.7	62.2	24.2	57.8	46.7	48.0	40.0
Some variety %		35.6	34.4	55.6	35.6	25.6	45.1	30.0	24.4	32.0	32.5
Wide variety %		56.6	16.7	38.8	11.1	12.2	29.7	12.2	28.9	16.7	26.4
**Missing Data %		**	**	**	5.6	**	1.0	**	**	3.3	1.1
Q9 Autonomy											
No Decision Making %		2.2	10.0	2.2	38.9	56.7	19.7	38.9	22.2	36.7	18.4
Some Decisions %		57.8	7.8	50.0	43.3	33.3	45.1	53.3	24.5	42.2	43.7

Variable		Students N=90	Chemical Engineers N=90	Self-Employed N=90	Teachers N=90	Tempo-rary N=90	Textile Workers N=90	Tool and Die N=91	White Collar N=90	Retired N=90	Unem-ployed N=90	National Sample N=973
My Own Decision	%	**	38.9	82.2	47.8	12.2	8.9	35.2	6.7	51.1	17.8	37.6
**Missing Data	%	100.0	1.1	**	**	5.6	1.1	**	1.1	2.2	3.3	0.3
Q10 Responsibility												
Mistakes-Little Conseq.	%	**	27.8	48.9	55.6	57.8	75.6	56.0	28.9	71.1	55.6	35.1
Some Consequences	%	**	27.8	32.2	33.3	25.6	20.0	27.5	60.0	20.0	26.7	39.2
Serious Consequences	%	**	43.3	18.9	6.7	8.9	4.4	16.5	8.9	5.6	13.3	24.0
**Missing Data	%	100.0	1.1	**	4.4	7.7	**	**	2.2	3.3	4.4	1.7
Q11 Learning Opportunity												
No Learning	%	**	2.2	31.1	2.2	14.4	56.7	26.4	26.7	34.4	34.4	24.8
Some Learning	%	**	24.4	33.3	16.7	50.0	24.4	41.8	46.6	25.6	37.8	31.6
Learn Many Things	%	**	73.4	35.6	80.0	30.0	17.8	31.8	26.7	38.9	24.4	43.1
**Missing Data	%	100.0	**	**	1.1	5.6	1.1	**	**	1.1	3.3	0.5
Q12 Work Interaction												
Work Alone	%	**	12.2	21.1	14.4	28.9	31.1	24.2	30.0	28.9	24.4	15.8
Work with Some	%	**	31.1	25.6	36.7	31.1	41.1	45.1	30.0	32.2	31.1	31.1
Work Much With Others	%	**	56.7	52.2	47.8	34.4	27.8	30.7	38.9	38.9	41.1	52.5
**Missing Data	%	100.0	**	1.1	1.1	5.6	**	**	1.1	**	3.3	0.6
Q13 Non-business Discussion Opportunity												
No Non-Business Talk	%	**	14.4	12.2	24.4	13.3	57.8	20.9	31.1	44.5	28.9	19.8
Some Non-Business Talk	%	**	53.4	36.7	56.7	44.4	21.1	56.0	47.8	28.9	37.8	43.9
Often Non-Business Talk	%	**	32.2	51.1	18.9	36.7	21.1	23.1	21.1	24.4	30.0	35.4
**Missing Data	%	100.0	**	**	**	5.6	**	**	**	2.2	3.3	0.9
Q14 Work in dangerous Circumstances												
Yes	%	**	63.3	10.0	5.6	3.3	20.0	53.8	**	23.3	35.6	25.0
No	%	**	35.6	89.9	93.3	96.7	80.0	42.9	100.0	76.7	61.1	70.9
**Missing Data	%	100.0	1.1	1.1	1.1	**	**	3.3	**	**	3.3	4.1

214

Q15 Work in unhealthy Circumstances

	%											
Yes	%	**	68.9	14.4	13.3	8.9	35.6	51.6	15.6	21.1	43.3	24.5
No	%	**	28.9	85.5	86.6	91.1	64.4	45.1	84.4	78.9	51.1	70.1
**Missing Data	%	100.0	2.2	1.1	1.1	**	**	3.3	**	**	5.6	5.4

Q16 Physical Overload

	%											
Never	%	**	41.1	27.8	36.7	66.7	20.0	12.1	68.9	36.7	21.1	38.6
Seldom	%	**	37.8	24.4	26.7	12.2	14.4	17.6	12.2	15.6	13.3	14.8
Sometimes	%	**	17.8	31.1	22.2	15.6	34.5	38.6	14.5	32.2	18.9	22.4
Often	%	**	2.2	16.7	13.3	4.4	31.1	31.9	4.4	13.3	42.2	22.5
**Missing Data	%	100.0	1.1	**	1.1	1.1	**	**	**	1.1	4.4	1.7

Q17 Mental Overload

	%											
Never	%	**	10.0	25.6	12.2	38.8	11.0	35.6	20.0	27.8	21.1	21.1
Seldom	%	**	7.8	14.4	13.3	22.2	25.6	27.4	26.7	17.8	20.0	13.5
Sometimes	%	**	42.2	35.6	27.8	33.3	25.6	24.2	24.4	38.9	22.2	29.7
Often	%	**	37.8	23.3	44.4	13.3	10.0	37.4	13.3	23.3	24.4	34.1
**Missing Data	%	100.0	2.2	1.1	2.2	2.2	**	**	**	**	5.6	1.6

Q18 Experience-Skill Use

	%											
Very Little	%	**	3.3	10.0	**	16.7	32.2	4.4	37.8	20.0	20.0	24.9
Little	%	**	14.4	21.1	8.9	22.2	27.8	18.7	23.3	18.9	25.6	38.7
A Lot	%	**	37.7	31.1	37.8	37.8	16.7	47.3	31.1	23.3	31.1	35.3
Almost All	%	**	44.4	37.8	52.3	23.3	22.2	28.6	7.8	36.7	21.1	**
**Missing Data	%	100.0	**	**	**	**	1.1	1.0	**	1.1	2.2	1.1

Q19 Decision Participation

	%											
No Inform.-Decisions	%	**	3.3	**	1.1	21.1	15.6	6.6	23.3	6.7	24.4	9.0
Inform.-After Decisions	%	**	7.8	1.1	17.8	33.3	45.6	16.5	37.9	16.7	25.6	19.1
Asks for Advice	%	**	31.1	1.1	21.1	14.4	22.2	29.7	14.4	17.8	10.0	19.0
Decide Jointly	%	**	41.1	3.3	46.7	21.1	13.3	30.8	21.1	30.3	24.4	27.9
I Decide	%	**	13.3	12.2	6.7	5.6	2.2	14.3	3.3	15.6	7.8	13.4
**Missing Data	%	100.0	3.3	82.3	6.7	4.4	1.1	2.2	**	12.2	7.8	11.6

Variable		Students N=90	Chemical Engineers N=90	Self-Employed N=90	Teachers N=90	Temporary N=90	Textile Workers N=90	Tool and Die N=91	White Collar N=90	Retired N=90	Unemployed N=90	National Sample N=973
Q20 Present Job is First Job												
Yes	%	**	32.2	35.6	68.9	27.8	33.3	33.0	58.9	51.1	46.7	47.7
No	%	**	62.1	47.7	23.3	67.8	56.7	61.3	33.3	45.6	47.7	46.3
**Missing Data	%	100.0	5.7	16.7	7.8	4.4	10.0	5.5	7.8	3.3	5.6	6.0
Q21D Tenure on first job												
	Mean	**	4.4	7.7	4.7	4.1	7.9	4.8	5.1	10.2	6.7	6.5
	SD	**	4.4	8.1	4.6	4.7	9.3	4.7	6.9	9.5	7.1	6.8
**Missing Data	%	100.0										
Q23A Reasons for choosing present job												
Good Pay	%	**	1.1	10.0	1.1	6.7	15.6	6.6	14.4	3.3	4.4	8.6
Good Working Conditions	%	**	7.8	5.6	5.6	8.9	4.4	7.7	6.7	5.6	**	4.5
Location	%	**	1.1	1.1	**	4.4	2.2	1.1	6.7	1.1	2.2	1.7
Hours	%	**	**	**	2.2	11.1	1.1	**	**	**	**	1.4
Interesting	%	**	42.2	17.8	55.6	8.9	7.8	12.1	17.8	14.4	15.6	26.6
Opportunity to Learn	%	**	**	1.1	1.1	1.1	1.1	2.2	1.1	**	1.1	0.9
Opportunity for Promotion	%	**	6.7	**	**	1.1	1.1	2.2	3.3	**	**	2.3
More Responsibility	%	**	**	1.1	1.1	**	**	**	**	**	**	0.1
Challenge	%	**	3.3	1.1	12.2	**	**	2.2	1.1	2.2	3.3	1.8
Trained for it	%	**	12.2	16.7	7.8	14.4	7.8	22.0	10.0	21.1	11.1	11.3
Job Security	%	**	1.1	**	1.1	**	1.1	**	2.2	2.2	3.3	0.7
Necessity	%	**	1.1	5.6	**	2.2	8.9	3.3	2.2	12.2	6.7	4.1
No Choice	%	**	5.6	4.4	1.1	14.4	32.2	16.5	16.7	12.2	14.4	13.9
Recommended	%	**	**	1.1	**	2.2	**	3.3	**	2.2	2.2	1.8
Parent Chose	%	**	1.1	13.3	**	1.1	1.1	**	**	3.3	3.3	2.9
Image of Firm	%	**	**	**	**	**	**	**	**	**	**	0.8
Independence	%	**	**	3.3	**	2.2	**	**	**	**	**	1.2

216

Military Draft	%	**	**	**	**	**	**	**	**	**	**	**
Health	%	**	**	1.1	**	**	1.1	**	1.1	**	**	0.9
Temp. to Fill Time	%	**	**	**	**	2.2	**	1.1	1.1	**	**	0.3
Temp. for Freedom	%	**	**	**	**	1.1	**	**	**	**	**	0.1
**Missing Data	%	100.0	16.7	17.8	11.1	17.8	14.4	19.8	15.6	20.0	32.2	13.8
Q23B Present job tenure	Mean	**	5.5	11.6	8.5	1.3	7.6	8.3	4.0	19.9	4.2	11.3
	SD	**	6.7	15.2	8.0	2.7	6.5	11.2	5.2	15.4	8.0	10.3
Q24 Level at which you started your work career												
Lower	%	**	10.0	24.4	14.4	11.1	30.0	16.5	13.3	15.6	21.1	19.6
Same	%	**	76.7	45.6	79.0	53.3	57.8	68.1	70.0	64.4	57.8	61.9
Higher	%	**	8.9	22.2	2.2	27.8	12.2	14.3	15.6	10.0	11.1	14.0
**Missing Data	%	100.0	4.4	7.8	4.4	7.8	**	1.1	1.1	10.0	10.0	4.5
Q25A Work career has ups and downs												
Yes	%	**	30.0	64.4	32.2	32.2	30.0	48.4	21.1	24.4	51.1	32.7
No	%	**	62.2	35.6	65.6	59.9	70.0	50.5	76.7	81.2	43.3	62.9
**Missing Data	%	100.0	7.8	**	2.2	7.8	**	1.1	2.2	4.4	5.6	4.4
Q25B Ups and Downs were												
Small	%	**	23.3	31.1	27.8	37.8	28.9	30.8	18.9	22.2	45.6	21.6
Large	%	**	12.2	34.4	11.1	6.7	4.4	20.9	8.9	10.0	17.8	14.3
**Missing Data	%	100.0	63.3	34.4	61.1	55.6	66.7	48.4	72.2	67.8	35.6	64.1
Q26 Degree of Improvement in Work History												
Some Decline	%	**	1.1	15.6	3.3	17.8	6.7	12.1	11.1	16.7	20.0	6.0
Same level	%	**	4.4	20.0	11.1	20.0	35.6	15.4	27.8	22.2	35.7	17.2
Some Improve	%	**	37.8	27.8	27.8	28.9	34.4	30.8	40.0	56.7	31.1	30.0
Much Improve	%	**	48.9	33.3	41.1	26.7	23.3	39.6	16.7	**	**	37.0
**Missing Data	%	100.0	7.8	3.3	16.7	6.7	**	2.2	4.4	4.4	12.2	9.8

Variable		Students N=90	Chemical Engineers N=90	Self-Employed N=90	Teachers N=90	Temporary N=90	Textile Workers N=90	Tool and Die N=91	White Collar N=90	Retired N=90	Unemployed N=90	National Sample N=973
Q27 Work History												
Satisfaction												
Dissatisfied	%	**	1.1	13.3	1.1	8.9	12.2	13.2	3.3	5.6	17.8	4.6
Some Dissatisfaction	%	**	6.7	10.0	2.2	5.6	7.8	7.7	13.3	2.2	11.1	7.3
Neutral	%	**	10.0	18.9	6.7	22.2	12.2	23.1	14.4	8.9	17.8	11.5
Some Satisfaction	%	**	60.0	32.2	55.6	44.4	45.6	29.6	56.7	43.3	26.7	45.2
Very Satisfied	%	**	18.9	22.2	25.6	15.6	22.2	15.4	10.0	38.9	17.8	25.9
**Missing Data	%	100.0	3.3	3.3	8.9	3.3	**	1.1	2.2	1.1	8.9	5.4
Valued Working Outcomes (assign 100 points)												
Q28A1 Status, Prestige	Mean	13.4	12.9	10.2	11.5	11.2	9.8	10.8	13.7	12.9	9.3	8.4
	S.D.	5.6	9.0	11.1	11.2	10.3	8.3	10.8	14.7	12.7	8.5	11.0
Q28A2 Income	Mean	18.9	22.8	30.3	12.9	21.8	32.5	29.8	27.3	18.9	23.6	30.5
	S.D.	6.6	12.9	20.7	9.9	16.2	16.7	20.3	20.8	16.9	17.0	23.7
Q28A3 Occupied	Mean	13.6	5.0	11.7	6.6	11.8	13.1	10.7	11.5	10.1	14.1	9.3
	S.D.	5.6	6.0	11.7	7.2	12.8	9.1	10.1	13.8	10.0	12.9	12.0
Q28A4 Interesting contacts	Mean	16.3	10.4	15.4	11.2	15.7	12.6	10.9	13.8	13.0	12.1	11.0
	S.D.	6.2	8.9	16.2	9.3	10.8	9.6	0.2	11.4	11.4	13.5	11.7
Q28A5 Serve society	Mean	16.6	13.1	8.0	19.8	9.90	9.5	11.8	10.1	15.9	11.7	13.3
	S.D.	5.3	11.4	12.3	12.0	10.5	8.5	13.7	9.1	13.2	10.4	15.4
Q28A6 Interesting and Satisfying	Mean	21.5	35.9	24.4	37.2	27.0	20.0	23.9	21.3	29.5	21.8	25.9
	S.D.	7.1	15.9	18.5	16.1	16.8	11.7	15.7	15.4	20.0	16.4	20.3

Q29 Importance of work in your total life

1: One of the Least	%	**	1.2	4.4	**	1.2	1.1	3.3	**	1.1	2.2	1.0
2: On 1-to-7-scale	%	2.2	**	2.2	**	2.2	1.2	2.2	1.1	**	**	0.9
3: On 1-to-7-scale	%	**	**	1.2	1.2	4.4	**	1.1	3.3	1.1	6.7	1.2
4: Of Medium Importance	%	17.8	7.8	16.7	22.2	40.0	13.3	24.2	37.8	7.8	14.4	21.8
5: On 1-to-7-scale	%	20.0	24.4	11.1	31.1	13.3	10.0	12.1	21.1	14.4	25.5	17.4
6: On 1-to-7-scale	%	30.0	34.4	22.2	13.3	13.3	27.8	11.0	15.6	24.4	15.6	22.8
7: One of the Most	%	28.9	31.1	34.4	32.2	20.0	43.3	44.0	20.0	35.6	20.0	29.2
**Missing Data	%	1.1	1.1	7.8	**	5.6	3.3	2.2	1.1	15.6	5.7	5.7

Relative importance of life areas (assign 100 points)

Q30A Leisure	Mean	23.9	17.4	19.4	15.2	24.2	14.3	20.5	22.6	18.7	21.6	17.9
	S.D.	7.9	13.0	19.0	9.6	15.6	12.6	17.1	17.4	18.8	18.7	15.7
Q30B Community	Mean	12.9	4.0	3.2	4.6	4.0	5.1	5.0	4.6	12.8	7.3	4.5
	S.D.	8.0	5.2	7.5	8.0	8.6	7.1	9.1	7.4	14.3	8.4	8.9
Q30C Work	Mean	24.6	36.0	37.3	31.2	25.6	32.0	20.1	28.3	11.7	24.0	27.8
	S.D.	9.0	13.8	25.0	13.1	12.6	14.4	15.9	17.0	15.6	17.7	18.7
Q30D Religion	Mean	10.9	3.9	8.0	4.9	1.6	7.8	5.6	8.7	5.4	7.2	4.8
	S.D.	8.8	7.7	18.2	10.2	4.5	9.1	12.1	12.7	8.9	10.3	11.5
Q30E Family	Mean	27.7	38.7	30.0	43.7	43.6	39.5	42.7	35.8	47.8	34.4	43.1
	S.D.	8.7	13.5	17.8	16.7	15.9	15.9	21.5	18.6	28.3	22.0	21.2
**Missing Data	%	**	**	**	**	1.0	1.3	6.1	**	4.2	5.5	1.9

Identification with work roles (1 = least, 6 = most)

Q31A Task Role	Mean	3.7	4.9	3.4	4.2	4.3	4.0	4.3	4.0	4.0	3.8	3.9
	S.D.	1.6	1.3	1.7	1.5	1.5	1.7	1.7	1.7	1.6	1.7	1.7
Q31B Company organization role	Mean	3.0	2.5	2.6	2.4	2.4	2.5	2.6	2.8	2.9	2.9	2.8
	S.D.	1.6	1.5	1.6	1.3	1.5	1.5	1.4	1.7	1.6	1.7	1.6

Variable		Students N=90	Chemical Engineers N=90	Self-Employed N=90	Teachers N=90	Temporary N=90	Textile Workers N=90	Tool and Die N=91	White Collar N=90	Retired N=90	Unemployed N=90	National Sample N=973
Q31C Product or service role	Mean	3.5	3.3	4.3	4.4	3.3	3.8	3.8	3.6	3.8	3.6	3.7
	S.D.	1.9	1.7	1.7	1.6	1.7	1.5	1.6	1.9	1.7	1.7	1.8
Q31D Type of People Role	Mean	3.3	2.9	3.7	3.5	3.6	2.8	2.8	3.6	3.6	3.5	3.5
	S.D.	1.5	1.4	1.5	1.4	1.6	1.5	1.4	1.5	1.6	1.6	1.5
Q31E Occupational or Profess. Role	Mean	4.2	4.3	3.6	4.3	3.9	3.4	3.4	3.4	3.6	3.6	3.7
	S.D.	1.9	1.7	1.6	1.6	1.6	1.8	1.6	1.6	1.7	1.8	1.7
Q31F Income Producing Role	Mean	3.4	3.3	3.7	2.5	3.9	4.5	4.3	3.6	3.1	3.6	3.8
	S.D.	1.6	1.5	2.0	1.5	1.7	1.6	1.7	1.7	1.8	2.0	1.8
Work Goals												
Q32A Opportunity to Learn	Mean	11.3	12.8	11.1	12.0	12.1	9.8	12.5	12.3	10.0	10.6	11.1
	S.D.	2.7	2.6	4.1	3.0	2.9	3.4	2.6	2.8	4.8	4.1	3.7
Q32B Good Interpersonnal relations	Mean	11.1	11.3	12.6	12.2	12.0	11.0	11.7	11.9	11.8	10.6	12.0
	S.D.	2.7	3.2	2.9	2.6	2.8	2.7	2.9	2.9	3.0	3.4	3.1
Q32C Good Opportunity for Promotion	Mean	11.5	10.8	9.4	8.4	11.2	11.9	11.9	11.8	9.7	10.2	10.4
	S.D.	2.8	3.4	4.8	3.9	3.3	2.7	2.8	2.9	4.7	3.5	3.9
Q32D Convenient Work Hours	Mean	10.0	8.4	11.2	11.4	11.3	10.0	10.9	10.4	9.9	11.2	10.9
	S.D.	2.6	3.3	4.1	3.2	3.2	3.4	3.3	3.1	3.9	3.8	3.5
Q32E Lot of Variety	Mean	10.2	11.5	11.4	11.3	11.0	9.9	10.1	10.7	9.2	9.8	10.7
	S.D.	3.1	2.8	5.0	2.7	3.2	3.5	3.1	3.1	3.6	3.6	3.5
Q32F Interesting Work	Mean	13.0	13.6	12.8	13.5	12.6	11.6	11.3	12.0	12.0	11.8	12.1
	S.D.	2.3	2.1	3.4	2.1	2.8	3.1	3.1	2.9	2.9	3.7	3.1
Q32G Good Job Security	Mean	10.5	8.9	11.5	10.4	9.3	11.6	10.2	9.9	10.9	10.6	10.5
	S.D.	3.0	3.6	4.2	3.6	3.2	2.6	3.3	3.2	2.9	3.6	3.9
Q32H Good Match Between Job Requirements and Abilities	Mean	10.9	10.8	12.0	11.8	10.7	10.6	10.2	10.7	11.0	9.3	11.0
	S.D.	3.0	3.2	3.3	3.3	3.6	3.1	3.3	2.9	2.9	3.6	3.2
Q32I Good Pay	Mean	11.5	11.2	12.6	10.1	11.5	13.2	12.0	10.7	10.7	12.1	11.9
	S.D.	2.7	2.8	3.3	3.8	3.2	2.6	3.4	3.3	3.4	3.6	3.1

		C1	C2	C3	C4	C5	C6	C7	C8	C9	C10	C11
Q32J Good Physical Working Conditions	Mean	10.2	8.7	11.5	10.2	9.5	12.3	10.0	8.7	10.0	10.0	10.5
	S.D.	3.0	3.5	3.8	3.7	3.6	2.9	3.9	3.6	3.5	4.0	3.5
Q32K A lot of Autonomy	Mean	10.5	11.4	12.6	11.5	11.2	10.1	11.0	9.9	9.4	10.2	11.4
	S.D.	3.6	3.0	3.3	3.5	3.5	3.4	3.8	3.9	3.9	4.2	3.4
Q33 Job Choice Number 1												
Prefer Job A	%	92.2	95.6	90.0	94.4	84.4	85.6	93.3	91.1	93.3	77.8	89.1
Prefer Job B	%	5.6	2.2	6.7	**	8.9	4.4	1.1	4.4	1.1	8.9	5.1
Either Job	%	2.2	1.1	3.3	2.2	3.3	10.0	4.4	2.2	4.4	12.2	4.1
**Missing Data	%	**	1.1	**	3.3	3.3	**	1.1	2.2	1.1	1.1	1.7
Q34 Job Choice Number 2												
Prefer Job A	%	82.2	96.7	88.9	91.1	80.0	50.0	86.8	80.0	87.8	68.9	81.2
Prefer Job B	%	10.0	**	1.1	3.3	7.8	42.2	9.9	12.2	8.9	17.8	9.6
Same	%	2.2	1.1	2.2	0.1	1.1	4.4	1.1	2.2	**	7.8	3.6
**Missing Data	%	5.6	2.2	7.8	5.5	11.1	3.3	2.2	5.6	3.3	5.6	5.7
Q35 Job Choice Number 3												
Prefer Job A	%	55.6	83.3	77.8	81.1	57.8	33.3	59.3	53.3	73.3	47.8	65.6
Prefer Job B	%	24.4	8.9	11.1	10.0	22.2	22.2	29.7	30.0	11.1	24.4	18.0
Same	%	3.3	5.6	1.1	1.1	3.3	3.3	2.2	2.2	2.2	7.8	3.0
**Missing Data	%	16.7	2.2	10.0	7.8	16.7	41.1	8.8	14.4	13.3	20.0	13.5
Q36 Job Choice Number 4												
Prefer Job A	%	38.9	54.4	54.4	68.9	42.2	23.3	36.3	34.4	60.0	35.6	50.4
Prefer Job B	%	14.4	28.9	23.3	20.0	22.2	22.2	30.8	25.6	14.4	24.4	19.9
Same	%	4.4	6.7	3.3	**	2.2	2.2	2.2	1.1	3.3	4.4	2.8
**Missing Data	%	42.2	10.0	18.9	11.1	33.3	52.2	30.8	38.9	22.2	35.6	26.9
Q37 Job Choice Number 5												
Prefer Job A	%	97.8	94.4	93.3	95.6	95.6	91.0	93.4	94.4	94.4	84.4	91.5
Prefer Job B	%	**	1.1	4.4	1.1	**	6.7	3.3	2.2	**	6.7	3.9
Same	%	2.2	1.1	2.2	**	2.2	2.2	2.2	1.1	2.2	7.8	2.8
**Missing Data	%	**	3.3	**	3.3	2.2	1.1	1.1	2.2	3.3	1.1	1.8
Q38 Job Choice Number 6												
Prefer Job A	%	91.1	96.7	91.1	93.3	93.3	57.8	90.1	88.9	86.7	77.8	84.9
Prefer Job B	%	7.8	**	3.3	1.1	3.3	34.4	8.8	7.8	8.9	10.0	7.5

221

Variable		Students N=90	Chemical Engineers N=90	Self-Employed N=90	Teachers N=90	Temporary N=90	Textile Workers N=90	Tool and Die N=91	White Collar N=90	Retired N=90	Unemployed N=90	National Sample N=973
Same	%	1.1	1.1	1.1	**	1.1	1.1	**	1.1	**	6.7	2.8
**Missing Data	%	**	2.2	4.4	5.6	2.2	6.7	1.1	2.2	4.4	5.6	4.8
Q39 Job Choice Number 7												
Prefer Job A	%	76.7	80.0	80.0	81.1	75.6	30.0	61.5	64.4	76.7	55.6	73.4
Prefer Job B	%	14.4	8.9	8.9	6.7	18.9	18.9	27.5	24.4	10.0	24.4	12.6
Same	%	1.1	3.3	3.3	1.1	**	2.2	3.3	1.1	**	6.7	3.0
**Missing Data	%	7.8	7.8	7.8	11.1	5.6	48.9	7.7	10.0	13.3	13.3	11.0
Q40 Job Choice Number 8												
Prefer Job A	%	52.2	75.6	64.4	76.7	57.8	**	41.8	48.9	64.4	42.2	59.1
Prefer Job B	%	22.2	14.4	18.9	15.6	21.1	24.0	28.6	21.1	11.1	21.1	16.6
Same	%	3.3	**	3.3	**	1.1	31.4	3.3	1.1	3.3	4.4	2.9
**Missing Data	%	22.2	10.0	13.3	7.8	20.0	44.6	26.4	28.9	21.1	32.2	21.4
Q41 Job Choice Number 9												
Prefer Job A	%	57.8	48.9	71.1	66.7	66.7	28.9	57.1	47.8	54.4	50.0	58.5
Prefer Job B	%	35.6	35.6	22.2	20.0	28.9	66.7	34.1	48.9	30.0	33.3	27.0
Same	%	5.6	11.1	5.6	8.9	1.1	4.4	5.5	2.2	8.9	12.2	8.7
**Missing Data	%	1.1	4.4	1.1	4.4	3.3	**	3.3	1.1	6.7	4.4	5.8
Q42 Job Choice Number 10												
Prefer Job A	%	35.6	26.7	52.2	52.2	46.7	10.0	29.7	26.7	41.1	27.8	41.1
Prefer Job B	%	26.7	32.2	25.6	27.8	25.6	31.1	35.2	33.3	17.8	32.2	24.9
Same	%	2.2	6.7	6.7	4.4	**	1.1	3.3	2.2	5.6	6.7	6.1
**Missing Data	%	35.6	34.4	15.6	15.6	27.8	57.8	31.9	37.8	35.6	33.3	28.9
Q43 Job Choice Number 11												
Prefer Job A	%	6.7	2.2	32.2	8.9	12.2	13.3	9.9	5.6	14.4	18.9	18.9
Prefer Job B	%	92.2	92.2	64.4	88.9	84.4	83.3	84.6	91.1	75.6	68.9	75.1
Same	%	**	2.2	2.2	1.1	**	3.3	1.1	1.1	3.3	10.0	4.0
**Missing Data	%	1.1	3.3	1.1	1.1	3.3	**	4.4	2.2	6.7	2.2	2.3
Q44 Job Choice Number 12												
Prefer Job A	%	4.4	2.2	25.6	7.8	6.7	5.6	6.6	5.6	10.0	14.4	13.4

Prefer Job B	%	10.0	28.9	22.2	50.0	15.6	13.3	16.5	23.3	20.0	16.7	22.1
Same	%	**	1.1	2.2	**	**	**	**	1.1	1.1	11.1	3.4
**Missing Data	%	85.2	67.8	50.0	42.2	77.8	81.1	76.9	70.0	68.9	57.8	61.2
Q45 Job Choice Number 13												
Prefer Job A	%	2.2	1.1	25.6	4.4	4.4	**	2.2	3.3	7.8	10.0	10.2
Prefer Job B	%	4.4	18.9	20.0	47.8	14.4	4.4	17.6	21.1	17.8	18.9	18.2
Same	%	**	**	2.2	**	**	1.1	**	1.1	1.1	5.6	2.3
**Missing Data	%	93.3	80.0	52.2	47.8	81.1	94.4	80.2	74.4	73.3	65.6	69.4
Q46 Job Choice Number 14												
Prefer Job A	%	6.7	1.1	26.7	2.2	12.2	8.9	6.6	4.4	.4	15.6	13.4
Prefer Job B	%	92.2	96.7	70.0	96.7	83.3	86.7	90.1	94.4	88.9	71.1	81.1
Same	%	1.1	**	1.1	**	1.1	3.3	**	1.1	2.2	7.8	3.7
**Missing Data	%	**	2.2	2.2	1.1	3.3	1.1	3.3	**	4.4	5.6	1.2
Societal Norms												
Q47A Employer should Retrain												
Strongly Disagree	%	1.1	1.1	3.3	**	2.2	**	1.1	1.1	2.2	6.7	1.4
Disagree	%	10.0	5.6	3.3	**	2.2	1.1	5.5	3.3	3.3	2.2	5.9
Agree	%	52.2	54.3	42.2	40.0	52.3	25.6	49.4	42.2	33.3	45.6	44.8
Strongly Agree	%	36.7	37.8	45.6	60.0	42.2	70.1	42.9	53.4	56.8	43.3	47.6
**Missing Data	%	**	1.1	5.6	**	1.1	2.2	1.1	**	4.4	2.2	0.3
Q47B Duty to Work												
Strongly Disagree	%	3.3	**	1.1	1.1	3.3	**	**	**	**	4.4	1.4
Disagree	%	17.8	11.1	3.3	10.0	14.4	4.4	1.1	7.8	2.2	8.9	9.5
Agree	%	42.2	46.7	30.0	42.2	50.1	34.4	50.0	47.8	28.9	37.8	41.5
Strongly Agree	%	36.7	41.1	65.6	45.6	32.2	57.8	46.2	43.3	68.9	46.7	47.2
**Missing Data	%	**	1.1	**	1.1	**	3.4	2.7	1.1	**	2.2	0.4
Q47C Society should Educate												
Strongly Disagree	%	**	1.1	2.2	**	2.2	**	**	**	**	4.4	0.6
Disagree	%	10.0	12.2	4.4	2.2	5.6	6.7	**	7.8	4.4	2.2	4.8

Variable		Students N=90	Chemical Engineers N=90	Self-Employed N=90	Teachers N=90	Temporary N=90	Textile Workers N=90	Tool and Die N=91	White Collar N=90	Retired N=90	Unemployed N=90	National Sample N=973
Agree	%	44.4	53.4	24.4	47.8	53.3	48.9	57.1	54.4	36.7	42.2	49.9
Strongly Agree	%	45.6	31.1	67.9	48.9	38.9	41.1	41.8	36.7	58.9	48.9	43.8
**Missing Data	%	**	2.2	1.1	1.1	**	3.3	1.1	1.1	**	2.3	0.9
Q47D Obligation to Save												
Strongly Disagree	%	1.1	**	3.3	**	3.3	6.7	1.1	**	**	8.9	1.3
Disagree	%	21.1	17.8	5.6	6.7	14.4	7.8	9.9	11.1	3.3	13.3	10.9
Agree	%	50.0	62.2	36.7	52.2	46.7	42.2	42.8	44.4	34.4	37.8	46.6
Strongly Agree	%	27.8	17.8	54.4	37.8	32.2	40.0	45.1	44.5	62.3	36.7	40.2
**Missing Data	%	**	2.2	**	2.2	3.4	3.3	1.1	**	**	3.3	1.0
Q47E Supervisor should Consult Workers												
Strongly Disagree	%	4.4	2.2	3.3	**	2.2	5.6	**	**	**	2.2	3.5
Disagree	%	15.6	22.2	15.6	3.3	10.0	17.8	11.0	4.4	13.3	8.9	10.5
Agree	%	37.8	47.8	44.5	37.8	48.9	37.8	39.6	46.7	30.0	55.6	49.6
Strongly Agree	%	42.2	26.7	33.3	58.9	38.9	35.6	48.4	48.9	55.6	31.1	35.8
**Missing Data	%	**	1.1	3.3	**	**	3.2	1.0	**	1.1	2.2	0.6
Q47F Obligation to Improve Work Methods												
Strongly Disagree	%	**	1.1	1.1	**	**	**	**	**	1.1	3.3	0.4
Disagree	%	5.6	2.2	**	3.3	5.6	1.1	3.3	2.2	1.1	6.7	3.6
Agree	%	42.2	54.4	27.8	31.1	46.7	47.8	35.2	50.0	27.8	43.3	44.6
Strongly Agree	%	52.2	40.0	70.0	65.6	45.6	47.8	59.3	47.8	68.9	44.4	50.4
**Missing Data	%	**	2.3	1.1	**	2.1	3.3	2.2	**	1.1	2.3	1.0
Q47G All Entitled to Meaningful Jobs												
Strongly Disagree	%	1.1	2.2	1.1	**	4.4	3.3	**	**	1.1	7.8	1.5
Disagree	%	13.3	14.4	6.7	8.9	12.2	12.2	5.5	13.3	5.6	11.1	9.1
Agree	%	46.7	51.1	45.6	33.3	40.0	44.4	47.3	45.6	43.3	36.7	45.1
Strongly Agree	%	37.8	30.0	46.6	56.7	42.2	36.7	45.0	38.9	48.9	42.2	43.1
**Missing Data	%	1.1	3.3	**	1.1	1.2	3.4	2.2	2.2	1.1	2.2	1.2

224

Q47H Monotonous Job OK if paid fairly											
Strongly Disagree	%	31.1	12.2	20.0	17.8	21.1	21.1	13.2	15.6	35.6	17.8	17.0
Disagree	%	42.2	44.4	39.0	48.9	44.4	26.7	54.9	48.9	31.1	28.9	39.5
Agree	%	20.0	37.9	31.1	25.6	25.6	30.0	24.2	27.8	15.6	27.8	34.1
Strongly Agree	%	5.6	3.3	7.8	6.7	8.9	20.0	5.5	7.7	14.4	23.3	8.4
**Missing Data	%	1.1	2.2	2.1	1.0	**	2.2	2.2	**	3.3	2.2	1.0
Q47I Job should be provided to all												
Strongly Disagree	%	2.2	1.1	2.2	1.1	4.4	**	**	**	**	1.1	0.7
Disagree	%	14.4	5.6	1.1	2.2	3.3	3.3	1.1	8.8	4.4	3.3	6.2
Agree	%	47.8	47.8	36.7	46.7	45.6	32.2	39.6	45.6	19.0	17.8	37.9
Strongly Agree	%	35.6	42.2	60.0	50.0	46.7	62.2	57.1	45.6	74.4	75.6	54.3
**Missing Data	%	**	3.3	**	**	**	2.3	2.2	**	2.2	2.2	0.9
Q47J Value any Work												
Strongly Disagree	%	14.4	8.9	13.3	7.8	14.4	5.6	3.3	17.8	8.9	5.6	10.7
Disagree	%	28.9	36.7	24.4	33.3	34.4	20.0	31.9	35.6	18.9	27.8	27.1
Agree	%	30.0	33.3	32.3	38.9	33.3	33.3	40.7	34.4	32.2	31.1	39.5
Strongly Agree	%	26.7	17.8	26.7	18.9	16.8	38.9	20.9	11.1	37.8	33.3	21.1
**Missing Data	%	**	3.3	3.3	1.1	1.1	2.2	3.2	1.1	2.2	2.2	1.6
Q48A If won Lottery or had Money												
Stop Working	%	1.1	4.4	5.6	2.2	10.0	18.9	8.8	5.6	6.7	12.2	12.1
Continue same Job	%	51.1	43.2	51.1	46.7	51.1	41.1	36.3	43.3	65.6	40.1	48.7
Cont. Diff. Conditions	%	47.8	52.4	38.9	51.1	38.9	40.0	52.7	47.8	22.2	43.3	36.1
**Missing Data	%	**	**	4.4	**	**	**	2.2	3.3	5.5	4.4	3.1
Work Definition												
Q49A If in Working Place												
No, Is not Work	%	76.7	81.1	52.2	82.2	76.7	50.0	68.1	63.3	72.2	82.2	70.8
Yes, Is Work	%	23.3	18.9	47.8	17.8	23.3	50.0	31.9	36.7	24.8	17.8	29.2

Variable		Students N=90	Chemical Engineers N=90	Self-Employed N=90	Teachers N=90	Temporary N=90	Textile Workers N=90	Tool and Die N=91	White Collar N=90	Retired N=90	Unemployed N=90	National Sample N=973
Q49B If told to do it												
No, Is not Work	%	94.4	94.4	93.3	96.7	90.0	85.5	86.8	90.0	94.4	80.0	86.2
Yes, Is Work	%	5.6	5.6	6.7	3.3	10.0	14.4	13.2	10.0	5.6	20.0	13.8
Q49C If Physically strenuous												
No, Is not Work	%	90.0	91.1	80.0	88.9	88.9	75.6	73.6	94.4	82.2	65.6	79.7
Yes, Is Work	%	10.0	8.9	20.0	11.1	11.1	24.4	26.4	5.6	17.8	34.4	20.2
Q49D If Part of Task												
No, Is not Work	%	44.4	44.4	56.7	36.7	52.2	68.9	56.0	51.1	37.8	53.3	49.6
Yes, Is Work	%	55.6	55.6	43.3	63.3	47.8	31.1	44.0	48.9	62.2	46.7	50.4
Q49E If Contributes to Society												
No, Is not Work	%	55.6	62.2	74.4	48.9	63.3	58.9	51.6	68.9	42.2	67.8	59.6
Yes, Is Work	%	44.4	37.8	24.4	51.1	36.7	41.1	48.4	31.1	57.8	32.2	40.4
Q49F If Feeling of Belonging												
No, Is not Work	%	63.3	73.3	82.8	63.3	70.0	81.1	74.1	78.9	76.7	73.3	76.1
Yes, Is Work	%	36.7	26.7	17.2	36.7	30.0	18.9	25.9	21.1	23.3	26.7	23.9
Q49G If Mentally strenuous												
No, Is not Work	%	68.9	63.3	71.1	63.3	74.4	93.3	71.4	65.6	74.4	80.0	74.8
Yes, Is Work	%	31.1	36.7	28.9	36.7	25.6	6.7	28.6	34.4	25.6	20.0	25.2
Q49H If at Certain Time												
No, Is not Work	%	73.3	87.8	72.2	85.6	68.9	66.7	87.9	77.8	84.4	82.2	84.0
Yes, Is Work	%	26.7	12.2	27.8	14.4	31.1	33.3	12.1	22.2	15.6	17.8	16.0
Q49I If it Adds Value												
No, Is not Work	%	75.2	56.7	83.3	65.6	76.7	76.7	87.9	78.9	85.2	80.0	77.8
Yes, Is Work	%	24.8	43.3	16.7	34.4	23.3	23.3	12.1	21.1	14.8	20.0	22.2
Q49J If not Pleasant												
No, Is not Work	%	98.9	98.9	97.8	100.0	100.0	98.9	98.9	96.7	96.7	98.9	98.6
Yes, Is Work	%	1.1	1.1	2.2	**	**	1.1	1.1	3.3	3.3	1.1	1.4

Q49K If you Get Money												
No, Is not Work	%	31.8	35.6	40.0	25.6	19.8	12.2	20.0	45.6	24.8	28.9	25.6
Yes, Is Work	%	68.2	64.4	60.0	74.4	80.2	87.8	80.0	54.4	75.2	71.1	74.4
Q49L If you Must Account												
No, Is not Work	%	87.6	92.2	91.1	83.3	87.9	96.7	91.1	93.3	85.6	86.7	87.8
Yes, Is Work	%	12.4	7.8	8.9	16.7	12.1	3.3	8.9	6.7	14.4	13.3	12.2
Q49M If you Must do It												
No, Is not Work	%	83.8	83.3	74.4	82.2	86.8	74.4	87.8	90.0	77.8	86.7	95.6
Yes, Is Work	%	16.2	16.7	25.6	17.8	13.2	25.6	12.2	10.0	22.2	13.3	4.4
Q49N If Others Profit												
No, Is not Work	%	66.4	76.7	65.3	61.1	59.3	66.7	62.2	54.4	66.7	61.1	52.2
Yes, Is Work	%	33.6	23.3	33.3	38.9	40.7	33.3	37.8	45.6	33.3	38.9	47.8
Q50A Choose Same Occupation again?												
Same	%	59.4	47.8	67.8	55.6	42.9	44.4	33.3	68.9	45.6	58.9	63.3
Different	%	37.6	47.8	26.6	43.3	53.8	54.5	60.0	30.0	50.0	37.8	33.4
**Missing Data	%	3.0	4.4	5.6	1.1	3.3	1.1	6.7	1.1	4.4	3.3	3.3
Q50B Recommend Occup. to children?												
Yes	%	31.0	21.1	37.8	60.0	76.9	87.8	68.9	45.6	70.0	57.8	**
No	%	73.9	76.7	57.8	26.7	24.0	12.2	24.4	45.5	26.7	33.9	**
**Missing Data	%	5.1	2.2	4.4	3.3	1.1	**	6.7	8.9	3.3	3.3	100.0
Q51A Attitudes toward Work will change in next 10 years												
Yes	%	47.1	58.9	57.8	43.3	47.3	37.8	41.1	44.4	58.9	37.8	43.3
No	%	44.8	37.8	28.9	51.1	50.5	54.4	48.9	51.2	36.7	57.8	54.5
**Missing Data	%	2.1	3.3	13.3	5.6	2.2	7.8	10.0	4.4	4.4	4.4	2.2
Q52 Preference, Job vs. Organization												
Stay with Different Job	%	45.9	**	**	94.5	52.7	76.7	46.7	5.6	3.3	39.9	**
Same Job Diff. Organiz.	%	28.6	**	**	4.4	41.8	23.3	28.9	8.9	2.2	51.0	**

Variable	%	Students N=90	Chemical Engineers N=90	Self-Employed N=90	Teachers N=90	Temporary N=90	Textile Workers N=90	Tool and Die N=91	White Collar N=90	Retired N=90	Unemployed N=90	National Sample N=973
**Missing Data	%	100.0	8.9	94.5	85.5	24.4	**	5.5	1.1	100.0	100.0	25.3
Q53 Leisure unrelated to work												
Never	%	6.7	2.2	8.9	1.1	10.0	18.9	13.2	14.4	**	**	10.0
Only Occasionally	%	8.9	3.3	6.7	5.6	3.3	4.4	6.6	12.2	**	**	10.1
Sometimes	%	28.9	21.1	23.3	35.6	15.6	22.2	26.4	21.2	**	**	26.0
Often	%	31.1	40.0	32.2	44.4	24.4	16.7	25.3	21.1	**	**	23.4
Very Often	%	22.2	32.3	27.8	13.3	45.6	37.8	27.5	30.0	**	**	29.4
**Missing Data	%	2.2	1.1	1.1	**	1.1	**	0.1	1.1	100.0	100.0	1.1
Q54 Participate in Company Activities?												
No	%	2.2	21.1	5.6	16.7	26.7	22.2	12.1	8.9	**	**	17.5
May Be	%	42.3	38.9	6.7	42.2	25.6	12.2	20.9	34.4	**	**	26.9
Yes	%	53.3	36.7	11.1	41.1	46.7	64.5	65.9	55.6	**	**	46.5
**Missing Data	%	2.2	3.3	76.6	**	1.1	1.1	1.1	1.1	100.0	100.0	9.1
Q55 Worry about Work in Free Time?												
Never	%	4.4	3.3	11.1	2.2	37.8	24.4	17.5	12.2	**	16.7	17.2
Only Occasionally	%	10.0	10.0	12.2	1.1	14.4	11.1	11.0	8.9	**	13.3	14.2
Sometimes	%	40.0	32.2	17.8	30.0	26.7	37.8	31.9	45.6	**	15.6	30.4
Often	%	36.7	37.8	28.9	50.0	8.9	18.9	25.3	23.3	**	18.8	21.2
Very Often	%	6.7	16.7	28.9	16.7	11.1	7.8	13.2	8.9	**	18.9	16.3
**Missing Data	%	2.2	**	1.1	**	1.1	**	1.1	1.1	100.0	16.7	0.7
Q56A Change Jobs next 12 Months?												
Yes	%	72.2	20.0	18.9	11.1	56.7	25.6	15.4	11.1	**	28.9	13.7
No	%	26.7	76.7	80.0	87.8	38.0	**	81.3	**	**	52.2	82.1
**Missing Data	%	1.1	3.3	1.1	1.1	5.6	74.4	3.3	89.9	100.0	18.9	4.2

Q57 Ease of Finding a similar job with another Employer?

Response		1	2	3	4	5	6	7	8	9	10	11
Difficult	%	6.7	21.1	**	10.0	8.9	52.2	22.0	25.6	**	28.9	24.0
Not So Easy	%	42.2	27.8	**	17.8	26.7	14.4	23.1	21.1	**	33.3	19.6
Somewhat Easy	%	21.1	7.8	**	15.6	13.3	4.4	7.7	11.1	**	5.6	9.8
Easy	%	21.1	16.7	**	32.2	31.1	15.6	25.2	23.3	**	12.2	17.7
Very Easy	%	7.8	15.5	**	10.0	14.4	7.8	14.3	10.0	**	4.4	9.6
**Missing Data	%	1.1	11.1	100.0	14.4	5.6	5.6	7.7	8.9	100.0	15.6	19.3

Q58 Willing to Train for a Different Job?

Response		1	2	3	4	5	6	7	8	9	10	11
Under No Conditions	%	17.8	28.9	55.6	36.7	22.2	38.9	33.0	25.6	**	17.8	44.1
Only if Forced to	%	31.1	25.6	18.9	17.8	18.9	33.3	29.7	18.9	**	26.7	22.3
Under Certain Conditions	%	43.3	44.4	22.2	42.2	46.7	27.8	35.2	51.1	**	36.7	30.2
**Missing Data	%	7.8	1.1	3.3	3.3	12.2	**	2.1	4.4	100.0	18.8	3.4

Q59 Retrain for a different Occupation this Year?

Response		1	2	3	4	5	6	7	8	9	10	11
Yes	%	**	4.4	8.9	10.0	30.0	20.0	9.9	18.9	**	34.4	11.1
No	%	**	93.4	84.4	84.4	68.9	80.0	86.8	81.1	**	48.9	86.9
**Missing Data	%	100.0	2.2	6.7	5.6	1.1	**	3.3	**	100.0	16.7	2.0

Q60 Intend to Retrain Present Job-this Year?

Response		1	2	3	4	5	6	7	8	9	10	11
Yes	%	85.6	28.9	11.1	33.3	24.4	21.1	37.4	48.9	**	28.9	33.8
No	%	14.4	70.0	86.6	66.7	73.4	75.6	59.3	47.8	**	50.0	64.5
**Missing Data	%	**	1.1	3.3	**	2.2	3.3	3.3	3.3	100.0	21.1	1.7

Q61 Try to be Promoted this Year?

Response		1	2	3	4	5	6	7	8	9	10	11
Yes	%	94.4	57.8	28.9	27.8	33.3	75.6	69.2	77.8	**	2.2	49.2
No	%	5.4	40.0	50.0	68.9	61.1	23.3	27.5	21.1	**	3.4	47.1
**Missing Data	%	2.2	2.2	21.1	3.3	5.6	1.1	3.3	1.1	100.0	94.4	3.7

<u>*Q62A Has Other Plans*</u>

229

		Students N = 90	Chemical Engineers N = 90	Self-Employed N = 90	Teachers N = 90	Temporary N = 90	Textile Workers N = 90	Tool and Die N = 91	White Collar N = 90	Retired N = 90	Unemployed N = 90	National Sample N = 973
Regarding Work?												
Yes	%	53.3	57.8	34.4	35.6	34.4	18.9	36.3	46.7	**	3.3	32.2
No	%	43.4	37.8	65.6	64.4	62.3	80.0	60.4	51.1	**	**	64.8
**Missing Data	%	3.3	4.4	**	**	3.3	1.1	3.3	2.2	100.0	96.7	3.0
Q63 Societal Development which will Endanger Employment Situation?												
Yes	%	47.8	30.0	38.9	11.1	24.4	30.0	19.8	8.9	**	25.6	21.5
No	%	51.1	68.9	55.5	86.7	73.4	65.6	75.8	90.0	**	52.2	73.7
**Missing Data	%	1.1	1.1	5.6	2.2	2.2	4.4	4.4	1.1	100.0	22.2	4.8
Q64 Societal Development which will Improve Employment Situation?												
Yes	%	60.0	47.8	31.1	44.4	38.9	41.1	34.1	38.9	**	33.3	37.9
No	%	34.4	48.9	61.1	43.4	50.0	56.7	59.4	56.7	**	40.0	55.6
**Missing Data	%	5.6	3.3	7.8	12.2	11.1	2.2	6.5	4.4	100.0	26.7	6.5
Q65 Relative Pay Expectations												
Go Down	%	4.5	3.3	16.7	4.4	5.6	8.9	7.7	2.2	**	7.8	5.9
Stay Same	%	37.8	58.9	48.9	34.4	43.3	51.1	31.9	31.1	**	34.4	46.8
Go up	%	54.4	35.6	27.8	61.2	50.0	37.8	58.2	66.7	**	41.1	45.2
**Missing Data	%	3.3	2.2	6.6	**	1.1	2.2	2.2	**	100.0	16.7	2.1
Q66A Future Work Importance												
Less Imp.	%	4.4	5.6	10.0	4.4	6.7	8.9	11.0	5.6	**	6.7	8.8
Equal in Imp.	%	37.8	80.0	66.7	85.6	50.0	52.2	60.4	67.7	**	38.9	67.8
More Imp.	%	57.8	13.3	20.0	10.0	43.3	37.8	25.3	26.7	**	37.7	20.2
**Missing Data	%	**	1.1	3.3	**	**	1.1	3.3	**	100.0	16.6	3.2

Q67 Alternative if Same Pay/Less Hours

More Holidays	%	10.0	23.3	26.7	17.8	30.0	17.8	14.3	13.3	**	16.7	19.9
Less Working Hours	%	32.2	21.1	28.9	27.8	40.0	37.8	35.1	53.6	**	38.9	36.7
Free Afternoon per Week	%	11.1	11.1	14.4	1.1	4.4	16.7	11.0	7.8	**	7.8	8.6
More Education pre-Work	%	14.4	7.8	5.7	6.7	6.7	5.6	5.5	12.2	**	6.7	4.7
Year of Study every 10 Years	%	18.9	30.0	3.3	16.7	12.2	7.8	13.2	7.8	**	5.6	11.0
Less Hours for older Workers	%	8.9	1.1	3.3	6.7	5.6	5.6	4.4	1.1	**	8.9	5.0
Early Retirement	%	3.3	5.6	13.3	22.2	1.1	7.7	15.4	2.2	**	1.1	10.2
**Missing Data	%	1.2	**	4.4	1.1	**	1.0	1.1	2.2	100.0	14.4	4.0

Q68 Less Hours/Less Pay Attitude

Against	%	48.9	56.7	57.8	33.3	37.8	56.6	70.3	32.2	**	52.3	47.4
Don't Care	%	23.3	13.3	22.2	32.2	24.4	15.6	12.1	17.8	**	20.0	22.1
Moderately in Favour	%	12.2	15.6	7.8	22.2	16.7	12.2	6.6	27.8	**	11.1	14.7
In Favour	%	14.4	13.3	11.1	11.1	20.0	15.6	6.6	21.1	**	3.3	14.2
**Missing Data	%	1.2	1.1	1.1	1.1	1.1	**	4.4	1.1	100.0	13.3	1.6

Q69 Age

	Mean	17.3	37.0	45.6	32.5	28.8	34.8	38.3	28.6	69.4	35.8	3.5
	SD	1.0	9.6	15.4	8.7	9.2	12.7	11.2	9.7	6.1	13.3	1.3

Q70 Highest Formal Education

Primary School	%	43.3	**	32.2	**	5.6	56.7	24.2	5.6	25.6	30.0	18.9
Secondary School	%	54.4	1.1	38.9	4.4	64.4	35.6	53.8	67.8	41.1	51.1	45.5
Some College or Votech	%	**	**	20.0	85.6	15.6	6.7	20.9	14.4	27.8	8.9	18.3
University Degree	%	**	98.9	8.9	10.0	14.4	**	1.1	12.2	4.4	4.4	16.1
**Missing Data	%	2.2	**	**	**	**	1.0	**	**	1.1	5.6	1.1

Q71 Religious Education

Yes	%	37.8	23.3	47.8	41.1	16.7	71.1	41.8	54.4	57.8	57.8	53.8
No	%	61.1	75.6	51.1	57.8	80.0	27.8	58.2	45.6	42.2	40.0	45.6
**Missing Data	%	1.1	1.1	1.1	1.1	3.3	1.1	**	**	**	2.2	0.8

Variable		Students N=90	Chemical Engineers N=90	Self-Employed N=90	Teachers N=90	Temporary N=90	Textile Workers N=90	Tool and Die N=91	White Collar N=90	Retired N=90	Unemployed N=90	National Sample N=973
Q72 Association with Religion												
No Contact	%	40.0	53.3	46.7	44.4	65.6	30.0	48.3	34.4	47.8	37.8	45.7
Loose Contact	%	56.7	31.1	46.7	35.6	32.2	51.1	46.2	38.9	42.2	42.2	39.9
Close Contact	%	3.3	14.4	5.6	20.0	1.1	17.8	4.4	26.7	10.0	18.9	14.1
**Missing Data	%	**	1.2	1.0	**	1.1	1.1	1.1	**	**	1.1	0.3
Q73 Father's Highest Education												
Primary School	%	53.3	38.9	51.2	45.6	43.3	74.4	62.6	42.2	52.2	56.7	46.7
Secondary School	%	41.1	30.0	24.4	27.8	36.7	15.6	23.1	36.7	23.3	18.9	27.4
Some College or Votech	%	1.1	11.1	3.3	12.2	7.7	1.1	3.3	6.7	5.6	3.3	4.7
University Degree	%	1.1	20.0	8.9	10.0	6.7	**	6.6	12.2	8.9	4.4	8.7
**Missing Data	%	3.4	**	12.2	4.4	5.6	8.9	4.4	2.2	10.0	16.7	12.4
Q73B Mother's Highest Education												
Primary School	%	52.2	38.9	51.1	50.0	48.9	75.6	72.5	54.4	68.9	58.9	52.9
Secondary School	%	36.7	38.9	25.6	35.6	34.4	10.0	16.5	38.9	15.6	20.0	24.5
Some College or Votech	%	4.4	6.7	1.1	4.4	4.4	**	2.2	2.2	3.3	1.1	4.7
University Degree	%	2.2	13.3	3.3	5.6	8.9	**	3.3	2.2	2.2	1.1	2.9
**Missing Data	%	2.2	2.2	18.9	4.4	3.3	14.4	5.5	2.2	10.0	18.9	15.0
Q74 Nature of Youth Community												
City	%	83.3	77.8	81.1	73.3	75.5	71.1	72.5	85.6	83.3	77.8	71.7
Village	%	16.7	10.0	8.9	10.0	16.7	16.7	18.7	10.0	14.4	11.1	14.5
Rural	%	**	12.2	8.9	16.7	7.8	12.2	6.6	4.4	3.3	8.9	12.8
**Missing Data	%	**	**	1.1	**	**	**	2.2	**	**	2.2	1.0
Q75 Nature of Present Community												
City	%	87.8	92.2	88.9	87.8	94.4	94.5	82.4	91.1	93.3	88.9	83.8

Village	%	10.6	10.0	6.7	6.7	17.6	1.1	2.2	3.3	7.8	6.7	12.2
Rural	%	5.0	**	**	2.2	**	4.4	2.2	8.9	3.3	1.1	**
**Missing Data	%	0.6	1.1	**	**	**	**	1.2	**	**	**	100.0
Q76A Marital Status/ Partnership?												
Yes	%	80.9	50.0	71.1	54.4	84.6	73.3	67.8	83.3	77.8	88.9	**
No	%	18.3	45.6	25.6	44.5	15.4	26.7	32.2	16.71	22.2	11.1	**
**Missing Data	%	0.8	4.4	3.3	1.1	**	**	**	**	**	**	100.0
Q76B Employment Status of Partner												
Not Employed	%	27.5	15.6	46.7	10.0	41.8	27.8	3.3	**	37.8	17.8	**
Part Time	%	11.2	5.6	5.6	5.6	17.6	4.4	8.9	2.2	16.7	30.0	**
Full Time	%	38.5	24.4	8.9	35.6	23.1	37.8	53.4	74.4	22.2	42.2	**
Other	%	2.3	3.3	4.4	3.3	2.2	1.1	3.3	5.6	1.1	**	**
**Missing Data	%	20.5	51.1	34.4	45.5	15.3	28.9	31.1	17.8	22.2	10.0	100.0
Q77 No. of Financially Dependent	Mean	1.6	1.8	2.1	1.7	1.6	1.4	2.0	2.1	1.8	2.0	**
	SD	0.9	1.3	0.6	0.9	0.7	0.9	1.1	1.1	0.8	0.7	**
Q78 General Life Satisfaction												
1: Very Dissatisfied	%	1.2	6.7	2.2	1.1	2.2	2.2	**	1.1	2.2	**	2.2
2: On 1-to-9-scale	%	0.2	3.3	1.1	**	**	2.2	**	**	2.2	1.1	1.1
3: On 1-to-9-scale	%	1.3	2.2	3.3	1.1	1.1	1.1	1.1	**	3.3	1.1	2.2
4: On 1-to-9-scale	%	1.7	6.7	2.2	2.2	**	6.7	2.2	4.4	4.4	1.1	**
5: On 1-to-9-scale	%	10.3	12.2	8.9	8.9	5.5	13.3	11.1	6.7	12.2	3.3	8.9
6: On 1-to-9-scale	%	8.9	7.8	15.6	8.9	11.0	6.7	4.4	5.6	17.8	7.8	10.0
7: On 1-to-9-scale	%	22.3	17.8	21.1	23.3	20.9	11.1	21.1	28.9	14.4	33.3	13.3
8: On 1-to-9-scale	%	21.6	12.2	18.9	21.1	19.8	23.3	20.0	16.7	8.9	36.7	27.8
9: Very satisfied	%	29.8	15.6	22.2	33.4	38.5	33.3	36.7	34.4	28.9	11.1	26.7
**Missing Data	%	2.9	14.5	5.6	**	1.0	1.2	3.4	2.2	5.7	4.5	7.8
Q79 Citizenship												
Yes	%	91.3	92.2	95.6	81.1	94.5	93.3	91.1	91.1	83.3	94.4	95.6

Variable		Students N = 90	Chemical Engineers N = 90	Self-Employed N = 90	Teachers N = 90	Tempo-rary N = 90	Textile Workers N = 90	Tool and Die N = 91	White Collar N = 90	Retired N = 90	Unem-ployed N = 90	National Sample N = 973
No	%	4.4	5.6	14.4	8.9	7.8	6.7	5.5	16.7	2.2	6.7	7.5
**Missing Data	%	**	**	2.3	**	1.1	**	**	2.2	2.2	1.1	1.2
Q81A Interview was conducted												
At Home	%	**	77.8	5.6	58.9	85.6	**	97.8	5.6	77.8	65.6	97.4
At Workplace	%	100.0	22.2	94.4	38.9	13.3	100.0	**	92.2	**	2.2	1.1
**Missing Data	%	**	**	**	2.2	1.1	**	2.2	2.2	22.2	32.2	1.5
Q82 Sex												
Male	%	46.7	90.0	87.8	**	4.4	66.7	94.5	50.0	43.3	53.3	56.8
Female	%	46.7	7.8	12.2	98.9	95.6	31.1	3.3	47.8	47.8	42.2	42.0
**Missing Data	%	6.6	2.2	**	1.1	**	2.2	2.2	2.2	8.9	4.5	1.2
Q83B Type of Self -Employment												
Craftsman	%	**	2.2	8.9	**	**	**	6.6	**	8.9	8.9	8.7
Service	%	**	7.8	23.3	36.7	17.8	**	3.3	30.0	30.0	28.9	26.4
Commercial	%	**	3.3	58.9	**	1.1	**	**	**	4.4	1.1	4.8
**Missing Data	%	100.0	86.7	8.9	63.3	81.1	100.0	90.1	70.0	56.7	61.1	59.9
Q84A Ownership of Work Organization												
Public	%	**	48.9	**	87.8	22.2	8.9	4.4	42.2	28.9	34.4	41.4
Private	%	**	26.7	97.8	1.1	56.7	55.6	52.7	56.7	21.1	25.6	36.7
**Missing Data	%	100.0	4.4	2.2	11.1	21.1	35.5	42.9	1.1	50.0	38.9	21.9
Q84B Size of Organization												
Under 100	%	**	17.8	96.7	72.2	41.2	**	40.7	47.8	37.8	36.7	47.2
100-299	%	**	21.1	**	10.0	13.3	**	15.4	25.6	6.7	12.2	10.8
300-999	%	**	24.4	**	1.3	11.1	35.6	25.5	2.2	4.4	7.8	10.3
Over 1000	%	**	31.1	**	14.4	22.2	64.4	15.4	20.0	20.0	6.7	26.7

**Missing Data

Q85 Length of Interview (in Minutes)	%	100.0	6.6	3.3	2.2	12.2	**	3.2	4.4	31.1	36.6	5.0
	Mean	41.1	42.1	50.0	52.9	41.6	48.4	40.5	39.4	60.5	45.4	43.8
	SD	10.0	10.0	21.7	50.1	10.7	44.1	11.0	10.1	77.0	37.3	24.8

** Indicates data missing and/or unavailable

References

Adams, J. S. Wages, inequities, productivity, and work quality. *Industrial Relations*, 1963, *3*, 6–16.

Adar, L., and C. Adler. *Education for Values in Schools for Immigrant Children*. Jerusalem: School of Education, Hebrew University, 1965 (Hebrew).

Agrell, G. *Work, Toil and Sustenance*. Verbun, Sweden: Hanan Ohlssons, 1976.

Akerman, A. *Zionism in Struggle: Policies of Settlement, Security and Contemplations, 1882–1982*. Jerusalem: Good Times, 1982.

Aldag, R. J., and A. F. Brief. Some correlates of work values. *Journal of Applied Psychology*, 1975, *60*, 757–760.

Allport, F. A structuronomic conception of behavior: Individual and collective. *Journal of Abnormal and Social Psychology*, 1962, *64*, 3–30.

Alon, G. *Studies in Jewish History* Tel Aviv: Hakibbutz, Hameuched, 1967 (Hebrew).

Anavi, V. Social and educational factors and work values of high school pupils. M.Sc. Thesis. Haifa: Technion–Israel Institute of Technology, 1982 (Hebrew).

Anderson, N. *Work and Leisure*. London: Routledge & Kegan Paul, 1961.

Arlosoroff, H. *Nation, Society and State*. Tel Aviv: Hakibbutz Hameuchad, 1984 (Hebrew).

Arnold, H. J., and D. C. Feldman. A multivariate analysis of the determinants of job turnover. *Journal of Applied Psychology*, 1982, *67*, 350–360.

Arvey, R. D. *Fairness in Selecting Employees*. Reading, MA: Addison-Wesley, 1979.

Ayali, M. *A Nomenclature of Workers and Artisans in the Talmudic and Midrashic Literature*. Tel Aviv: Hakibbutz Hameuchad, 1984 (Hebrew).

———. *Workers and Craftsmen: Their Work and Status in Hazal's Literature*. Tel Aviv: Masada, 1987 (Hebrew).

Bacon, A. W. Leisure and the alienated worker: A critical reassessment of three radical theories of work and leisure. *Journal of Leisure Research*, 1975, *7*, 179–190.

Barfield, R. E. *The Automobile Worker and Retirement: A Second Look*. Ann Arbor, MI: Institute for Social Research, 1970.

Barker, R. *Ecological Psychology*. Stanford, CA: Stanford University Press, 1968.

Bartal, G. *Histadrut—Structure and Activities*. Tel Aviv: Histadrut—General Federation of Labor, 1978 (Hebrew).

Bar-Tzuri, R., and T. Batzri. *Strikes in Israel, 1974–1984*. Tel Aviv: Economic and Social Research Institute, General Federation of Labor, 1985 (Hebrew).

Bass, B. M. *Organizational Psychology*. Boston: Allyn & Bacon, 1965.

Bass, B. M. and L. Eldridge. Accelerated managers' objectives in twelve countries. *Industrial Relations*, 1973, *12*, 158–171.

Beehr, T. A., and N. Gupta. A note on the structure of employee withdrawal. *Organizational Behavior and Human Performance*, 1978, *21*, 73–79.

Ben-David, Y. *Work and Education in the Kibbutz: Reality and Aspirations*, Rehovot: The Center for Studies on Rural and Urban Settlements, 1975 (Hebrew).

Ben-Gurion, D. *Bama'aracha*. Tel Aviv: Davar, 1949 (Hebrew).

Ben-Meir, J., and P. Kedem. Index of religiosity of the Jewish population in Israel. *Megamot*, 1978, *24*, 353–362 (Hebrew).

Beutell, N. I., and O. C. Brenner. Sex differences in work value. *Journal of Vocational Behavior*, 1986, *28*, 29–41.

Bigoness, W. J., and G. Hofstede. A cross national study in managerial work goals: A quasi-longitudinal investigation. Paper presented at the annual Academy of Management meeting, 1987.

Blood, M. R. Work values and job satisfaction. *Journal of Applied Psychology*, 1969, *53*, 456–459.

Braude, L. *Work and Workers: A Sociological Analysis*. New York: Praeger, 1975.

———. Work: A theoretical clarification. *Sociological Quarterly*, 1963/1964, *4*, 343–348.

Brenner, O. C., and J. Tomkiewicz. Job orientation and females: Are sex differences declining? *Personnel Psychology*, 1979, *32*, 741–750.

Bridgman, P. *The Logic of Modern Physics*. New York: Macmillan, 1927.

Buchholz, R. An empirical study of contemporary beliefs about work in American society. *Journal of Applied Psychology*, 1978, *63*, 219–227.

Campbell, A., P. E. Converse, and W. L. Rodgers. *The Quality of American Life*. New York: Russell Sage Foundation, 1976.

Centers, R., and P. Bugental. Intrinsic and extrinsic job motivations among different segments of the working population. *Journal of Applied Psychology*, 1966, *50*, 193–197.

Cherrington, D. J. *The Work Ethic: Working Values and Values that Work*. New York: Amacom, 1980.

Chestang, L. W. Work personal change and human development. In S. H. Akabas and P. A. Kurzman (Eds.), *Work, Workers and Work*. Englewood Cliffs, NJ.: Prentice Hall, 1982.

Chusmir, L. H. Job commitment and the organizational woman. *Academy of Management Review*, 1982, *7*, 595–602.

Cohen, E. Changes in the social structure of work in the kibbutz. *Economic Quarterly* (Riv'on Lekalkala), 1963, *10*, 378–388 (Hebrew).

Coleman, J. Foundations for a theory of collective decisions. *The American Journal of Sociology*, 1966, *71*, 615–627.

Cook, J. D., and T. D. Wall. New work attitude measures of trust, organizational commitment and personal need fulfilment. *Journal of Occupational Psychology*, 1980, *53*, 39–52.

Cragin, J. The nature of importance perceptions: A test of a cognitive model. *Organizational Behavior and Human Performance*, 1983, *31*, 262–276.

Crawford, J. Career development and career choice in pioneer and traditional women. *Journal of Vocational Behavior*, 1978, *12*, 129–139.

Davis, L. E. Individuals and the organization. *California Management Review*, 1980, *22*, 5–14.

Doeringer, P., and M. Piore. *Internal Labor Markets and Manpower Analysis*. Lexington, MA: D. C. Heath 1971.

Donald, M., and R. Havighurst. The meaning of leisure. *Social Forces*, 1959, *37*, 357–360.

Dowling, P. J., and T. W. Nagel. Nationality and work attitudes: A study of Australian and American business majors. *Journal of Management*, 1986, *12*, 121–128.

Dubin, R. Industrial workers' worlds: A study of the "central life interest" of industrial workers. *Social Problems*, 1956, *3*, 131–142.

————. *The World of Work*. Englewood Cliffs, NJ: Prentice Hall, 1958.

————. Work in modern society. In R. Dubin (Ed.), *Handbook of Work, Organization and Society,* pp. 5–35. Chicago: Rand McNally, 1976.

Dubin, R., J. Champoux, and L. Porter. Central life interests and organizational commitment of blue collar and clerical workers. *Administrative Science Quarterly*, 1975, *20*, 311–421.

Dubin, R., R. A. Headley, and T. C. Taveggia. Attachment to work. In R. Dubin (Ed.), *Handbook of Work, Organization and Society,* pp. 281–341. Chicago: Rand McNally, 1976.

Dunham, R. B. Shiftwork: A review and theoretical analysis. *The Academy of Management Review*, 1977, *2*, 624–634.

————.*Organizational Behavior*. Homewood, IL: Richard D. Irwin, 1984.

Durkheim, E. *The Division of Labor in Society*. Paris: F. Alcan, 1893.

Dyer, L., and D. F. Parker. Classifying outcomes in work motivation research: An examination of intrinsic-extrinsic dichotomy, *Journal of Applied Psychology*, 1975, *60*, 455–458.

Eisenstadt, S. N. The social conditions for the development of the voluntary organization in Israel. In S. N. Eisenstadt, N. Adler, H. Bar-Yosef, and R. Kahana (Eds.), *The Social Structure of Israel* (2nd ed.). Jerusalem: Academon, 1969 (Hebrew).

————. *The Development of the Ethnic Problem in Israeli Society*. Jerusalem: The Jerusalem Institute for Israel Studies, 1986.

Elizur, D. Facets of work values: A structural analysis of work outcomes. *Journal of Applied Psychology*, 1984, *69*, 379–389.

Enav, D. Factors related to intergenerational agreement on work values. M.Sc. thesis. Haifa: Technion Institute of Technology, 1984 (Hebrew).

England, G. W. Managers and their value systems: A five country comparative study. *Columbia Journal of World Business*, 1978, *13*, 35–44.

England, G. W., and I. Harpaz. Some methodological and analytic considerations in cross-national comparative research. *Journal of International Business Studies*, 1983, *14*, 49–59.

————. How working is defined: National contexts and demographic and organizational role influences. *Journal of Organizational Behavior* (forthcoming).

Erez, M. Professional orientations and incentives for engineers and scientists in industry. *Organization and Administration*, 1974, *20*, 25–32 (Hebrew).

Erez, M., and Y. Rim. Motivation to work: Engineers and scientists in industry. *Megamot*, 1975, *21*, 179–193 (Hebrew).

Erikson, E. H. *Childhood and Society* (2nd ed.). New York: Norton, 1963.

Etzioni, A. *A Comparative Analysis of Complex Organizations*. New York: The Free Press, 1961.

———. Work in the American future: Reindustrialization or quality of life. In C. J. Kerr and M. Rosow (Eds.), *Work in America: The Decade Ahead*. New York: Van Nostrand, 1979.

Evans, A. *Hours of Work in Industrialized Countries*. Geneva: International Labor Office, 1975.

Facts about Israel. Jerusalem: Ministry of Foreign Affairs, 1985.

Faderbush, S. *The Law of the Kingdom in Israel* (2nd ed.). Jerusalem: Mossad Harav Kook, 1973 (Hebrew).

Farris, G. F. A predictive study of turnover. *Personnel Psychology*, 1971, *24*, 311–328.

Firth, R. Anthropological background to work. *Occupational Psychology*, 1948, *22*, 94–102.

Fogel, Y. The value of work in Chazal's writings. *Zerae'em*, 1978, *140*, 6–7 (Hebrew).

Foreign Press Center Japan (Ed.). *The Women of Japan—Past and Present*. Tokyo: Foreign Press Center, 1977.

Fox, M., and S. Hesse-Biber. *Women at Work*. Palo Alto, CA: Mayfield, 1984.

Friedlander, F. Relationships between the importance and satisfaction of various environmental factors. *Journal of Applied Psychology*, 1965, *49*, 160–164.

Friedman, E., and R. Havighurst. *The Meaning of Work and Retirement*. Chicago: University of Chicago Press, 1954.

Friedman, G. *The Anatomy of Work*. London: Heinemann, 1961.

Fyindling, M. *Labor Laws: Sources of Labor Laws According to Torah Laws with Comments and Editions from Torah Scholars in Eretz Israel*. Jerusalem: Moshe Sryber, 1945 (Hebrew).

Galin, A., and A. Harel. *Development and Trends in Israeli Industrial and Labor Relations Systems*. Tel Aviv: Massada, 1978 (Hebrew).

Garson, B. *All the Livelong Day: The Meaning and Demeaning of Routine Work*. New York: Penguin, 1977.

Gechman, A., and Y. Weiner. Job involvement and satisfaction as related to mental health and personal time devoted to work. *Journal of Applied Psychology*, 1975, *60*, 521–523.

Gerth, H., and C. Mills. *From Max Weber: Essays in Sociology*. New York: Oxford University Press, 1946.

Glaser, B. G. *Organizational Scientists: Their Professional Careers*. Indianopolis, IN: Bobbs-Merrill, 1964.

Goldberg, A. I. The relevance of cosmopolitan/local orientations to professional values and behavior. *Sociology of Work and Occupations*, 1976, *3*, 331–356.

Gouldner, A. W. Cosmopolitans and locals: Toward an analysis of latent social roles—I. *Administrative Science Quarterly*, 1957, *2*, 281–306.

Greenberg, H. *Israel: Social Problems*. Tel Aviv: Dekel Academic Press, 1979.

Guttman, L. A general nonmetric technique for finding the small coordinate space for a configuration of points, *Psychometrika*, 1968, *33*, 469–506.

Hackman, J. R., and G. R. Oldham. Development of job diagnostic survey. *Journal of Applied Psychology*, 1975, *60*, 159–170.

Haire, M., E. E. Ghiselli, and L. W. Porter. *Managerial Thinking: An International Study*. New York: Wiley, 1966.

Hall, D. T. A theoretical model of career subidentity development in organizational settings. *Organizational Behavior and Human Performance*, 1971, *6*, 50–76.

———. *Careers in Organizations*. Santa Monica, CA: Goodyear, 1976.

Hall, D. T., and L. W. Foster. A psychological success cycle and goal setting: Goals, performance and attitudes. *Academy of Management Journal*, 1977, *20*, 290.

Hall, D. T., J. G. Goodale, S. Rabinowitz, and M. A. Morgan. Effects of top-down departmental and job change upon perceived employee behavior and attitudes: A natural field experiment. *Journal of Applied Psychology*, 1978, *62*, 62–72.

Hall, D. T., B. Schneider, and H. T. Nygren. Personal factors in organizational identification. *Administrative Science Quarterly*, 1970, *15*, 176–190.

Hall, R. H. *Dimensions of Work*. Beverly Hills, CA: Sage, 1986.

Hardin, E., Reif, H., and Heneman, H., Jr. Stability of job preferences of department store employees. *Journal of Applied Psychology*, 1951, *35*. 256–259.

Harpaz, I. *Job Satisfaction: Theoretical Perspective and Longitudinal Analysis*, New York: Libra, 1983.

———. The Importance of Work Goals: An International Perspective. *Journal of International Business Studies* 1990, *21*, 75–93.

Hartigan, J. A. *Clustering Algorithms*. New York: Wiley, 1975.

Hayashi, C., S. Nishira, T. Suzuki, K. Muzuno, and Y. Sakamoto (Eds.). *Changing Japanese values—Statistical surveys and analyses*. Tokyo: Institute of Mathematical Statistics, 1977.

Hearnshaw, L. S. Attitudes to work. *Occupational Psychology*, 1954, *28*, 129–139.

Hedges, J., and E. Sekscenski. Workers on late shifts in a changing economy. *Monthly Labor Review*, 1979, *102*, 14–22.

Heider, F. *The Psychology of Interpersonal Relations*. New York: Wiley, 1958.

Hendrick, I. The discussion of the instinct to master. *Psychoanalytic Quarterly*, 1943, *12*, 561–565.

Hepworth, S. Moderating factors of the psychological impact of unemployment. *Journal of Occupational Psychology*, 1980, *53*, 139–145.

Hertzel, B. Z. *The Jewish State—Altnoiland*. Tel Aviv: Neuman, 1960 (Hebrew).

Herzberg, A. *The Zionist Idea*. Jerusalem: Keter, 1970 (Hebrew).

Herzberg, F., B. Mausner, R. Peterson, and D. Capwell. *Job Attitudes: Review of Research and Opinion*. Pittsburgh: Psychological Service of Pittsburgh, 1957.

Herzberg, F., B. Mausner, D. Capwell, and B. Snyderman. *The Motivation to Work*. New York: Wiley, 1959.

Hess, M. *General Writings*. Jerusalem: The Jewish Agency, 1956 (Hebrew).

Hinrichs, J. R. A replicated study of job satisfaction dimensions. *Personnel Psychology*, 1968, *21*, 479–503.

Hoff, E., and Gruneisen, V. Arbeitserfahrungen, Erziehungseinstellungen, und Erziehungsverhalten von Eltern. In H. Lukesch and K. Schneewind (Eds.), *Familiäre Sozialisation: Probleme, Ergebnisse, Perspektiven*, pp. 65–89. Stuttgart (W. Germany): Klett-Cotta, 1978.

Hofstede, G. H. The color of collars. *Columbia Journal of World Business*, 1972, *7*, 72–80.

———. Nationality and espoused values of managers. *Journal of Applied Psychology*, 1976, *61*, 148–155.

————. *Culture's Consequences: International Differences in Work Related Values.* Beverly Hills, CA: Sage, 1980.

Holvoet, M. *MOW Data Treating.* Ghent, Belgium: Laboratory for Applied Psychology, 1984.

Homans, G. C. *The Human Group.* New York: Harcourt, Brace and World, 1950.

————. *Social Behavior: Its Elementary Forms.* New York: Harcourt, Brace and World, 1961.

Hulin, C., and H. Triandis . Meanings of work in different organization environments. In P. Nystrom and W. Starbuck (Eds.), *Handbook of Organization Design,* Vol. 2, pp. 336–357. New York: Oxford University Press, 1981.

Huse, E. F. *The Modern Manager.* St. Paul: West, 1979.

ILO (International Labor Organization). *Year Book of Labour Statistics,* Geneva, 1983.

Iso-Ahola, S., and K. Buttimer. The emergence of work and leisure ethic from early adolescence to early adulthood. *Journal of Leisure Research,* 1981, *13,* 282–288.

Izraeli, D. N. Women in the world of work. In A. Friedman, R. Shrift, and D. N. Izraeli (Eds.), *The Double Bind: Women in Israel,* p. 113–172. Tel Aviv: Hakibbutz Hameuchad, 1982 (Hebrew).

Jabotinsky, Z. *The Question of Work.* Jerusalem: Organization of Tzhar and Baytar Workers, 1933 (Hebrew).

Jacques, E. Preliminary sketch of a general structure of executive strata. In W. Brown and E. Jacques (Eds.), *Glacier Project Papers.* London: Heinemann, 1965.

Jahoda, M. The psychological meanings of unemployment. *New Society,* 1979, *49,* 492–495.

Jakubowski, T. *Meanings of work among middle-managers.* Amherst: University of Massachusetts, 1968 (Unpublished).

Jauch, R., F. Glueck, and N. Osborn. Organizational loyalty, professional commitment and academic research productivity. *Academy of Management Journal,* 1978, *21,* 84–92.

Juzanek, J. The work ethic: What are we measuring? *Relations Industrielles,* 1978, *33,* 666–677.

Kanungo, R. N. The concept of alienation and involvement revisited. *Psychological Bulletin,* 1979, *56,* 119–138.

————. *Work Alienation: An Integration Approach,* New York: Praeger, 1982a.

————. Measurement of job and work involvement. *Journal of Applied Psychology,* 1982b, *67,* 341–349.

Kanungo, R. N., and R. W. Wright. A cross-cultural comparative study of managerial job attitudes. *Journal of International Business Studies,* 1983, *14,* 115–129.

Kaplan, H. R., and C. Tausky. The meaning of work among the hard-core unemployed. *Pacific Sociological Review,* 1974, *17,* 185–198.

Karasek, R. Job demands, job decision latitude and mental strain: Implications for job redesign. *Administrative Science Quarterly,* 1979, *24,* 285–308.

Katz, E., and M. Gurevitch. *The Culture of Leisure in Israel.* Tel Aviv: Am Oved, 1973 (Hebrew).

Katzanelson, B. *Writings.* Tel-Aviv: Davar, 1949 (Hebrew).

Katzell, R. A. Changed attitudes toward work. In C. Kerr and J. M. Rosow (Eds.), *Work in America in the Decade Ahead.* New York: Van Nostrand, 1979.

Kelley, H. H. Attribution theory in social psychology. In D. Levine (Ed.), *Nebraska Symposium on Motivation.* Lincoln, NB: University of Nebraska Press, 1967, 192–240.

————. The process of causal attribution. *American Psychologist*, 1974, *28*, 107–128.

Kelley, L., and R. Worthley. The role of culture in comparative management: A cross-cultural perspective. *Academy of Management Journal*, 1981, *24*, 164–173.

Kerr, C. Introduction: Industrialism with a human face. In C. Kerr & J. M. Rosow (Eds.), *Work in America in the Decade Ahead*, pp. ix-xxvii. New York: Van Nostrand, 1979.

Kilpatrick, F., M. Cummings, Jr., and M. Jennings. *Source Book of a Study of Occupational Values and the Image of the Federal Service*. Washington, D.C.: Brookings Institute, 1964.

Klecka, W. R. Discriminant analysis. In N. Nie et al. (Eds.), *Statistical Package for the Social Sciences* (2nd ed.). New York: McGraw-Hill, 1975.

Koch, J. L., and R. M. Steers. Job attachment, satisfaction and turnover among public sector employees. *Journal of Vocational Behavior*, 1978, *12*, 119–128.

Kohlberg, L. The development of children's orientations toward moral order: I. Sequence in the development of human thought. *Vita Humana*, 1963, *6*, 11–33.

————. From is to ought: How to commit the naturalistic fallacy and get away with it in the study of moral development. In T. Mischel (Ed.), *Cognitive Development and Epistemology*. New York: Academic Press, 1971.

Kohn, M., and C. Schooler. *Work and Personality: An Inquiry into the Impact of Social Stratification*. Norwood, NJ: Albex, 1983.

Kornhauser, W. *Scientists in Industry: Conflict and Accommodation*, Berkeley, CA: University of California Press, 1962.

Krau, E. Commitment to work in immigrants: Its functions and peculiarities. *Journal of Vocational Behavior*, 1984, *24*, 329–339.

Kraut, A.I. Some recent advances in cross-national management research. *Academy of Management Journal*, 1975, *18*, 538–549.

Kraut, A. I., and S. Ronen. Validity of job facets importance: A multinational, multicriteria study. *Journal of Applied Psychology* 1975, *60*, 671–677.

Kremer, J., and E. Weiner. *Attitudes of Industrial and Service Employees towards Retirement*. Haifa: Society for Planned Retirement, 1974 (Hebrew).

Kuethe, J., and B. Levenson. Concepts of organization worth. *American Journal of Sociology*, 1964, *70*, 342–348.

Lacy, W., J. Bokemeier, and J. Shepard. Job attributes preferences and work commitment of men and women in the United States. *Personnel Psychology*, 1983, *36*, 315–329.

Lantos, B. Metaphysical considerations on the concept of work. *International Journal of Psychoanalysis*, 1952, *44*, 549–554.

Lawler, E. E., III. *Pay and Organizational Effectiveness: A Psychological View*. New York: McGraw-Hill, 1971.

————. *Motivation in Work Organizations*. Monterey, CA: Brooks/Cole, 1973.

Lawler, E. E., III, and D. T. Hall. Relationship of job characteristics to job involvement, satisfaction, and intrinsic motivation. *Journal of Applied Psychology*, 1970, *54*, 305–312.

Lawler, E. E., III, and L. W. Porter. Perceptions regarding management compensation. *Industrial Relations*, 1963, *3*, 41–49.

Ledvinka, J. *Federal Regulation of Personnel and Human Resource Management*. Belmont, CA: Kent, 1982.

Le'Sham, H. Work and craft in the Jewish thought. *Mahanayim*, 1964, *91*, 28–29 (Hebrew).

Leviatan, U. *Work Life for the Older Person in the Kibbutz*. Givat Haviva: The Institute for the Study of the Kibbutz Society, 1975 (Hebrew).

————. The place of work in the life of the Kibbutz female member. *The Kibbutz*, 1976, *3–4*, 92–109 (Hebrew).

————. *Work and Age: Centrality of Work in the Life of Older Kibbutz Members*. Haifa: Kibbutz University Center, University of Haifa, 1980.

————. *Human Nature or Environmental Effect? Why Men Are Different than Women in Their Work Centrality*. Haifa: Kibbutz University Center, University of Haifa, 1985 (Hebrew) No. 63.

Leviatan, U., Z. Am-Ad, and G. Adar. *Aging in the Kibbutz: Satisfaction with Life and Its Antecedents*. Haifa: Institute for Kibbutz Research, University of Haifa, 1982.

Levin, M. *The Alienated Voter*. New York: Holt, Rinehart & Winston, 1960.

Levinson, D. J., C. Darrow, E. Klein, M. Levinson, and B. McKee. The psychological development of man in early adulthood and the mid-life transition. In D. T. Ricks, A. Thomas, and M. Roff (Eds.). *Life Span Research in Psychopathology*. Minneapolis: University of Minnesota Press, 1974.

Levitan, S. A., and C. M. Johnson. *Second Thoughts on Work*. Kalamazoo, MI: Upjohn Institute for Employment Research, 1982.

————. The survival of work. In P. J. Andrisani et al. (Eds.). *The Work Ethic: A Critical Analysis*. Madison, WI: Industrial Relations Research Association, 1983.

Levitan, S. A., G. L. Mangum, and R. Marshall. *Human Resources and Labor Markets* (3rd ed.). New York: Harper & Row, 1981.

Lingoes, J. C. A general survey of the Guttman-Lingoes nonmetric program series. In R. N. Shepard et al. (Eds.). *Multidimensional Scaling*, Vol. 1. New York: Seminar Press, 1972.

Locke, E. What is job satisfaction? *Organizational Behavior and Human Performance*, 1969, *4*, 309–336.

————. The nature and causes of job satisfaction. In M.D. Dunnette (Ed.), *Handbook of Industrial and Organizational Psychology*, pp. 1279–1349. Chicago: Rand McNally, 1976.

Locke, E., and D. Schweiger. Participating in decision-making: One more look. In B. Staw (Ed.), *Research in Organization Behavior*, Vol. I, pp. 265–339. Greenwich, CT: JAI Press, 1979.

Lodahl, T., and M. Kejner. The definition and measurement of work involvement. *Journal of Applied Psychology*, 1965, *49*, 24–33.

Maccoby, E., and C. Jacklin. *The Psychology of Sex Differences*. Stanford, CA: Stanford University Press, 1974.

McClelland, D. *The Achieving Society*. Princeton, NJ: Van Nostrand, 1961.

McClelland, D., J. Sturr, R. Knapp, and H. Wendt. Obligations to self and society in the United States and Germany. *Journal of Abnormal and Social Psychology*, 1958, *56*, 245–255.

Mae, M. Japanische familien-struktur and sozialisation. In S. Yoshijima (Ed.), *Sozialisation und literatur. Ein interkultureller und interdisziplinaer versuch. Inter universitatsseminar fur deutsche und Japanische Kultur*. Tokyo: Sansyusya Verlag, 1981.

Mahoney, T. Another look at job satisfaction and performance. In T. A. Mahoney (Ed.), *Compensation and Reward Perspectives*, pp. 322–334. Homewood, IL: Irwin, 1979a.

————. Organizational hierarchy and position worth. *Academy of Management Journal*, 1979b, *22*, 726–737.

Mannheim, B. A comparative study of work centrality, job rewards and satisfaction. *Sociology of Work and Occupations*, 1975, *2*, 79–101.

————. Job satisfaction, work role centrality and work place preference of male and female industrial workers. *Behavioral Sciences Mimeograph Series* (Rep. No. 30). Haifa: Center for the Study of Man at Work, Technion Research and Development Foundation, 1980.

————. Social background, schooling and parental job attitudes as related to adolescents' work values. *Youth and Society*, 1988, *19*, 269–293.

Mannheim, B., and O. Angel. Pay systems and work-role centrality of industrial workers. *Personnel Psychology*, 1986, *39*, 359–377.

Mannheim, B., J. Chomsky, and A. Cohen. *Work centrality, rewards and role strains of Israeli male occupational groups*. Haifa: Center for the Study of Man at Work, Technion Research and Development Foundation, 1972.

Mannheim, B., and A. Cohen. Multivariate analysis of factors affecting work centrality of occupational categories. *Human Relations*, 1978, *31*, 525–533.

Mannheim, B., and R. Dubin. Work role centrality of industrial workers as related to organizational conditions, task autonomy, managerial orientations and personal characteristics. *Journal of Occupational Behavior*, 1986, *7*, 107–124.

Mannheim, B., and J. Rein. Work centrality of different age groups. Paper presented at the Tenth International Congress of Gerontology, Jerusalem, June 1975.

————. Work centrality and different age groups and the wish to discontinue work. *International Journal of Aging and Human Development*, 1981, *13*, 221–232.

Mannheim, B., and M. Schiffrin. Family structure, job characteristics, rewards and strains as related to work-role centrality of employed and self-employed professional women with children. *Journal of Occupational Behavior*, 1984, *5*, 83–101.

Marx, K. Economic and philosophical manuscripts. *Marx-Engels Gesamtausgabe*, Vol. 3. Berlin: Marx-Engels Institute, 1932. (Originally published in 1844.)

Maslow, A. *Motivation and Personality*. New York: Harper & Row, 1954.

Maurer, J. Work as a "central life interest" of industrial supervisors. *Academy of Management Journal*, 1968, *11*, 329–339.

Menninger, W. C. The meaning of work in Western society. In H. Borow, (Ed.), *Man in a World at Work*. Boston: Houghton Mifflin, 1964.

Middleton, R. Alienation, race and education. *American Sociological Review*, 1963, *28*, 973–977.

Miller, G. The interpretation of nonoccupational work in modern society: A preliminary discussion and typology. *Social Problems*, 1980, *27*, 381–391.

Mintzberg, H. *The Nature of Managerial Work*. New York: Harper & Row, 1973.

Mirels, H. L., and J. B. Garrett. The Protestant ethic as a personality variable. *Journal of Consulting and Clinical Psychology*, 1971, *36*, 40–44.

Moch, M. K. Job involvement, internal motivation and employees' integration into networks of work relationships. *Organizational Behavior and Human Performance*, 1980, *25*, 15–31.

Morrow, P. C. Concept redundancy in organizational research: The case of work commitment. *Academy of Management Journal*, 1983, *8*, 486–500.

Morse, N. C., and R. C. Weiss. The function and meaning of work and the job. *American Sociological Review*, 1955, *20*, 191–198.

Mosse, C. *The Ancient World at Work*. New York: Norton, 1969.

MOW-International Research Team. The meaning of working. In C. Dlugos and K. Weirmair (Eds.), *Management under Differing Value Systems—Managerial Philosophies and Strategies in a Changing World*, pp. 565–630. Berlin/New York: Walter De Gruyter, 1981.

―――. *The Meaning of Working*. London: Academic Press, 1987.

Mowday, R. T., R. M. Steers, and L. W. Porter. The measurement of organizational commitment. *Journal of Vocational Behavior*, 1979, *4*, 224–247.

Murphy, J., and C. Gilligan. Moral development in late adolescence and adulthood: A critique and reconstruction of Kohlberg's theory. *Human Development*, 1980, *23*, 77–104.

Myers, M. S., and S. S. Myers. Towards understanding the changing work ethic. *California Management Review*, 1974, Spring, 7–19.

Naoi, A., and C. Schooler. *Occupational conditions and psychological functioning in Japan*. Paper presented at the annual meeting of the American Sociological Association, 1981.

Neal, A., and A. Rettig. Dimensions of alienation among manual workers and non-manual workers. *American Sociological Review*, 1963, *28*, 599–608.

Near, J. P., R. W. Rice and R. G. Hunt. The relationship between work and non-work domains: A review of empirical research. *Academy of Management Review*, 1980, *5*, 415–429.

Nedava, J. *Zeev Jabotinsky—The Man and His Doctrine*. Tel Aviv: Misrad Habitachon, 1980 (Hebrew).

Neff, W. S. *Work and Human Behavior*. New York: Atherton, 1968.

―――. Work and human behavior. *Humanitas*, 1971, *7*, 177–191.

―――. *Work and Human Behavior* (2nd ed.). Chicago: Aldine, 1977.

Northrop, F. *The Logic of Modern Physics*. New York: Macmillan, 1959.

Oates, W. E. *Confession of a Workaholic*. Nashville: Abinedon, 1978.

Olafson, F. *Society, Law and Morality*. Englewood Cliffs, NJ: Prentice Hall, 1961.

Olson, M. *The Logic of Collective Action: Public Goods and the Theory of Groups*. Cambridge, MA: Harvard University Press, 1965.

Orzack, L. H. Work as a "central life interest" of professionals. *Social Problems*, 1959, *7*, 73–84.

Parker, S. R. Work and non-work in three occupations. *Sociological Review*, 1965, *13*, 65–75.

―――. *The Future of Work and Leisure*. London: MacGibbon & Kee, 1971.

Parker, S. R., and M. Smith. Work and leisure. In R. Dubin (Ed.). *Handbook of Work, Organization and Society*, pp. 37–62. Chicago: Rand McNally, 1976.

Parnes, H., and R. King. Middle-aged job losers. *Industrial Gerontology*, 1977, *4*, 77–95.

Parsons, T., and E. Shils. (Eds.). *Toward a General Theory of Action*. Cambridge, MA: Harvard University Press, 1952.

Patchen, M. *Participation, Achievement and Involvement on the Job*. Englewood Cliffs, NJ: Prentice Hall, 1970.

Peres, Y., and R. Katz. Stability and centrality: The nuclear family in modern Israel. *Social Forces*, 1981 *59*, 687–704.

―――. The working mother and her family. Unpublished research report to the office of Labor and Welfare. 1984 (Hebrew).

Perlman, M. *Labor Union Theories in America*. Westport, CT: Greenwood Press, 1976.

Pharr, S. Japan: Historical and contemporary perspectives. In J. Hiele and A. Smock (Eds.). *Women: Roots and Status in Eight Countries.* New York: Wiley, 1977.

Piaget, J. *The Moral Development of the Child.* Glencoe, IL: The Free Press 1965. (Originally published in 1932.)

Pinsker, Y. L. *The Autoemancipation—A Manifest to his People—Published by a Russian Jew.* Tel Aviv: Dvir, 1967 (Hebrew).

Porat, R. (Ed.). *A Laboratory Manual for the Guttman-Lingoes Nonmetric Computer Programs,* Vol. 1. Jerusalem: Israel Institute of Applied Social Research, 1974.

Porter, L. W. *Organizational Patterns of Managerial Job Attitudes.* New York: American Foundation for Management Research, 1964.

Porter, L. W., and E. E. Lawler III. Properties of organizational structure in relation to job attitudes and job behavior. *Psychological Bulletin,* 1965, *64,* 23–51.

Porter, L. W., E. E. Lawler III, and J. R. Hackman. *Behavior in Organizations.* New York: McGraw-Hill, 1975.

Presser, H. B., and W. Baldwin. Child care as a constraint on employment: Prevalence correlates and bearing on the work and fertility nexus. *American Journal of Sociology,* 1980, *85,* 1202–1213.

Psathas, G. Toward a theory of occupational choice for women. *Sociology and Social Research,* 1968, *52,* 253–268.

Quinn, R. P. What workers want: The relative importance of job facets to American workers. Ann Arbor, MI: Survey Research Center, 1971. Mimeo.

Quinn, R. P., and W. Cobb. What workers want: Factor analysis of importance ratings of job facets. Ann Arbor, MI: Survey Research Center, 1971. Mimeo.

Quinn, R. P., and G. L. Staines. *The 1977 Quality of Employment Survey.* Ann Arbor, MI: Institute for Social Research, University of Michigan, 1979.

Rabinowitz, S. An examination of influence of individual difference variables and perceived job stimulation. Master's thesis. Michigan State University, 1975.

Rabinowitz, S., and D. T. Hall. Organizational research on job involvement. *Psychological Bulletin,* 1977, *83,* 265–288.

Rein, J. The community as a moderator factor of the organizational environment. Ph.D. thesis. Haifa: Technion-Israel Institute of Technology, 1977.

Reines, C. W. *Ethics and Life.* Jerusalem: Rubin Mass, 1979 (Hebrew).

Rest, J. *Development in Judging Moral Issues.* Minneapolis: University of Minnesota Press, 1979.

Reynolds, L. R. *Labor Economics and Labor Relations* (6th ed.). Englewood Cliffs, NJ: Prentice Hall, 1974.

Reynolds, L. R., S. H. Masters and C. H. Moser. *Labor Economics and Labor Relations* (9th ed.). Englewood Cliffs, NJ: Prentice Hall, 1986.

Rim, Y. Significance of work and personality. *Journal of Occupational Psychology,* 1977, 50, 135–138

Ritzer, G. *Man and His Work: Conflict and Change.* Englewood Cliffs, NJ: Prentice Hall, 1972.

———. *Working: Conflict and Change* (2nd ed.). Englewood Cliffs, NJ: Prentice Hall, 1977.

Robinson, J. P. *How Americans Use Time: A Social Psychological Analysis of Everyday Behavior.* New York: Praeger, 1977.

Ronan, W. W. Relative importance of job characteristics. *Journal of Applied Psychology,* 1970, *54,* 192–200.

Ronen, S. Personal values: A basis for work motivational set and work attitude. *Orga-*

nizational Behavior and Human Behavior Performance, 1978, *21*, 80–107.

Ronen, S., and O. Shenkar. Clustering countries on attitudinal dimensions: A review and synthesis. *Academy of Management Review*, 1985, *10*, 435–454.

Rosenstein, E. The Israeli industrial relations system. In IDE International Research Group. *European Industrial Relations*. London: Oxford University Press, 1981.

———. The structure and function of the Israeli industrial relations system. *Economics Quarterly*, 1984, *121*, 205–208 (Hebrew).

Rosner, M. Work in the kibbutz and the status of its people. *Hedim*, 1960, *64*, 84–98 (Hebrew).

———. Difficulties and rewards in the role of branch manager. *Hedim*, 1963, *46* (Hebrew).

———. *The Quality of Life in the Kibbutz*. Haifa: Kibbutz University Center, University of Haifa, 1980. No. 24.

———. *The Quality of Working Life in the Kibbutz*. Haifa: Kibbutz University Center, University of Haifa, 1982 (Hebrew).

Rosner, M., Y. Ben-David, A. Ovnat. N. Cohen, and U. Leviatan. *The Second Generation: Between Continuity and Change*. Tel Aviv: Sifriat Poalim, 1978 (Hebrew).

Rosow, J. M. *The Worker and the Job: Coping with Change*, Englewood Cliffs, NJ: Prentice Hall, 1974.

Rotenstreich, N. *Perspectives on Current Times and the Israeli Society*. Tel Aviv: Am Oved, 1980 (Hebrew).

Rousseau, J. *The Social Contract and Discourses*. London: Dent & Sons, 1916.

Rundquist, E., and R. Sletto. *Personality in the Depression*. Minneapolis: University of Minnesota Press, 1936.

Saal, F. E. Job involvement: A multivariate approach. *Journal of Applied Psychology*, 1978, *63*, 53–61.

Saleh, S. D., and T. G. Grygier. Psychodynamics of intrinsic and extrinsic job orientation. *Journal of Applied Psychology*, 1969, *53*, 446–450.

Saleh, S. D., and M. Lalljee. Sex differences in job satisfaction: A re-examination. *Personnel Psychology*, 1969, *31*, 537–547.

Salz, B. R. The human element in industrialization. *Economic Development and Cultural Change*, 1955, *4*, 96 (special supplement).

Schaie, K. A general model for the study of developmental problems. *Psychological Bulletin*, 1965, *64*, 92–107.

Schein, E. *Organizational Psychology* (3rd ed.). Englewood Cliffs, NJ: Prentice Hall, 1980.

Schiffrin, M. *Work centrality, rewards and job strains of women in academic professions*. M.S. thesis. Haifa: Technion-Israel Institute of Technology, 1979.

Schuler, R. S. Sex, organizational level, and outcome of importance: Where the differences are. *Personnel Psychology*, 1975, *28*, 365–375.

Seashore, S. E. Job satisfaction: A dynamic predicator of adaptive and defensive behavior. *Studies in Personnel Psychology*, 1973, *5*, 7–20.

Seeman, M. Alienation studies. *Annual Review of Sociology*, 1975, *1*, 91–123.

Sela, A. Work values in labor relations and their institutionalization, according to the Judaic sources (oral Torah) M.A. thesis, Haifa: Technion–Israel Institute of Technology, 1984.

Selye, H. *Stress without Distress*. Philadelphia: Lippincott, 1974.

Shamir, B. Protestant work ethic, work involvement and the psychological impact of unemployment. *Journal of Occupational Behaviour*, 1986a, *7*, 25–38.

————. Work Commitment and Work Centrality in the Israeli Society: Survey Data and Some Comments. In A. Globerson, A. Galin, and E. Rosenstein, *Human Resources and Industrial Relations in Israel: New Horizons*, pp. 287–309. Tel Aviv: Ramot, 1990 (Hebrew).

Shapira, Y. *Democracy in Israel*. Ramat Gan: Masada, 1977 (Hebrew).

Shapira, Z. *Factors Effecting Employee Work Values: Evidence about Industrial Workers in Israel*. Tel Aviv: Institute for Social and Labour Research, Tel Aviv University, 1983.

Shechter, J. *The Doctrine of A. D. Gordon*. Tel Aviv: Dvir, 1957 (Hebrew).

Shefi, N. *The meaning of work of registered nurses in government hospital institutes*. M.A. thesis. Haifa: University of Haifa, 1986 (Hebrew).

Shepher, J. Motivation work and social activity in kibbutz society. *Proceedings of the International Symposium of Cooperative Rural Communities*, 1968, *1*, 205–207.

Sheppard, H. L., and A. H. Belitsky. *The Job Hunt: Job Seeking Behavior of Unemployed Workers in a Local Economy*. Baltimore: Johns Hopkins Press, 1966.

Sheppard, H. L., and N. Herrick. *Where Have All the Robots Gone?* New York: The Free Press, 1972.

Shimmin, S. Concepts of work. *Occupational Psychology*, 1966, *40*, 195–201.

Shirom, A. *Introduction to Labor Relations in Israel*. Tel Aviv: Am Oved, 1983 (Hebrew).

Shostak, A. B. *Blue-Collar Stress*. Reading, MA: Addison-Wesley, 1980.

Siegel, A. L., and Ruh, R. A. Job involvement, participation in decision making, personal background and job behavior. *Organizational Performance*, 1973, *9*, 318–327.

Simon, H. *Administrative Behavior*. New York: Macmillan, 1947.

Sirota, D., and M. J. Greenwood. Understand your overseas work force. *Harvard Business Review*, 1971, *49*, 53–60.

Slocum, J. W. Motivation in managerial levels: Relationship of need satisfaction to job performance. *Journal of Applied Psychology*, 1967, *51*, 411–416.

Soliman, H. Motivation-hygiene theory of job attitudes: An empirical investigation and an attempt to reconcile both the one and the two factor theories of job attitudes. *Journal of Applied Psychology*, 1970, *54*, 452–461.

Special Task Force. *Work in America*. Cambridge, MA: MIT Press, 1973.

Stafford, E., Jackson, P., and Banks, M. Employment, work involvement and mental health in less-qualified young people. *Journal of Occupational Psychology*, 1980, *53*, 291–304.

Statistical Abstract of Israel. Jerusalem: Government Publications, 1982.

Statistical Abstract of Israel. Jerusalem: Government Publications, 1985.

Steers, R. Antecedents and outcomes of organizational commitment. *Administrative Science Quarterly*, 1977, *22*, 46–56.

Steers, R., and L. Porter. *Motivation and Work Behavior*. New York: McGraw-Hill, 1975.

————. *Motivation and Work Behavior* (3rd ed.). New York: McGraw-Hill, 1983.

Stracevich, M. M. Job factor importance for job satisfaction and dissatisfaction across different occupation levels. *Journal of Applied Psychology*, 1972, *56*, 467–471.

Stumpf, S. A., M. Greller, and R. Freedman. Equal employment opportunity regulation and change in compensation practices. *Journal of Applied Behavioral Science*, 1980, *16*, 29–40.

Super, D. E. *The Psychology of Careers*. New York: Harper & Row, 1957.

———. Career development: Exploration and planning. *Annual Review of Psychology*, 1978, *29*, 333–372.

Takeuchi, H. Man and occupation. In R. Iwauchi (Ed.), *The Sociology of Occupation*. Tokyo: Gakubun Sha, 1975.

Tannenbaum, A. S. *Social Psychology of the Work Organization*. Belmont, CA: Brooks/ Cole, 1966.

Tausky, C. Meaning of work among blue collar men. *Pacific Sociological Review*, 1969, *12*, 49–55.

Tausky, C., and E. Piedmont. The meaning of work and unemployment: Implication for mental health. *International Journal of Social Psychology*, 1967, *14*, 44–49.

Terborg, J. R., and D. R. Ilgen. A theoretical approach to sex discrimination in traditionally masculine occupations. *Organizational Behavior and Human Performance*, 1975, *13*, 352–376.

Thompson, J. *Organizations in Action*. New York: McGraw-Hill, 1968.

Tilgher, A. Work through the ages. In S. Nosow and H. Form (Eds.), *Man, Work and Society*. New York: Basic Books, 1962.

Triandis, H. *The Analysis of Subjective Culture*. New York: Wiley, 1972.

Trommsdorff, G. Vergleich von sozialisations bedingungen in Japan und der Bundesrepublik. Paper presented at the Tagung fur Familiensoziologie, Arnoldshain, November 1981.

———. Value change in Japan. *International Journal of Intercultural Relations*, 1983, *7*, 37–360.

Tuma, N. B., and Grimes, A. J. A comparison of models of role orientations of professionals in a research oriented university. *Administrative Science Quarterly*, 1981, *26*, 187–206.

Turner, A., and P. Lawrence. *Industrial Jobs and the Worker*. Boston: Harvard University Press, 1965.

Turner, R. H. Role taking, role standpoint, and reference group behavior. *American Journal of Sociology*, 1956, *61*, 316–328.

Vecchio, R. P. The function and meaning of work and the job: Morse and Weiss (1955) revisited. *Academy of Management Journal*, 1980, *23*, 361–367.

Vroom, V. H. Ego involvement, job satisfaction, and job performance. *Personnel Psychology*, 1962, *15*, 159–177.

———. *Work and Motivation*. New York: Wiley, 1964.

Warr, P. B. A study of psychological well-being. *British Journal of Psychology*, 1978, *69*, 111–121.

———. Psychological aspects of employment and unemployment. *Psychological Medicine*, 1981, *12*, 7–11.

———. A national study of non-financial employment commitment. *Journal of Occupational Psychology*, 1982, *55*, 297–312.

———. Work and unemployment. In P. Drenth, H. Thierry, P. Willems, and C. deWolff (Eds.). *Handbook of Work and Organization Psychology*. London: Wiley, 1984.

Warr, P., and P. Jackson. Self-esteem and unemployment among young workers. *Le Travail humain*, 1983, *46*, 355–366.

Warr, P. B., and D. J. Lovatt. Retraining and other factors associated with job finding after redundancy. *Journal of Occupational Psychology*, 1977, *50*, 67–84.

Weber, M. *The Protestant Ethic and the Spirit of Capitalism*. London: George, Allen & Unwin, 1930.

Weick, K. *The Social Psychology of Organizing* (2nd ed.). Reading, MA: Addison-Wesley, 1979.

Weisfeld, I. H. *Labor Legislation in the Bible and Talmud*. New York: Yeshiva University Press, 1974.

Weiss, D., R. Dawis, G. England, and L. Lofquist. Minnesota Studies in vocational rehabilitation: XVIII. *Construct Validation Studies of the Minnesota Importance Questionnaire,* Bulletin 41. Minneapolis: Industrial Relations Center, University of Minnesota, 1964.

Weiss, R. S., and R. L. Kahn. Definitions of work and occupations. *Social Problems,* 1960, *8,* 142–151.

Weller, L. *Sociology in Israel*. Westport, CT: Greenwood Press, 1974.

Wiersma, U. *Differences between What Women and Men Want from a Job and Why*. Paper presented at the Academy of Management annual meeting, 1987.

Wilensky, H. Orderly careers and social participation: The impact of work history on social integration in the middle class. *American Sociological Review,* 1961, *26,* 521–539.

―――. Varieties of work experience. In H. Borow (Ed.). *Man in a World of Work*. Boston: Houghton Mifflin, 1964.

Wollack, S., N. Goodale, J. Wijting, and P. Smith. Development of the survey of work values. *Journal of Applied Psychology,* 1971, *55,* 331–338.

Yankelovich, D. The meaning of work. In Rosow, J. M. (Ed.). *The Worker and the Job*. Englewood Cliffs, NJ: Prentice Hall, 1974.

―――. Work, values, and the new breed. In C. Kerr and J. M. Rosow (Eds.). *Work in America: the Decade Ahead*. New York: Van Nostrand, 1979.

―――. *New Rules: Searching for Self-fulfillment in a World Turned Upside Down*. New York: Random House, 1981.

Youth Bureau, Prime Minister's Office of Japan (Ed.). *The Youth of the World and Japan: The Findings of the Second World Youth Survey*. Tokyo: Prime Minister's Office, 1978.

Yuchtman-Yaar, E. *Economic Culture in Post Industrial Society: Orientation toward Growth, Technology and Work*. Tel Aviv: The Pinhas Sapir Center for Development, Tel Aviv University, Discussion paper No. 6–84. 1984.

Yuchtman-Yaar, E., and M. Semyonov. Ethnic inequality in Israeli schools and sports: An expectation-states approach. *American Journal of Sociology,* 1979, *85,* 576–590.

Index

ABOUT THE AUTHOR

ITZHAK HARPAZ (Ph.D., 1977, Industrial Relations, University of Minnesota) is a senior lecturer of human resources management at the University of Haifa, Haifa, Israel. His areas of specialization include organizational behavior, personnel and human resources management, and cross-cultural comparative research focusing on work and organizations. He has published articles and chapters on the above topics in professional journals and books. He is the author of a book on job satisfaction and has co-authored a book on the meaning of working in eight countries.